PRE-COLUMBIAN AMERICA

AMERICA

EMPIRES OF THE NEW WORLD

THE BRITANNICA GUIDE TO ANCIENT CIVILIZATIONS

PRE-COLUMBIAN AMERICA

EMPIRES OF THE NEW WORLD

EDITED BY KATHLEEN KUIPER, MANAGER, ARTS AND CULTURE

Britannica
Educational Publishing

IN ASSOCIATION WITH

ROSEN
EDUCATIONAL SERVICES

Published in 2011 by Britannica Educational Publishing
(a trademark of Encyclopædia Britannica, Inc.)
in association with Rosen Educational Services, LLC
29 East 21st Street, New York, NY 10010.

Distributed exclusively by Rosen Educational Services.
For a listing of additional Britannica Educational Publishing titles, call toll free (800) 237-9932.

First Edition

Britannica Educational Publishing
Michael I. Levy: Executive Editor
J.E. Luebering: Senior Manager
Marilyn L. Barton: Senior Coordinator, Production Control
Steven Bosco: Director, Editorial Technologies
Lisa S. Braucher: Senior Producer and Data Editor
Yvette Charboneau: Senior Copy Editor
Kathy Nakamura: Manager, Media Acquisition
Kathleen Kuiper: Manager, Arts and Culture

Rosen Educational Services
Jeanne Nagle: Senior Editor
Nelson Sá: Art Director
Cindy Reiman: Photography Manager
Matthew Cauli: Designer, Cover Design
Introduction by Janey Levy

3 1969 01996 5986

Library of Congress Cataloging-in-Publication Data

Kuiper, Kathleen.
Pre-Columbian America : empires of the New World / Kathleen Kuiper.
  p. cm. -- (The Britannica guide to ancient civilizations)
"In association with Britannica Educational Publishing, Rosen Educational Services."
Includes bibliographical references and index.
ISBN 978-1-61530-150-8 (library binding)
1. America—Civilization. 2. Indians—History. 3. Indians—Social life and customs. I. Title.
E58.K85 2010
970—dc22

2010013770

Manufactured in the United States of America

On the cover: Templo las Inscripciones ("Temple of the Inscriptions"), a famous Mayan
burial monument in Palenque, Mexico.*Peter Adams/Photographer's Choice/Getty Images*

On pages 15, 37, 72, 107, 142 : A woven mat from the pre-Columbian archeological
site Chavín de Huántar, in Peru's Andean highlands. *Herman du Plessis/Gallo Images/
Getty Images*

CONTENTS

18

30

53

CHAPTER 3: THE TOLTEC AND THE AZTEC, POST-CLASSIC PERIOD (900–1519) 72

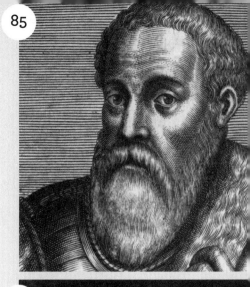

85

103

105

112

163

167

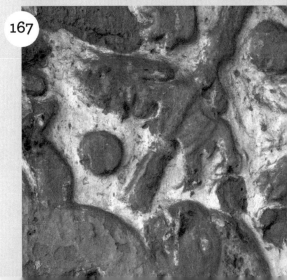

los á aqui naciá awon de Buahen.
tu hombre mal awon de mocyr en
la guerra

Because educational curricula in the West typically emphasize European civilization and cultural traditions, pre-Columbian civilizations are, at best, a peripheral concept for many people today. Perhaps the best-known features of pre-Columbian civilizations are architectural, namely the Mayan and Aztec pyramids and the Inca ruins at Machu Picchu, and ritualistic, such as a penchant for human sacrifice. Yet these isolated elements provide only a fragmented, and thus distorted, picture of the cultures to which they belonged. These elements alone cannot convey the size, richness, and complex history of pre-Columbian civilizations.

Details found in this book mark an attempt to rectify that situation. Readers will come to a deep understanding of the cultures, traditions, accomplishments, and belief systems of the Mesoamerican and Andean peoples.

The term "pre-Columbian" refers to a time in the Americas before European explorers and settlers arrived. It derives from one of Western history's most familiar explorers, Christopher Columbus, and owes its invention to Columbus's traditional albeit somewhat inaccurate designation as the discoverer of this "New World." While pre-Columbian can apply to life in both North and South America, when scholars speak of pre-Columbian civilizations, they are referring to the great civilizations of Mexico, Central America, and the Andes. The Maya, Aztec, and Inca are the best known of these. Maya and Aztec civilizations flourished in the area known as Mesoamerica, which includes about half of Mexico, all of Guatemala and Belize, and parts of Honduras and El Salvador. The Inca realm in the South American Andes covered parts of the modern nations of Ecuador, Peru, Bolivia, Chile, and Argentina.

Scholars once believed that the Americas were sparsely populated at the time of European arrival a vast wilderness paradise ripe for the taking, abundant with animals, natural resources, and perhaps gold beyond one's wildest imaginings. While the continents' natural riches have never been questioned, the notion of an almost-uninhabited land is no longer viewed as accurate. Some scholars have estimated that the population of the Americas could have been as high as 112 million when Columbus arrived. In contrast, Europe's population at the time has been estimated at 70 million to 88 million. It has also been estimated that more than 25 million of the Americas' inhabitants lived in central Mexico. That figure is more than two and a half times the combined population of Spain and Portugal in Columbus's day.

Supporting the thesis of burgeoning populations are archeological finds such

Symbols and characters from an Aztec syllabary, which provides a key to the Aztec written language. Hulton Archive/Getty Images

as the tools, approximately 13,000 years old, found near Clovis, New Mexico, in the 1930s. Archaeologists unearthed a site at Monte Verde, Chile, that was occupied at least 12,800 years ago. These provided clear evidence of humans in the Americas, and for much of the 20th century, it was believed that these people represented the continents' earliest inhabitants. According to the most popular theory, they had reached the Americas by crossing the Bering Strait on a land bridge, created by lower sea levels during the Ice Age, that connected what is now Siberia and Alaska. From Alaska, these people, called paleo-Indians, and their descendants spread across both North and South America.

Later in the century, new discoveries challenged earlier thinking. In Mexico, archaeologists found evidence of even earlier human habitation. At Tlapacoya, near Mexico City, they found tools dated at about 23,000 years old. Tools almost 24,000 years old were uncovered near Puebla, Mexico. What the Mexican discoveries meant was that people were living and thriving in the Americas at a time when northern Europe was still covered by ice sheets.

The earliest inhabitants of Mesoamerica occupied a world very different from the one that exists today. Temperatures were much colder. Cool, wet grasslands covered the highland valleys, where large herds of mammals grazed. In this environment, paleo-Indians were nomads who lived a successful hunter-gatherer lifestyle. Then, about 7000 BC, temperatures rose, the immense ice sheets covering the northern part of the planet shrank, and many of the large animals hunted by paleo-Indians became extinct. The new world and new climate demanded a new lifestyle. By about 6500 BC, the people of Mexico were farming, growing and harvesting crops that included squash. They were raising corn (maize) by 5000 BC and beans after 3500 BC. Semipermanent homes and villages accompanied farming.

The era from 1500 BC to 100 AD is known as the Formative period, a time when permanent villages appeared, then cities arose. Also at this time the Olmec civilization emerged in southern Mexico. The Olmec, probably best known today for their huge sculptures of human heads, had an extensive trading network, a complex religion, and great ceremonial centres. Theirs has been considered the first great Mesoamerican civilization.

The Zapotec civilization also emerged during the Formative period, at Monte Albán, near Oaxaca, Mexico. Hieroglyphs and calendrical notations on carvings at Monte Albán reveal that the Zapotec civilization was the first in Mesoamerica to develop writing and a calendar.

Mayan-speaking people appeared in the Valley of Guatemala, near modern Guatemala City, during the Formative period as well. Their exact origin is uncertain. The great Maya civilization characterized by cities, ceremonial centres, and towering pyramids still lay in the future, but after about 600 BC, these early Mayan speakers began building small ceremonial centres and pyramidal platforms. By the end of the Formative period, Maya civilization had begun to take shape. Architecture was advanced, and carvings containing hieroglyphs and notations following the Maya sacred calendar began to appear.

Scholars term the next period in the region's history the Classic period. Teotihuacán, north of present-day Mexico City, was the largest Early Classic city in pre Columbian Mesoamerica and the major manufacturing centre for pottery and figurines. Its population around 600 AD may have numbered as many as 150,000. The powerful and far-reaching impact of its cultural traditions, language, export of goods, and reputation as the "City of the Gods" made Teotihuacán an enduring influence on the entirety of Mesoamerica.

The great Maya civilization blossomed during the Classic period. In dense forests, the Maya built roads and maintained contact with distant sites through an extensive trading network. They constructed ceremonial and political centres such as Tikal, Copán, Palenque, Uxmal, and Kabah—sites that served as government, religious, and trade centres for tens of thousands of people in surrounding hamlets. These centres are noteworthy for their temple pyramids. At Tikal one temple pyramid reached a height of 230 feet (70 metres),

believed to be the tallest structure ever built by early Mesoamericans.

The Maya are also noted for their intellectual accomplishments. By at least 200 BC, they had developed a hieroglyphic writing system, the only such system in the pre-Columbian Americas. They also developed a mathematical system that utilized place value and zero and devised a complex calendrical system incorporating three calendars—a sacred year, a solar year, and the Long Count, which involved a series of cycles.

For reasons that are not fully understood, the Maya civilization collapsed around 900 AD. The people themselves, however, did not disappear. Maya still live in modern Mesoamerica.

The collapse of the Maya civilization marked the end of the Classic period and the beginning of the Postclassic. An abundance of historical documentation distinguishes the Postclassic from earlier periods. According to these historical annals, 900 AD was approximately when the city of Tula was founded and the rise of the Toltec began. The annals credit the Toltec with the first great Mesoamerican empire. Numerous questions, however, surround both the Toltec and Tula. It is not certain that the modern city of Tula is identical with the Toltec city of that name. There is even some question whether the Toltec actually existed as a people.

No such questions surround the great Postclassic civilization of the Aztec. The annals record that, in 1325, the Aztec founded their capital of Tenochtitlán, where present-day Mexico City stands. In 1426, Tenochtitlán began the conquests that formed the Aztec empire.

Aztec society had a complex social and political organization. The basic unit was the nuclear family. Several related families occupied a single household, and several households formed a *calpulli*. The unit above the *calpulli* was the state.

Aztec society was divided into three castes: the *pipiltin*, or nobles; the *macehual*, or commoners; and the *mayeques*, or serfs. Numerous social classes existed within each caste. Aztec society also included pawns, who were similar to indentured servants, and slaves, who served mainly as human sacrifices.

The magnificent capital of Tenochtitlán covered more than 5 square miles (13 square kilometers) and had a population of perhaps 200,000. When Spanish conquistador Hernán Cortés and his soldiers entered the city in 1519, they were overwhelmed by its splendour, especially that of the palace of Montezuma II. In letters Cortés described the palace and city in superlative terms.

Cortés conquered Tenochtitlán in 1521. With that, the Aztec empire fell, and the Postclassic period came to an end. However, in the South American Andes, the great Inca civilization still flourished.

In the Andes region, desert stretches for thousands of miles along the Pacific coast. A few miles inland, running parallel to the coast, rise the Andes. The people who inhabited this region overcame harsh climate and difficult terrain to develop some remarkable cultures.

People had settled the Andes long before the rise of the Inca. Fishermen occupied coastal areas by 3500 BC. Early settlements were seasonal, but by approximately 2500 BC there were permanent fishing villages. Ceremonial buildings and pyramids existed by 2000 BC. Some scholars believe the Andes highlands were occupied at a much earlier date, perhaps as early as 15,000 BC. Crops were being cultivated by 3000 BC. Pottery, one of the primary Andean arts, appeared about 2000 BC. Before long, the heddle loom, a device for weaving cloth, was in use.

The earliest cultures developed in small pockets, isolated from each other. The first highly developed culture in pre-Columbian Peru was Chavín, which flourished from about 900 BC to about 200 BC. For the first time, a common ideology or religion unified many local or regional cultures. Chavín eventually covered most of northern and central Peru, and its influence extended south along the coast.

The Moche culture, which emerged along the northern coast after 200 BC, represented a cultural peak. Lively, realistic scenes of people and things decorated Moche pottery, providing valuable information about Moche life. The Moche also had elaborate architecture and highly developed irrigation systems.

The remarkable Tiwanaku civilization appeared on the southern shore of Lake Titicaca in Bolivia at least by 200 BC. At its greatest extent, the influence of Tiwanaku stretched across much of Bolivia, northwestern Argentina, northern Chile, and southern Peru. Yet little is known about Tiwanaku. It was long thought to be a ceremonial site, but discoveries in the late 20th century revealed that it was actually the capital city of a great civilization. Tiwanaku's influence can be attributed largely to its highly productive agricultural system. Its raised-field system consisted of raised planting areas separated by small irrigation ditches.

The Inca had reached Cuzco, Peru, by the 13th century. Little is known about them with certainty before that. They are famous today for their great empire and remarkable technology. The Inca had no writing system, but they did have an ingenious accounting and record-keeping method that utilized the *quipu*, a long rope with cords hanging from it. Knots and colours conveyed information. Some scholars believe the quipus were also used for historical records.

These devices are just one example of the central role of textiles in Inca civilization. Woven cloths were used for burial, sacrifice, calendars, and even suspension bridges. Cloth was so highly valued that it was used to pay Inca soldiers in the field.

Another tremendous Inca technological accomplishment was their highway system. It contained at least 15,500 miles (24,945 km) of highway. The Andes route, where the roadway was some 25 feet (about 8 metres) wide and traversed the highest peaks, was especially noteworthy.

After the Inca established themselves at Cuzco, they began forcing their neighbours to pay tribute. In the 14th century, they began taking control of more land. These "conquests" were essentially raids for plunder, since the Inca took no steps to establish rule over the "conquered" groups. That changed in the 15th century, and they began building their empire. Conquests continued into the 16th century, along with turmoil within the empire triggered largely by disputes over succession to the throne.

By 1532 the Inca ruled an empire that extended to northern Ecuador, west-central Argentina, and central Chile. The empire contained more than 12 million people who spoke at least 20 languages. However, turmoil continued within the empire, and Spanish conquistador Francisco Pizarro took advantage of that. With just a small group of soldiers that included four of his brothers, Pizarro kidnapped and executed the Incan leader Atahuallpa, marched on the royal capital, and installed what amounted to a dummy government, which allowed him to enjoy the spoils of war for years to come. With these acts Pizarro had managed to topple the last of the great pre-Columbian empires.

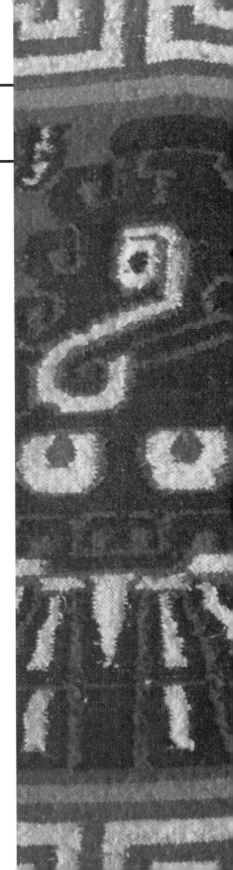

CHAPTER 1

MESOAMERICAN CIVILIZATIONS

Mesoamerica is a term that applies to the area of Mexico and Central America that was civilized in pre-Spanish times. In many respects, the American Indians who inhabited Mesoamerica were the most advanced native peoples in the Western Hemisphere. The northern border of Mesoamerica runs west from a point on the Gulf Coast of Mexico above the modern port of Tampico, then dips south to exclude much of the central desert of highland Mexico, meeting the Pacific coast opposite the tip of Baja (Lower) California. On the southeast, the boundary extends from northwestern Honduras on the Caribbean across to the Pacific shore in El Salvador. Thus, about half of Mexico, all of Guatemala and Belize, and parts of Honduras and El Salvador are included in Mesoamerica.

Geographically and culturally, Mesoamerica consists of two strongly contrasted regions: highland and lowland. The Mexican highlands are formed mainly by the two Sierra Madre ranges that sweep down on the east and west. Lying athwart them is a volcanic cordillera stretching from the Atlantic to the Pacific. The high valleys and landlocked basins of Mexico were important centres of pre-Spanish civilization. In the southeastern part of Mesoamerica lie the partly volcanic Chiapas–Guatemala highlands. The lowlands are primarily coastal. Particularly important was the littoral plain extending south along the Gulf of Mexico, expanding to include the Petén-Yucatán Peninsula, homeland of the Mayan peoples.

Agriculture in Mesoamerica was advanced and complex. A great many crops were planted, of which corn, beans, and squashes were among the most important. In the highlands, hoe cultivation of more or less permanent fields was the rule, with such intensive forms of agriculture as irrigation and *chinampas* (the so-called floating gardens reclaimed from lakes or ponds) practiced in some regions. In contrast, lowland agriculture was frequently of the shifting variety. A patch of jungle was first selected, felled and burned toward the end of the dry season, and then planted with a digging stick in time for the first rains. After a few years of planting, the field was abandoned to the forest, as competition from weeds and declining soil fertility resulted in diminishing yields.

There is good evidence, however, that the slash-and-burn system of cultivation was often supplemented by "raised-field" cultivation in the lowlands. These artificially constructed earthen hillocks built in shallow lakes or marshy areas were not unlike the *chinampas* of the Mexican highlands. In addition, terraces were constructed and employed for farming in some lowland regions. Nevertheless, the demographic potential for agriculture was probably always greater in the highlands than it was in the lowlands, and this was demonstrated in the more extensive urban developments in the former area.

The extreme diversity of the Mesoamerican environment produced what has been called symbiosis among its subregions. Interregional exchange of agricultural products, luxury items, and other commodities led to the development of large and well-regulated markets in which cacao beans were used for money. It may have also led to large-scale political unity and even to states and empires. High agricultural productivity resulted in a nonfarming class of artisans who were responsible for an advanced stone architecture, featuring the construction of stepped pyramids, and for highly evolved styles of sculpture, pottery, and painting.

The Mesoamerican system of thought, recorded in folding-screen books of deerskin or bark paper, was perhaps of even greater importance in setting them off from other New World peoples. This system was ultimately based upon a calendar in which a ritual cycle of 260 (13 × 20) days intermeshed with a "vague year" of 365 days (18 × 20 days, plus five "nameless" days), producing a 52-year Calendar Round. Religious life was geared to this cycle, which is unique to them. The Mesoamerican pantheon was associated with the calendar and featured an old, dual creator god; a god of royal descent and warfare; a sun god and moon goddess; a rain god; a culture hero called the Feathered Serpent; and many other deities. Also characteristic was a layered system of 13 heavens and nine underworlds, each with its presiding god. Much of the system was under the control of a priesthood that also maintained an advanced knowledge of astronomy.

As many as 14 language families were found in Mesoamerica. Nahuatl, the official tongue of the Aztec empire, was the most important of these. Another large family is Mayan, with a number of mutually unintelligible languages, at least some of which were spoken by the inhabitants of the great Maya ceremonial centres. The other languages that played a great part in Mesoamerican civilization were Mixtec and Zapotec, both of which had large, powerful kingdoms at the time of the Spanish conquest. Still a linguistic puzzle are such languages as Tarascan, mother tongue of an "empire" in western Mexico that successfully resisted Aztec encroachments. It has no sure relatives, although some linguistic authorities have linked it with the Quechua language of distant Peru.

EARLY HUNTERS
(TO 6500 BC)

The time of the first peopling of Mesoamerica remains a puzzle, as it does for that of the New World in general. It is widely accepted that groups of peoples entered the hemisphere from northeastern Siberia, perhaps by a land bridge that then existed, at some time in the Late Pleistocene, or Ice Age. There is abundant evidence that, by 11,000 BC, hunting peoples had occupied most of the New World south of the glacial ice cap covering northern North America. These peoples hunted such large grazing mammals as mammoth, mastodon, horse, and camel, armed with spears to which were attached finely made, bifacially chipped points of stone. Finds in Mesoamerica, however, confirm the existence of a "prebifacial-point horizon," a stage known to have existed elsewhere in the Americas, and suggest that it is of very great age. In 1967 archaeologists working at the site of Tlapacoya, southeast of Mexico City, uncovered a well-made blade of obsidian associated with a radiocarbon date of about 21,000 BC. Near Puebla, Mexico, excavations in the Valsequillo region revealed cultural remains of human groups that were hunting mammoth and other extinct animals, along with unifacially worked points, scrapers, perforators, burins, and knives. A date of about 21,800 BC has been suggested for the Valsequillo finds.

More substantial information on Late Pleistocene occupations of Mesoamerica comes from excavations near Tepexpan, northeast of Mexico City. The excavated skeletons of two mammoths showed that these beasts had been killed with spears fitted with lancelike stone points and butchered on the spot. A possible date of about 8000 BC has been suggested for the two mammoth kills. In the same geologic layer as the slaughtered mammoths was found a human skeleton; this Tepexpan "man" has been shown to be female and rather a typical American Indian of modern form. While the association with the mammoths was first questioned, fluorine tests have proved them to be contemporary.

A casting made from the remains of a human female found in Tepexpan, near Mexico City. An initial mistake in gender attribution led to the remains being erroneously labeled "Tepexpan man." Francis Miller/Time & Life Pictures/Getty Images

The environment of these earliest Mesoamericans was quite different from that existing today, for volcanoes were then extremely active, covering thousands of square miles with ashes. Temperatures were substantially lower, and local glaciers formed on the highest peaks. Conditions were ideal for the large herds of grazing mammals that roamed Mesoamerica, especially in the highland valleys, much of which consisted of cool, wet grasslands not unlike the plains of the northern United States. All of this changed around 7000 BC, when worldwide temperatures rose and the great ice sheets of northern latitudes began their final retreat. This brought to an end the successful hunting way of life that had been followed by Mesoamericans, although man probably also played a role in bringing about the extinction of the large game animals.

INCIPIENT AGRICULTURE (6500–1500 BC)

The most crucial event in the prehistory of Mesoamerica was man's capture of the food energy contained in plants. This process centred on three plants: Indian corn (maize), beans, and squashes. Since about 90 percent of all food calories in the diet of Mesoamericans eventually came from corn, archaeologists for a long time have sought the origins of this plant—which has no wild forms existing today—in order to throw light on the agricultural basis of Mesoamerican civilization.

The search for Mesoamerican agricultural origins has been carried forward most successfully through excavations in dry caves and rock shelters in the modern southern Mexican states of Puebla and Oaxaca. Sequences from these archaeological sites show a gradual transition from the Early Hunting to the Incipient Cultivation periods. At the Guila Naquitz cave, in Oaxaca, there are indications that the transition began as early as 8900 BC. Finds from caves in the Tehuacán valley of Puebla, however, offer more substantial evidence of the beginnings of plant domestication at a somewhat later time. There, the preservation of plant remains is remarkably good, and from these it is evident that shortly after 6500 BC the inhabitants of the valley were selecting and planting seeds of chili peppers, cotton, and one kind of squash. Most important, between 5000 and 3500 BC they were beginning to plant mutant forms of corn that already were showing signs of the husks characteristic of domestic corn.

One of the problems complicating this question of the beginnings of early corn cultivation is related to a debate between paleobotanists on wild versus domesticated strains. One school of thought holds that the domesticated races of the plant developed from a wild ancestor. The other opinion is that there was never such a thing as wild corn, that instead corn (*Zea mays*) developed from a related grass, teosinte (*Zea mexicana* or *Euchlaena mexicana*). In any event, by 5000 BC corn was present and being used as a food, and between 2,000 and 3,000 years after that it had developed rapidly as a food plant. It has been estimated that there is more energy present in a single kernel of some modern races than there was in an ear of this ancient Tehuacán corn. Possibly some of this was popped, but a new element in food preparation is seen in the *metates* (querns) and *manos* (handstones) that were used to grind the corn into meal or dough.

Beans appeared after 3500 BC, along with a much improved race of corn. This enormous increase in the amount of plant food available was accompanied by a remarkable shift in settlement pattern. In place of the temporary hunting camps and rock shelters, which were occupied only seasonally by small bands, semipermanent villages of pit houses were constructed on the valley floor. Increasing sedentariness is also to be seen in the remarkable bowls and globular jars painstakingly pecked from stone, for pottery was as yet unknown in Mesoamerica.

In the centuries between 3500 and 1500 BC, plant domestication began in what had been hunting-gathering contexts, as on the Pacific coast of Chiapas and on the Veracruz Gulf coast and in some lacustrine settings in the Valley of Mexico. It seems probable that early domesticated plants from such places as the Tehuacán valley were carried to these new environmental niches. In many cases, this shift of habitat resulted in genetic improvements in the food plants.

Pottery, which is a good index to the degree of permanence of a settlement (because of its fragility it is difficult to transport), was made in the Tehuacán valley by 2300 BC. Fired clay vessels were made as early as 4000 BC in Ecuador and Colombia, and it is probable that the idea of their manufacture gradually diffused north to the increasingly sedentary peoples of Mesoamerica.

The picture, then, is one of man's growing control over his environment through the domestication of plants. Animals played a very minor role in this process, with only the dog being surely domesticated before 1500 BC. At any rate, by 1500 BC the stage was set for the adoption of a fully settled life, with many of the sedentary arts already present. The final step was taken only when native agriculture in certain especially favoured subregions became sufficiently effective to allow year-round settlement of villages.

EARLY FORMATIVE PERIOD (1500–900 BC)

It is fairly clear that the Mexican highlands were far too dry during the much warmer interval that prevailed from 5000 to 1500 BC for agriculture to supply more than half of a given population's energy needs. This was not the case along the alluvial lowlands of southern Mesoamerica, and it is no accident that the best evidence for the earliest permanent villages in

TEOSINTE

Teosinte is a tall, stout, solitary annual or spreading perennial grass of the family Poaceae, native to Mexico, Guatemala, Honduras, and Nicaragua. There are four species of teosinte. Corn, or maize (Z. mays mays), is a worldwide cultigen that probably was derived from the "Balsas" teosinte (Z. mays parviglumis) of southern Mexico in pre-Columbian times more than 5,000 years ago.

Annual teosintes strongly resemble subspecies mays in their large terminal, plumelike, male inflorescences (the tassels). However, they differ strongly in their small, 5–12-seeded female ears, which are hidden in clusters in the leaf axils. Nonetheless, both the perennial and annual species readily cross with corn, and in the 1980s attempts were made to produce a perennial variety of corn. Teosintes have a high resistance to both viral and fungal diseases of corn as well as corn insect pests.

Mesoamerica comes from the Pacific littoral of Chiapas (Mexico) and Guatemala, although comparable settlements also have been reported from both the Maya lowlands (Belize) and the Veracruz Gulf coast.

EARLY VILLAGE LIFE

The Barra (c. 1800–1500 BC), Ocós (1500–1200 BC), and Cuadros (1100–900 BC) phases of the Pacific coasts of Chiapas and Guatemala are good examples of early village cultures. The Barra phase appears to have been transitional from earlier preagricultural phases and may

not have been primarily dependent upon corn farming, but people of the Ocós and Cuadros phases raised a small-eared corn known as *nal-tel*, which was ground on metates and manos and cooked in globular jars. From the rich lagoons and estuaries in this area, the villagers obtained shellfish, crabs, fish, and turtles. Their villages were small, with perhaps 10 to 12 thatched-roof houses arranged haphazardly.

Ocós pottery is highly developed technically and artistically. Something of the mental life of the times may be seen in the tiny, handmade clay figurines produced by the Ocós villagers. These, as in

Formative cultures generally throughout Mesoamerica, represent nude females and may have had something to do with a fertility cult. The idea of the temple-pyramid may well have taken root by that time, for one Ocós site has produced an earthen mound about 26 feet (8 metres) high that must have supported a perishable building. The implication of the site is that, with increasing prosperity, some differentiation of a ruling class had taken place, for among the later Mesoamericans the ultimate function of a pyramid was as a final resting place for a great leader.

Eventually, effective village farming with nucleated settlements occupied throughout the year appeared in the highlands. But perhaps from the very beginning of Formative life there were different cultural responses directed toward both kinds of environment. In the highlands, divided into a number of mutually contrasting environments no one of which could have provided sufficient resources for the subsistence of a single settlement, villages were presumably linked to each other symbiotically. In the lowlands, particularly in the littoral, one especially favourable environment, such as the lagoon–estuary system, may have been so rich in resources that villages within it would have been entirely self-sufficient. In effect, the former would have resulted in a cultural integration based upon trade, while the latter would have been integrated, if at all, by a unity of likeness. The two kinds of civilization that eventually arose in each region—the highlands definitely urban, the lowlands less so—reflect the same contrast.

Early Religious Life

Early religious phenomena can only be deduced from archaeological remains. Numerous clay figurines found in tombs afford little evidence of religious beliefs during the agricultural Pre-Classic periods of Zacatenco and Ticomán (roughly 1500 to the 1st century BC). It is possible, however, that terra-cotta statuettes of women were meant to represent an agricultural deity, a goddess of the crops. Two-headed figurines found at Tlatilco, a site of the late Pre-Classic, may portray a supernatural being. Clay idols of a fire god in the form of an old man with an incense burner on his back date from the same period.

The first stone monument on the Mexican plateau is the pyramid of Cuicuilco, near Mexico City. In fact, it is rather a truncated cone, with a stone core; the rest is made of sun-dried brick with a stone facing. It shows the main features of the Mexican pyramids as they were developed in later times. It was doubtless a religious monument, crowned by a temple built on the terminal platform and surrounded with tombs. The building of such a structure obviously required a protracted and organized effort under the command of the priests.

The final phase of the Pre-Classic cultures of the central highland forms a transition from the village to the city,

The pyramid at Cuicuilco. A forerunner of Mesoamerican pyramids built through the ages, Cuicuilco is a rather squat structure built of sun-dried brick and stone. Omar Torres/AFP/ Getty Images

from rural to urban life. This was a far-reaching social and intellectual revolution, bringing about new religious ideas together with new art forms and theocratic regimes. It is significant that Olmec statuettes have been found at Tlatilco with late Pre-Classic material.

THE RISE OF OLMEC CIVILIZATION

It was once assumed that the Formative stage was characterized only by simple farming villages. It is now realized, however, that coexisting with these peasantlike cultures was a great civilization, the Olmec, that had arisen in the humid lowlands of southern Veracruz and Tabasco, in Mexico.

The Olmec were perhaps the greatest sculptors of ancient Mesoamerica. Whether carving tiny jade figures or gigantic basalt monuments, they worked with a great artistry that led a number of archaeologists to doubt their considerable antiquity, although radiocarbon dates from the type site of La Venta showed that Olmec civilization was indeed Formative, its beginning dating to at least 1,000 years before the advent of Maya civilization.

San Lorenzo is now established as the oldest known Olmec centre. In fact, excavation has shown it to have taken on the appearance of an Olmec site by 1150 BC and to have been destroyed, perhaps by invaders, around 900 BC. Thus, the Olmec achieved considerable cultural heights within the Early Formative, at a time when the rest of Mesoamerica was at best on a Neolithic level. The reasons for its precocious rise must have had something to do with its abundant rainfall and the rich alluvial soil deposited along the broad, natural levees that flank the waterways of the southern Gulf coast. Thus, the ecological potential for corn farmers in this counterpart of Mesopotamia's Fertile Crescent was exceptionally high. The levee lands, however, were not limitless, and increasingly dense populations must inevitably have led to competition for their control. Out of such conflicts would have crystallized a dominant landowning class, perhaps a group of well-armed lineages. It was this elite that created the Olmec civilization of San Lorenzo.

In appearance, the San Lorenzo site is a compact plateau rising about 160 feet (49 metres) above the surrounding plains. Cutting into it are deep ravines that were once thought to be natural but that are now known to be man-made, formed by the construction of long ridges that jut out from the plateau on the northwest, west, and south sides. Excavations have proved that at least the top 25 to 35 feet (8 to 11 metres) of the site was built by human labour. There are about 200 small mounds on the surface of the site, each of which once supported a dwelling house of pole and thatch, which indicates that it was both a ceremonial centre, with political and religious functions, and a minuscule town.

San Lorenzo is most noted for its extraordinary stone monuments. Many of these, perhaps most, were deliberately smashed or otherwise mutilated about 900 BC and buried in long lines within the ridges and elsewhere at the site. The monuments weighed as much as 44 tons (40 metric tons) and were carved from basalt from the Cerro Cintepec, a volcanic flow in the Tuxtla Mountains about 50 air miles (80 km) to the northwest. It is believed that the stones were somehow dragged down to the nearest navigable stream and from there transported on rafts up the Coatzacoalcos River to the San Lorenzo area. The amount of labour involved must have been enormous and so would have the social controls necessary to see the job through to its completion.

The central theme of the Olmec religion was a pantheon of deities; each of which usually was a hybrid between jaguar and human infant, often crying or snarling with open mouth. This "were-jaguar" is the hallmark of Olmec art, and it was the unity of objects in this style that first suggested to scholars that they

THE OLMEC COLOSSAL HEADS

Olmec colossal basalt head, c. 1st century BC; in Parque La Venta, Tabasco, Mex. Height 8 feet (2.4 metres). George Holton/Photo Researchers

Most striking of the Olmec sculptures are the "colossal heads," human portraits on a stupendous scale. The first of these were found by the American anthropologist Matthew W. Stirling (1896–1975) at La Venta. Several of these are now known from San Lorenzo, the largest of which is nine feet (3 metres) high. The visages of these heads are flat-faced, with thickened lips and staring eyes. Their rounded facial forms exhibit broad features, heavy-lidded eyes, and a down-turned mouth. Each one wears headgear resembling an early form of football helmet, and some have suggested that these "helmets" were in fact protective coverings in a rubber-ball game that is known from Olmec figurines to have been played at San Lorenzo. Later interpretations suggest that these heads might represent leaders of the Olmec people.

were dealing with a new and previously unknown civilization. There is actually a whole spectrum of such were-jaguar forms in Olmec art, ranging from the almost purely feline to the human in which only a trace of jaguar can be seen.

These Olmec monuments were generally carved in the round with great technical prowess, even though the only methods available were pounding and pecking with stone tools. Considerable artistry can also be seen in the pottery figurines of San Lorenzo, which depict nude and sexless individuals with were-jaguar traits.

Exotic raw materials brought into San Lorenzo from distant regions suggest that the early Olmec controlled a large trading network over much of Mesoamerica. Obsidian, used for blades, flakes, and dart points, was imported from highland Mexico and Guatemala. Most items were obviously for the luxury trade, such as iron ore for mirrors and various fine stones like serpentine employed in the lapidary industry. One material that is conspicuously absent, however, is jade, which does not appear in Olmec sites until after 900 BC and the fall of San Lorenzo.

There is evidence that the Olmec sent groups from their Gulf coast "heartland" into the Mesoamerican highlands toward the end of the Early Formative, in all likelihood to guarantee that goods bound for San Lorenzo would reach their destination. San Lorenzo-type Olmec ceramics and figurines have been found in burials at several sites in the Valley of Mexico, such as Tlapacoya, and in the state of Morelos. The Olmec involvement with the rest of Mesoamerica continued into the Middle Formative and probably reached its peak at that time.

San Lorenzo is not the only Olmec centre known for the Early Formative. Laguna de los Cerros, just south of the Cerro Cintepec in Veracruz, appears to have been a large Olmec site with outstanding sculptures. La Venta, just east of the Tabasco border, was another contemporary site, but it reached its height after San Lorenzo had gone into decline.

MIDDLE FORMATIVE PERIOD (900–300 BC)

Once ceramics had been adopted in Mesoamerica, techniques of manufacture and styles of shape and decoration tended to spread rapidly and widely across many cultural frontiers. These rapid diffusions, called horizons, enable archaeologists to link different cultures on the same time level. Good horizon markers for the Early Formative are colour zones of red pigment set off by incised lines; complex methods of rocker stamping (a mode of impressing the wet clay with the edge of a stick or shell); the *tecomate*, or globular, neckless jar; and Olmec excised pottery. The beginning of the Middle Formative over much of Mesoamerica is marked by the diffusion of a very hard, white pottery, decorated with incised lines, and by solid pottery figurines with large, staring eyes formed by a punch. The people who replaced and probably overthrew the Olmec of San Lorenzo about 900 BC had such pottery and figurines, the ultimate origins of which are still a puzzle.

During the Middle Formative, cultural regionalism increased, although the Olmec presence can be widely detected. The transition to fully settled life had taken place everywhere, and burgeoning populations occupied hamlets, villages, and perhaps even small towns throughout Mesoamerica, both highland and lowland.

OLMEC CIVILIZATION AT LA VENTA

La Venta was located on an almost inaccessible island, surrounded at that time by the Tonalá River; the river now divides the states of Veracruz and Tabasco. As San Lorenzo's fortunes fell, La Venta's rose, and between 800 and 400 BC it was the most important site in Mesoamerica.

At the centre of La Venta is a 100-foot-high mound of earth and clay that may well house the tomb of a great Olmec ruler. Immediately north of the Great Mound is a narrow north–south plaza flanked by a pair of long mounds. Beyond the plaza is a ceremonial enclosure surrounded by a "fence" made entirely of upright shafts of columnar basalt. A low, round mound on the north side of the ceremonial enclosure contained several tombs, one of which was surrounded and covered by basalt columns. In this tomb were found the bundled remains of two children, accompanied by magnificent ornaments of jade. Offerings were not only placed with the dead but were also deposited as caches in the site, especially along the north–south axis of the ceremonial centre.

Among the most beautiful objects manufactured by the Olmec were the concave mirrors of iron ore, which were pierced to be worn around the neck. These could throw pictures on a flat surface and could probably start fires on hot tinder. Olmec leaders at La Venta, whether they were kings or priests, undoubtedly used them to impress the populace with their seemingly supernatural powers. Olmec sculptors continued to produce the basalt monuments, including colossal heads and "altars," that have been found at La Venta. Significantly, an increasing number of monuments were carved in relief, and some of these were stelae (standing stone slabs) with rather elaborate scenes obviously based upon historical or contemporary events.

OLMEC COLONIZATION IN THE MIDDLE FORMATIVE

From the Middle Formative there are important Olmec sites located along what appears to have been a highland route to the west to obtain the luxury items that seemed to have been so desperately needed by the Olmec elite—e.g., jade, serpentine, iron ore for mirrors, cinnabar, and so forth. Olmec sites in Puebla, the Valley of Mexico, and Morelos are generally located at the ends of valleys near or on major passes; they were perhaps trading stations garrisoned by Olmec troops. The largest of these sites is Chalcatzingo, Morelos, a cult centre located among three denuded volcanic peaks rising from a plain. On a talus slope at the foot of the middle peak are huge boulders on which have been carved Olmec reliefs in La Venta style. The principal relief shows an Olmec woman, richly garbed, seated within the mouth of a cave; above her, cumulus clouds pour down rain.

Similar Olmec reliefs, usually narrative and often depicting warriors brandishing clubs, have been located on the Pacific plain of Chiapas (Mexico) and Guatemala. Since about 1960, spectacular Olmec cave paintings have been found in Guerrero, offering some idea of what the Olmec artists could do when they worked with a large spectrum of pigments and on flat surfaces.

Olmec culture or civilization did not spread eastward from its Veracruz-Tabasco centres into the Maya lowlands, but occasional Olmec artifacts have been found in Formative Maya contexts, such as at Seibal, in southern Petén, Guatemala. Maya Formative Period occupations, represented by settled farming villages and well-made ceramics, date to c. 1000 BC in the lowlands of Guatemala and Belize. It seems reasonably certain, however, that at this early date great ceremonial centres, comparable to those of Olmec San Lorenzo or La Venta, were never constructed in the Maya lowlands.

It was formerly thought that the Olmec worshiped only one god, a rain deity depicted as a were-jaguar, but study has shown that there were at least 10 distinct gods represented in Olmec art. Surely present were several important deities of the later, established Mesoamerican pantheon, such as the fire god, rain god, corn god, and Feathered Serpent. Other aspects of mental culture are less well-known; some Olmec jades and a monument from La Venta have non-calendrical hieroglyphs, but none of this writing has been deciphered.

To sum up the Olmec achievement, not only was this the first high culture in Mesoamerica—one that had certainly achieved political statehood—but either it or cultures influenced by it lie at the base of every other Mesoamerican civilization.

EARLY MONTE ALBÁN

Monte Albán is a prominent series of interconnected hills lying near Oaxaca, Mexico. One of these was completely leveled off in Middle Formative times to serve as the base for a site that was to become the Zapotec people's most important capital. Prior to that time, the Early Formative ancestral Zapotec had lived in scattered villages and at least one centre of some importance, San José Mogote. San José Mogote shows evidence of Olmec trade and contacts dating to the time of San Lorenzo.

At Monte Albán, during the earliest, or Monte Albán I, epoch of that site's history, a peculiar group of reliefs was carved on stone slabs and affixed to the front of a rubble-faced platform mound and around a contiguous court. The reliefs are usually called *danzantes*, a name derived from the notion that they represent human figures in dance postures. Actually, almost all of the *danzante* sculptures show Olmecoid men in strange, rubbery postures as though they were swimming in honey. From their open mouths and closed eyes, it is assumed that they are meant to represent dead persons. On many *danzantes* one or more unreadable hieroglyphs appear near the heads of the figures, most likely standing for the names of the sacrificed lords of groups beaten in combat by the Zapotec. Several slabs also bear calendrical notations, and it can be stated that the Middle Formative elite of Monte Albán were the first in Mesoamerica to develop writing and the calendar (at least in written form).

A dancer stands frozen in a stone relief at Monte Albán, near Oaxaca, Mex. Shutterstock.com

THE VALLEY OF MEXICO IN THE MIDDLE FORMATIVE

The cultures of central Mexico tended to lag behind those of southern Mexico in the development of political and religious complexity. The presence of Olmec figurines and ceramics in Early Formative burials in the Valley of Mexico has been noted, but the local communities of that time were of a modest village sort, as were those of the succeeding Middle Formative. On the western shores of the

great lake filling the Valley of Mexico, for instance, remains of several simple villages have been uncovered that must have been not unlike small settlements that can be found in the Mexican hinterland today. The people who lived at El Arbolillo and Zacatenco had simply terraced off village refuse to make platforms on which their pole-and-thatch houses were built. Metates and manos are plentiful. Pottery is relatively plain—featuring the abundant hard, white-slipped ware of the Middle Formative—and small female figurines are present by the thousands.

Subsistence was based upon corn farming and upon hunting. In some Middle Formative sites, however, such as Tlatilco, there is evidence of Olmec influence, as in the previous Early Formative Period. There are also indications that ceremonial pyramid construction began in the latter part of the Middle Formative at Cuicuilco, a site in the southern part of the valley, which was to become a major centre in the succeeding Late Formative Period.

THE MAYA IN THE MIDDLE FORMATIVE

In the Maya highlands, the key archaeological region has always been the broad, fertile Valley of Guatemala around present-day Guatemala City. The earliest occupation is known as the Arevalo phase, a village culture of the Early to Middle Formative. It was followed by Las Charcas, a Middle Formative culture known largely from the contents of

Architectural digs have revealed many Maya treasures, such as this sculpted urn.
Authenticated News/Hulton Archive/Getty Images

bottle-shaped pits found dug into the subsoil on the western edge of the modern city. Extremely fine ceramics have been excavated from them, including red-on-white bowls with animal figures, effigy vessels, three-footed cups, and peculiar three-pronged incense burners. Solid female figurines are also present.

The earliest Middle Formative cultures of the Maya lowlands are called, collectively, the Xe horizon. They apparently developed from antecedent Early Formative cultures of the Maya lowlands that have been discussed above. The problem of the origin of the Mayan-speaking people has not been solved. It may be that they were Olmec people who had been forced out of their homeland to the west by the collapse of San Lorenzo. There were already peoples in the Maya lowlands in Early Formative times, however, and if the early Maya were Olmec, they brought little of their Olmec culture with them. Another hypothesis is that the earliest Maya descended to their lowland homelands from the Guatemalan highlands.

In the Maya lowlands the Mamom cultures developed out of those of Xe times. Mamom shares many similarities with the highland Maya at Las Charcas: pottery is almost entirely monochrome—red, orange, black, and white—and figurines are female with the usual punched and appliquéd embellishments. Toward the end of the Middle Formative, or after about 600 BC, Mamom peoples began building small ceremonial centres and modest-sized pyramidal platforms.

LATE FORMATIVE PERIOD (300 BC–AD 100)

Probably the most significant features of the Late Formative are (1) the transformation of Olmec civilization in southeastern Mesoamerica into something approaching the earliest lowland Maya civilization and (2) the abrupt appearance, toward the end of the Late Formative, of fully urban culture at Teotihuacán in the Valley of Mexico. Most of the distinctive cultures that were to become the great Classic civilizations began to take shape at this time. There was no unifying force in the Late Formative comparable to the earlier Olmec; rather, regionalism and local cultural integration were the rule. There were, however, horizon traits, particularly in pottery, that were almost universal. Ceramics became elaborate in shape, often with composite or recurved outlines, hollow, bulbous feet, and flangelike protrusions encircling the vessel. The use of slips of a number of different colours as pottery decoration at times approached the elaborate polychromes of Classic times.

The idea of constructing temple-pyramids was probably also a general trait. It was a Mesoamerican custom to bury a dead person beneath the floor of his own house, which was often then abandoned by the bereaved. As an elite class of noble lineages became distinguished from the mass of the people, the simple house platforms serving as sepulchres might have become transformed into more imposing structures, ending in the huge pyramids of the Late Formative and Classic, which surely had funerary functions. The deceased leader or the gods from which he claimed descent, or both, would then have been worshiped in a "house of god" on the temple summit. These pyramids became the focal point of Mesoamerican ceremonial life, as well as the centres of settlement.

VALLEY OF MEXICO

The Cuicuilco-Ticomán culture succeeded the Middle Formative villages of the valley but retained many of their traits, such as the manufacture of solid handmade figurines. Of considerable interest is the type site of Cuicuilco, located on the southwestern edge of the valley. Lava from a nearby volcano covers all of Cuicuilco, including the lower part of the round "pyramid" for which it is best known. Ceramic analysis and radiocarbon dating have proved that the flow occurred at about the time of Christ. Rising up in four tiers, the Cuicuilco pyramid has a clay-and-rubble core faced with broken lava blocks. The summit was reached by ramps on two sides. Circular temples were traditionally dedicated in Mesoamerica to Quetzalcóatl, the Feathered Serpent, and he may have been the presiding deity of Cuicuilco.

In the Valley of Teotihuacán, a kind of side pocket on the northeastern margin of the Valley of Mexico, Cuicuilco-Ticomán culture eventually took on a remarkable outline, for there is evidence that by the beginning of the Christian Era

a great city had been planned. There is little doubt that by the Proto-Classic stage (AD 100–300) it had become the New World's first urban civilization.

VALLEY OF OAXACA

Occupation of the Monte Albán site continued uninterrupted, but ceramic evidence for Monte Albán II culture indicates that cultural influences from southeastern Mexico were reaching the Zapotec people. On the southern end of the site's main plaza is a remarkable stone structure called Building J, shaped like an arrow pointing southwest and honeycombed with galleries. Some believe it to have been an astronomical observatory. Incised slabs are fixed to its exterior. These include some older *danzantes* as well as depictions of Zapotec place glyphs from which are suspended the inverted heads of dead chiefs—surely again the vanquished enemies of Monte Albán. Dates are given in the 52-year Calendar Round, with coefficients for days and months expressed by bar-and-dot numerals, a system that is first known for Monte Albán I and that became characteristic of the Classic Maya. Throughout its long Formative and Classic occupation, the dominant ware of Monte Albán is a fine gray pottery, elaborated in Monte Albán II into the usual Late Formative shapes.

VERACRUZ AND CHIAPAS

La Venta suffered the fate of San Lorenzo, having been destroyed by violence around 400 BC. Olmec civilization subsequently disappeared or was transformed into one or more of the cultures of the southeastern lowlands.

One centre that retained a strong Olmec tradition, however, was Tres Zapotes, near the Tuxtla Mountains in the old Olmec "heartland." Its most famous monument, the fragmentary Stela C, is clearly epi-Olmec on the basis of a jaguar-monster mask carved in relief on its obverse. On the reverse is a column of numerals in the bar-and-dot system, which was read by its discoverer, Matthew W. Stirling, as a date in the Maya calendar corresponding to 31 BC. This is more than a century earlier than any known dated inscription from the Maya area itself. Thus, it is highly probable that this calendrical system, formerly thought to be a Maya invention, was developed in the Late Formative by epi-Olmec peoples living outside the Maya area proper.

IZAPAN CIVILIZATION

Izapa, type site of the Izapan civilization, is a huge temple centre near modern Tapachula, Chiapas, on the hot Pacific coast plain. Its approximately 80 pyramidal mounds were built from earth and clay faced with river boulders. A large number of carved stone stelae have been found at Izapa, almost all of which date to the Late Formative and Proto-Classic. Typically, in front of each stela is a round altar, often crudely shaped like a toad.

These stelae are of extraordinary interest, for they contain a wealth of information on Late Formative religious concepts prevalent on the border of the Maya area. Izapan stelae are carved in relief with narrative scenes derived from mythology and legend; among the depictions are warfare and decapitation, ceremonies connected with the sacred world tree, and meetings of what seem to be tribal elders. Many deities are shown, each of which seems derived from an Olmec prototype.

Sites with Izapan-style sculpture are distributed in a broad arc extending from Tres Zapotes in the former Olmec region, across the Isthmus of Tehuantepec into coastal Chiapas and Guatemala, and up into the Guatemalan highlands. Izapan civilization is clearly the intermediary between Olmec and Classic Maya in time and in cultural content, for the following early Maya traits are foreshadowed by it: (1) the stela–altar complex, (2) long-lipped deities, (3) hieroglyphic writing and Long Count dates on some monuments, (4) such iconographic elements as a U-shaped motif, and (5) a cluttered, baroque, and painterly relief style that emphasizes narrative. An important site pertaining to this Izapan culture is Abaj Takalik, on the Pacific slopes of Guatemala, to the east of Izapa. Three sculptural styles are represented there: Olmec or Olmecoid, Izapan, and Classic Maya. Among the latter is one stela with a date read as AD 126, earlier than any monuments discovered in the Maya lowlands.

Perhaps it was not Izapa itself but the great site of Kaminaljuyú, on the western

Izapan stelae frequently are carved in such a way that they tell a story beyond what these artifacts reveal about Mesoamerican life in general. Mexican School/Chiapas State, Mexico/ Jean-Pierre Courau/The Bridgeman Art Library

edge of Guatemala City, that transmitted the torch of Izapan civilization to the lowland Maya. This centre once consisted of more than 200 earth and clay mounds, most of which have been destroyed. The major occupation is ascribed to the Miraflores phase, the Late Formative culture of the Valley of Guatemala. Some of these huge Miraflores mounds contained log tombs of incredible richness. In one, the deceased lord was accompanied by sacrificed followers or captives. As many as 340 objects were placed with him, including jade mosaic masks, jade ear spools and necklaces, bowls of chlorite schist, and pottery vessels of great beauty. Also present in the tombs are peculiar "mushroom stones," which may actually have been used in rites connected with hallucinogenic mushrooms.

THE EARLIEST MAYA CIVILIZATION OF THE LOWLANDS

By the Late Formative, the lowland Maya had begun to shape a civilization that was to become the greatest in the New World. The Petén-Yucatán Peninsula lacks many raw materials and has a relatively low agricultural potential. But what it does have in limitless quantities is readily quarried limestone for building purposes and flint for stonework. Cement and plaster could easily be produced by burning limestone or shells.

The heart of the Maya civilization was always northern Petén, in Guatemala, where the oldest dated Maya stelae are found, although this presents something of a problem in cultural-historical interpretation, since the earliest prototypes for these stelae have been found in Pacific-littoral and highland Guatemala. The Late Formative culture of Petén is called Chicanel, evidence of which has been found at many Maya centres. Chicanel pottery includes dishes with wide-everted and grooved rims, bowls with composite silhouette, and vessels resembling ice buckets. Figurines are curiously absent.

Architecture was already quite advanced and had taken a form peculiar to the Maya. Temple platforms were built by facing a cemented-rubble core with thick layers of plaster. At the site of Uaxactún, Structure E-VII-sub affords a good idea of a Chicanel temple-platform. It is a four-sided, stucco-covered, stepped pyramid with pairs of stylized god masks flanking stairways on each side. On its summit was a thatched-roof temple. At Tikal, the giant among Maya ceremonial centres, the so-called Acropolis was begun in Chicanel times, and there was a great use of white-stuccoed platforms and stairways, with flanking polychromed masks as at Uaxactún.

Most important, there is evidence from Tikal that the Maya architects were already building masonry superstructures with the corbel vault principle—i.e., with archlike structures the sides of which extend progressively inward until they meet at the top. The large sizes of Chicanel populations and the degree of political centralization that existed by this time are further attested to by the discovery in the

WORLD TREE

A widespread motif in many myths and folktales among various preliterate peoples, especially in Asia, Australia, and North America, is the concept of the world tree or cosmic tree, which is the centre of the world. (Some may recognize this concept in filmmaker James Cameron's Avatar [2009], in which an enormous tree is the centre of life among the native Pandorans, the Na'vi.) The world tree is the means by which those peoples understand the human and profane condition in relation to the divine and sacred realm. Two main forms are known, and both employ the notion of the world tree as centre. In the one, the tree is the vertical centre binding together heaven and earth. In the other, the tree is the source of life at the horizontal centre of the earth. Adopting biblical terminology, the former may be called the tree of knowledge; the latter, the tree of life.

In the vertical, tree-of-knowledge tradition, the tree extends between earth and heaven. It is the vital connection between the world of the gods and the human world. Oracles and judgments or other prophetic activities are performed at its base.

In the horizontal, tree-of-life tradition, the tree is planted at the centre of the world and is protected by supernatural guardians. It is the source of terrestrial fertility and life. Human life is descended from it; its fruit confers everlasting life; and if it were cut down, all fecundity would cease. The tree of life occurs most commonly in quest romances in which the hero seeks the tree and must overcome a variety of obstacles on his way.

20th century of the huge site of El Mirador, in the extreme northern part of Petén. The mass of El Mirador construction dwarfs even that of Tikal, although El Mirador was only substantially occupied through the Chicanel phase.

Chicanel-like civilization is also known in Yucatán, where some temple pyramids of enormous size are datable to the Late Formative. An outstanding site is the cave of Loltún in Yucatán, where a relief figure of a standing leader in pure Izapan style is accompanied by a number of unreadable hieroglyphs as well as a notation in the 260-day count.

This inscription raises the question of writing and the calendar among the lowland Maya in the Late Formative. In the early 21st century archaeologists discovered Maya hieroglyphs dating from as early as *c.* 300 BC at the site of San Bartolo in northeastern Guatemala. The finding suggests that several important intellectual innovations considered to be typically Mayan were developed beyond the Maya area proper and appeared there before the close of the Formative. Izapan civilization nevertheless appears to have played a crucial role in this evolutionary process.

CHAPTER 2

THE MAYA: CLASSIC PERIOD

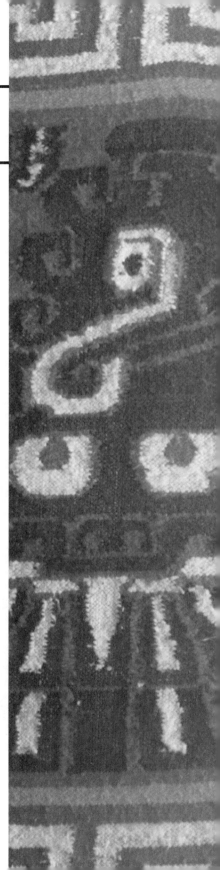

In the study of the Classic stage, there has been a strong bias in favour of the Maya. This is not surprising in view of the fact that the Maya have been studied far longer than any other people in Mesoamerica. But the concept of a "Classic" period is a case of the Maya tail wagging the Mesoamerican dog, since the usual span given to that stage—AD 250–900—is the period during which the Maya were erecting dated stone monuments. This brackets the Maya apogee, but for most areas of non-Maya Mesoamerica only the first half of the period may be accurately called a "golden age." While the famous and yet mysterious Maya collapse took place at about AD 900, in many other regions this downfall occurred almost three centuries earlier.

EARLY CLASSIC PERIOD (AD 100–600)

Qualitatively, there is little to differentiate the Classic from the Late Formative that preceded it. Various tendencies that were crystallizing in the last centuries before the Christian Era reached fulfillment in the Classic. Two cultures stand out beyond all others. One is that of Teotihuacán, which during the Early Classic played a role in Mesoamerica similar to that which Olmec had performed in the Early Formative. The second is the lowland Maya civilization, which during its six centuries of almost unbroken evolution in the humid forests reached cultural heights never achieved before or since by New World natives. The contrast between the two— one urban and expansionist, the other less urban and non-expansionist—exemplifies well the cultural results of the ecological possibilities offered by highland and lowland Mesoamerica.

TEOTIHUACÁN

Teotihuacán, which was located in the Valley of Teotihuacán, a pocketlike extension of the Valley of Mexico on its northeastern side, was probably the largest city of the New World before the arrival of the Spaniards. At its height, toward the close of the 6th century AD, it covered about eight square miles (13 square km) and may have housed more than 150,000 inhabitants. The city was divided into quarters by two great avenues that crosscut each other at right angles, and the entire city was laid out on a grid plan oriented to these avenues. The Avenue of the Dead, the main north–south artery of the city, is aligned to a point 16° east of true north, which may have had astrological meaning.

The Maya built the Pyramid of the Sun, a prominent feature of the landscape in Teotihuacán, Mex. Archive Photos/Getty Images

Because irrigation plays some part in the present-day agricultural economy of the Valley of Teotihuacán, it has been suggested that the Early Classic city also was based upon this subsistence system. It is almost inconceivable, however, that a city of such proportions could have relied upon the food production of its own valley or even upon the Valley of Mexico, whether irrigated or not.

Planning and construction of Teotihuacán began, according to radiocarbon dates, about the beginning of the Christian Era, in the Tzacualli phase. At this time, the major avenues were laid out and construction of the major ceremonial structures along the Avenue of the Dead began. Figurines and potsherds extracted from fill inside the 200-foot-high Pyramid of the Sun, the most prominent feature of Teotihuacán, prove that this was erected by the end of the Tzacualli phase. The pyramid rises in four great stages, but there is a fifth and much smaller stage between the third and fourth. An impressive stairway rises dramatically on its west side, facing the Avenue of the Dead. Reexamination suggests the presence of a huge tomb at its base, but this has never been excavated.

On the northern end of the Avenue of the Dead is the Pyramid of the Moon, very similar to that of the Sun, but with an additional platform-temple jutting out on the south. This exhibits the *talud-tablero* architectural motif that is typical of Teotihuacán culture; on each body or tier of a stepped pyramid is a rectangular frontal panel (*tablero*), supported by a sloping batter (*talud*). The *tablero* is surrounded by a kind of projecting frame, and the recessed portion of the panel usually bears a polychrome mural applied to the stuccoed surface.

Near the exact centre of the city and just east of the Avenue of the Dead is the Ciudadela ("Citadel"), a kind of sunken court surrounded on all four sides by platforms supporting temples. In the middle of the sunken plaza is the so-called Temple of Quetzalcóatl, which is dated to the second phase of Teotihuacán, Miccaotli. Along the balustrades of its frontal stairway and undulating along the *talud-tablero* bodies of each stage of this stepped pyramid are sculptured representations of Quetzalcóatl, the Feathered Serpent. Alternating with the Feathered Serpents on the *tableros* are heads of another monster that can be identified with the Fire Serpent—bearer of the Sun on its diurnal journey across the sky.

On either side of the Avenue of the Dead are residential palace compounds (probably occupied by noble families), which also conform to the Teotihuacán master plan. Each is a square, 200 feet (61 metres) per side, and is surrounded by a wall. The pedestrian would have seen only the high walls facing the streets, pierced by inconspicuous doors. Within the compounds, however, luxury was the rule. Roofs were flat, constructed of large cedar beams overlaid by brush and mortar. Interior walls were plastered and magnificently painted with ritual processions of gods and various mythological narratives. Interconnected apartments were arranged around a large, central, open-air court.

These dwellings were the residences of Teotihuacán's elite. Toward the periphery of Teotihuacán, however, the social situation may have been quite different. One excavation on the eastern side of the city disclosed a mazelike complex of much tinier and shoddier apartments that recall the poorer sections of Middle Eastern cities. It may be guessed that there lay the crowded dwellings of the artisans and other labourers who made the city what it was. There is also evidence that certain peripheral sections were reserved for foreigners.

Teotihuacán must have been the major manufacturing centre of the Early Classic, for the products of its craftsmen were spread over much of Mesoamerica. The pottery, particularly during the Xolalpan phase, which represents the culmination of Teotihuacán as a city and empire, is highly distinctive. The hallmark of the city is the cylindrical vessel with three slab legs and cover, often stuccoed and then painted with scenes almost identical to those on the walls of buildings. There are also vessels shaped like modern flower vases and cream pitchers. Thin Orange ware is a special ceramic type produced to Teotihuacán specifications, perhaps in southern Veracruz, and exported by its own traders. Figurines were produced by the tens of thousands in pottery molds.

Among its many commercial specializations, obsidian was probably preeminent, for the Teotihuacanos had gained control of the mines of green obsidian above the present-day city of Pachuca, in Hidalgo. They also had a local but poorer quality source. Millions of obsidian blades, as well as knives, dart points, and scrapers, were turned out by Teotihuacán workshops for export.

The name Teotihuacán meant "City of the Gods" (or, "Where Men Became Gods") in Aztec times, and although the city had been largely deserted since its decline, the Aztec royal house made annual pilgrimages to the site. Teotihuacán culture exerted a profound influence on all contemporary and later Mesoamerican cultures. Many Aztec gods, such as Tlaloc, his consort Chalchiuhtlicue, and Quetzalcóatl, were worshiped by the Teotihuacanos. Like the Aztec, the Teotihuacanos generally cremated their dead. In fact, there are so many congruences between Teotihuacán practices and those of the later Toltec and Aztec that some authorities believe them to have been speakers of Nahuatl language and the precursors of those people. Some linguistic authorities, however, believe that the Teotihuacanos spoke a Totonac language, similar to what was spoken by the inhabitants of central Veracruz. It is not known whether the people of the city, like the Maya, were literate.

Teotihuacán was the greatest city of Mesoamerica, indeed, of all pre-Columbian America. Authorities are divided as to whether it was the capital of a great political empire. Some believe that Teotihuacán's expansion was carried by

QUETZALCÓATL

Aztec round dance for Quetzalcóatl and Xolotl (a dog-headed god who is Quetzalcóatl's companion), detail from a facsimile Codex Borbonicus (folio 26), c. 1520; original in the Chamber of Deputies, Paris. Courtesy of the Newberry Library, Chicago

One of the major deities of the ancient Mesoamerican pantheon, Quetzalcóatl is the Feathered Serpent. His name is from Nahuatl quetzalli, "tail feather of the quetzal bird [Pharomachrus mocinno]," and coatl, "snake." Representations of a feathered snake occur as early as the Teotihuacán civilization (3rd to 8th century AD) on the central plateau. At that time, Quetzalcóatl seems to have been conceived as a vegetation god—an earth and water deity closely associated with the rain god Tlaloc.

With the immigration of Nahua-speaking tribes from the north, Quetzalcóatl's cult underwent drastic changes. The subsequent Toltec culture (9th through 12th centuries), centred at the city of Tula, emphasized war and human sacrifice linked with the worship of heavenly bodies. Quetzalcóatl became the god of the morning and evening star, and his temple was the centre of ceremonial life in Tula.

In Aztec times (14th through 16th centuries) Quetzalcóatl was revered as the patron of priests, the inventor of the calendar and of books, and the protector of goldsmiths and other craftsmen; he was also identified with the planet Venus. As the morning and evening star, Quetzalcóatl was the symbol of death and resurrection. With his companion Xolotl, a dog-headed god, he was said to have descended to the underground hell of Mictlan to gather the bones of the ancient dead. Those bones he anointed with his own blood, giving birth to the men who inhabit the present universe.

One important body of myths describes Quetzalcóatl as the priest-king of Tula, the capital of the Toltecs. He never offered human victims, only snakes, birds, and butterflies. But the god of the night sky, Tezcatlipoca, expelled him from Tula by performing feats of black magic. Quetzalcóatl wandered down to the coast of the "divine water" (the Atlantic Ocean) and then immolated himself on a pyre, emerging as the planet Venus. According to another version, he embarked upon a raft made of snakes and disappeared beyond the eastern horizon.

force of arms, while others believe its power to have been largely economic and religious. In either case, at its height in the 6th century Teotihuacán was the greatest civilization in Mesoamerica, with an influence that far outstripped that of the later Aztec empire. For the archaeologist, the universal spread of Teotihuacán ceramic and other traits constitutes an Early Classic horizon.

Cholula

The broad, fertile plains surrounding the colonial city of Puebla, to the southeast of the snowcapped volcanoes that border the Valley of Mexico, were from very ancient times an important centre of pre-Hispanic population. The modern traveler, approaching the city, sees to its west, in the distance, what looks like a sizable hill rising from the plain. This is actually the pyramid of Cholula, the largest single structure in Mexico before the Spanish conquest.

Archaeological exploration of the Cholula pyramid has shown that it was built from adobe in four great construction stages. In its final form, the pyramid measured 1,083 feet by 1,034 feet (330 metres by 315 metres) at the base and was about 82 feet (25 metres) high. By Late Post-Classic times the pyramid had been abandoned for so long that the Spaniards who subdued (and massacred) the residents of Cholula considered it a natural prominence. All four superimposed structures within the pyramid were carried out according to strict Teotihuacán architectural ideas. The earliest structure, for instance, has the usual *talud-tablero* motif, with stylized insectlike figures painted in black, yellow, and red appearing in the *tableros*. Similar decoration, also in Teotihuacán style, is to be found in the later structures.

Great quantities of ceramics and pottery figurines have been recovered from the excavations, and these demonstrate a near archaeological identity between Early Classic Teotihuacán and Cholula. Because of the staggering size and importance of its pyramid, it has been suggested that Cholula was some kind of sister city to Teotihuacán. Cholula was surely part of the Teotihuacán cultural sphere and may well have participated in the administration of its empire. Excavations at the base of the pyramid have produced a previously unsuspected cultural element. Several enormous slabs were uncovered, two of which were a kind of altar, while the third was set upright as a stela. All are rectangular but with borders carved in low relief in the complex interlace motif that is the hallmark of the Classic Central Veracruz style.

Classic Central Veracruz

The Mesoamerican ball game was played throughout the area and still survives in attenuated form in northwestern Mexico. On the eve of the conquest, games took place in a rectangular court bordered on the long sides by walls with both sloping and vertical rebound surfaces. There were two teams, each composed of a small number of players. The ball was of solid rubber, of substantial size, and traveled with considerable speed around the court. It could not be hit or touched with the open hands or with the feet; most times the player tried to strike it with the hip. Consequently, fairly heavy protective padding was necessary to avoid injuries, which in some cases were fatal. Leather padding was worn over the hips, and pads were placed on the elbows and knees. A heavy belt was tied around the waist built up from wood and leather, while in some parts of the Maya region and in Late Formative Oaxaca, gloves and something resembling jousting helmets were worn.

The Classic Central Veracruz style is almost purely devoted to the paraphernalia of the ball game and to the ball courts themselves. At the site of El Tajín, which persisted through the end of the Late Classic, elaborate reliefs on the walls of the courts furnish details on how this equipment was used. *Yugos* ("yokes") were the stone counterparts of the heavy protective belts. During the postgame ceremonies, which may have featured the sacrifice of the captain and other players on the losing side, these U-shaped objects were worn about the waists of the participants. On the front of the *yugo* was placed an upright stone object that may originally have functioned as a ball-court marker and that took two forms: *hachas* ("axes"), or thin stone heads, and *palmas* ("palms"). All are carved in an elaborate low-relief style in which life forms are enmeshed in undulating and interlaced scroll designs with raised borders. All of these items,

and the style itself, may have evolved out of late Olmec art on the Gulf coast.

Very often the *yugos* represent the marine toad, a huge amphibian with swollen poison glands on the head; in its jaws is a human head. The earliest *hachas*, which were characteristically notched to fit on the *yugos*, were quite thick human heads and may well date to the Late Formative or Proto-Classic. In time, these become very thin and represent human heads wearing animal headgear. *Palmas* are paddle-shaped stone objects with tri-lobed bases and exhibit a much richer subject matter than either *hachas* or *yugos*, quite often illustrating brutal scenes of sacrifice and death, two concepts that were closely associated with the ball game on the Gulf coast.

Despite the definite presence of the style at Teotihuacán and Cholula, Classic Central Veracruz is focused upon north central Veracruz, where the type site of El Tajín is located, and contiguous parts of Puebla. Today, this region is dominated by speakers of Totonac, a distant relative of Mayan, and the Totonac themselves claim that they built El Tajín. Whether or not Classic Central Veracruz culture was a Totonac achievement, the style persisted through the Classic Period and strongly influenced developments in distant regions.

SOUTHERN VERACRUZ

On the southern Gulf coast plain, Olmec traditions seemed to have lasted into the Early Classic and merged with

Teotihuacán artistic canons to produce new kinds of art. Cerro de las Mesas, lying in the plains of the Papaloápan River not far from the coast, is one of these hybrid sites. Dozens of earthen mounds are scattered over the surface in a seemingly haphazard manner, and the archaeological sequence is long and complex. The site reached its apogee in the Early Classic, when the stone monuments for which it is best known were carved. Most important are a number of stelae, some of which are carved in a low-relief style recalling Late Formative Tres Zapotes, early lowland Maya, and Cotzumalhuapa (on the Pacific coast of Guatemala).

Cerro de las Mesas pottery, deposited in rich burial offerings of the Early Classic, is highly Teotihuacanoid, with slab-legged tripods predominating. At this and other sites in southern Veracruz, potters also fashioned large, hollow, handmade figures of the gods. An especially fine representation of the Old Fire God was found at Cerro de las Mesas. The most spectacular discovery, however, was a cache of some 800 jade objects. Many of the specimens in this treasure trove are of Olmec workmanship, obviously heirlooms from the much earlier Olmec civilization, while some are clearly Early Classic Maya.

The entire coastal plain from Cerro de las Mesas north to the borders of Classic Central Veracruz culture is famed for Remojadas-style pottery figurines, which must have been turned out in incredible quantity for use as burial goods. The Remojadas tradition dates to the Late Formative and lasts until the Early Post-Classic. Figurines are hollow and largely mold-made in the Late Classic, while they were fashioned by hand in the Early Classic. The best-known Classic representations are the "smiling figures" of grinning boys and girls wearing loincloths, skirts, or nothing at all. All kinds of genre scenes are represented, including even lovers in swings, as well as more grim activities such as the heart sacrifice of victims tied down in what look like beds.

CLASSIC MONTE ALBÁN

The cultural phases designated as Monte Albán III-A and III-B mark the Classic occupation of this major site in the Valley of Oaxaca. There can be little doubt that the people of Monte Albán were Zapotec speakers, who during Classic times had unequaled opportunity to develop their civilization unaffected by the major troubles that disturbed Teotihuacán and the Maya at the close of the Early Classic. Instead of the 18 or 19 sites known for the valley during the Late Formative, there now were more than 200, a testimony to Zapotec prosperity.

The Monte Albán Classic Period (III-A and III-B) lasted from AD 250 to 700. During the earlier (III-A) part of the period (250–450) the site shows considerable influence from Teotihuacán. The Early Post-Classic Period at Monte Albán (IV; 700–1000) was a time of significant cultural change. It is still uncertain, however, whether the Mixtec replaced the Zapotec at that time.

The Classic site of Monte Albán is quite spectacular. Stone-faced platforms are fronted by stairways with flanking balustrades and exhibit a close counterpart of the *talud-tablero* motif of Teotihuacán. The temple superstructures had colonnaded doorways and flat beam-and-mortar roofs. One of the best-preserved ball courts of Mesoamerica can be seen at Monte Albán, with a ground plan fashioned in the form of a capital "I." Spectators watched the game from stone grandstands above the sloping playing surfaces.

Subsurface tombs were dug in many parts of the site as the last resting places of Monte Albán's elite. The finest are actually miniature replicas of the larger temples on the surface, complete with facade and miniature painted rooms. The style of the funerary wall paintings is quite close to Teotihuacán, in which areas of flat colour are contained within very finely painted lines in red or black. Teotihuacán presence can also be seen in the finer pottery of Classic Monte Albán, but the manufacture is local as can be proved from the predominance of the fine gray ware that has always typified Monte Albán.

The tradition of literacy dates to Monte Albán I. By Classic times, inscriptions are abundant, appearing on stelae, lintels, slabs used as doors, and wall paintings. The 52-year Calendar Round was the only form of writing dates. The subject matter of these inscriptions can be related to the scenes that they accompany: quite often it is a bound captive standing on a place-glyph, presumably an enemy leader taken in war—an old Monte Albán preoccupation.

The Zapotec of Monte Albán, like the Maya, never exerted much cultural or other pressure on peoples beyond their lands. They did, however, control lands from the Tehuacán Valley in Puebla as far south as the Pacific shore of Oaxaca. Whether they themselves were also controlled by Teotihuacán has not been demonstrated.

THE MAYA HIGHLANDS AND PACIFIC COAST

Little is known about the Guatemalan highlands between the demise of the Late Formative Miraflores culture and the onset of the Early Classic. But at the ancient site of Kaminaljuyú, on the western side of Guatemala City, a group of invaders from Teotihuacán built a miniature replica of their capital city. This happened about AD 400, when Teotihuacán was at the height of its power.

This implanted Teotihuacán culture is called Esperanza. Mexican architects must have accompanied the elite, for Kaminaljuyú structures copy the older prototypes down to the last detail, including the support of the lower moldings around *tableros* with slate slabs. The abundant volcanic building stone, however, so freely used at Teotihuacán, was not present, so that Esperanza temple platforms are built from clay instead.

Each temple platform was rebuilt several times, the later structures being raised over the earlier. Within the stairways fronting each successive platform a great leader was buried. The rich burial furniture in the tombs is informative, for it included three classes of goods: (1) items such as Thin Orange pottery manufactured in Teotihuacán or in one of its satellite areas, (2) hybrid Teotihuacán-Maya pottery and other objects, probably made in Kaminaljuyú, and (3) pottery imported from Petén and of Early Classic Maya manufacture. Also discovered in one tomb was a slate mirror carved in Classic Central Veracruz style. Jade objects occur in abundance in the Esperanza tombs, and in one structure an enormous boulder was recovered; it had been imported from the Maya source along the Motagua River in the southeastern lowlands. The Esperanza elite were enormously wealthy.

What were they doing in the Maya highlands in the first place? Were they an army of imperial conquest? Or were their interests more in the realm of trade? Or both? It is not possible to be definite in these interpretations; but it is known that among the Aztec of the Late Post-Classic there was an institution called the *pochteca*, a hereditary guild of armed merchants who traveled into distant lands looking for luxury goods to bring back to the royal house. Quite often the *pochteca* would seize lands of

hostile peoples through which they passed, or they would provoke incidents that led to the intervention of the regular Aztec army.

It has been suggested that the Teotihuacanos in Kaminaljuyú were also *pochteca*. They had clear access to the Petén-Yucatán Peninsula and may have exercised political control over it. Kaminaljuyú may have been one of their principal bases of operations in the inclusion of the Maya, both highland and lowland, within the Teotihuacán state.

Within a zone only 75 miles (121 km)long and 30 miles (48 km) wide, on the Pacific coast plain of Guatemala, is a cluster of nine compactly built ceremonial centres that together form the Cotzumalhuapa civilization. It forms a puzzle, for there are strong affiliations with most other contemporary civilizations in Mesoamerica. Stylistic influence from the lowland Maya, Classic Central Veracruz, and Teotihuacán can be detected among others. While Cotzumalhuapa took form by the Early Classic, it continued into the Late Classic; but there are great problems in dating individual sculptures.

The problem of Cotzumalhuapa has been linked with that of the Pipil, a shadowy people living in the same region on the eve of the Spanish conquest, who spoke Nahua rather than Maya. It is possible that these Classic sites were actually Pipil capitals, but the case cannot be proved. There is some hieroglyphic writing on Cotzumalhuapa sculptures, mainly dates within what seems to be a 52-year Calendar Round, the glyphs for

days being Mexican rather than Maya. There are no real texts, then, to help with the problem.

CLASSIC CIVILIZATION IN THE MAYA LOWLANDS: TZAKOL PHASE

Archaeologists have divided the entire area occupied by speakers of Mayan languages into three subregions: (1) the Southern Subregion, essentially the highlands and Pacific Coast of Guatemala, (2) the Central Subregion, which includes the department of Petén in northern Guatemala and the immediately adjacent lowlands to the east and west, and (3) the Northern Subregion, consisting of the Yucatán Peninsula north of Petén proper. Between 250 and 900 the most brilliant civilization ever seen in the New World flourished in the forested lowlands of the Central and Northern subregions.

Lowland Maya civilization falls into two chronological phases or cultures: Tzakol culture, which is Early Classic and began shortly before AD 250, and the Late Classic Tepeu culture, which saw the full florescence of Maya achievements. Tepeu

Large stone stele carved with the Maya calendar, discovered in Tikal, Guatemala. Travel Ink/Gallo Images/Getty Images

culture began about 600 and ended with the final downfall and abandonment of the Central Subregion about 900. These dates, based on the correlation of the Long Count system of the Maya calendar with the Gregorian calendar, are the most generally accepted, but there is a slight chance that a rival correlation espoused by the American archaeologist Herbert J. Spinden may be correct, which would make these dates 260 years earlier.

One of the earliest objects inscribed with the fully developed Maya calendar is the Leiden Plate, a jade plaque, now housed in the National Museum of Ethnology, Leiden, Neth., depicting a richly arrayed Maya lord trampling a captive underfoot. On its reverse side is a Long Count date corresponding to 320. Although it was found in a very late site on the Caribbean coast, stylistic evidence suggests that the Leiden Plate was made at Tikal, in the heart of northern Petén. In the mid-20th century the University of Pennsylvania's ambitious field program at the Tikal site produced Stela 29, erected 28 years before, in 292. Both objects and, in fact, almost all early Tzakol monuments draw heavily upon a heritage from the older Izapan civilization of the Late Formative, with its highly baroque, narrative stylistic content.

Because of the Maya penchant for covering older structures with later ones, Tzakol remains in the Central Subregion have to be laboriously dug out from their towering Late Classic overburdens. Nevertheless, it is clear that at sites like Tikal, Uaxactún, and Holmul, Maya civilization had reached something close to its final form. Enormous ceremonial centres were crowded with masonry temples and "palaces" facing onto spacious plazas covered with white stucco. The use of the corbel vault for spanning rooms—a trait unique to the lowland Maya—was by this time universal. Stelae and altars (a legacy from Izapa) are carved with dates and embellished with the figures of men and perhaps gods. Polychrome pottery, the finest examples of which were sealed in the tombs of honoured personages, emphasizes stylized designs of cranes, flying parrots, gods, and men. These often occur on bowls with a kind of apron or basal flange encircling the lower vessel. Along with these purely Maya ceramics are vessels that show the imprint of distant Teotihuacán: the cylindrical vase supported by three slab legs, the "cream pitcher," and the *florero* ("flower vase").

Wall painting had already reached a high degree of perfection in the Central Subregion, as attested by an extremely fine mural at Uaxactún depicting a palace scene in which two important lords confer with each other. This mural art is quite different from that of Teotihuacán, being very naturalistic instead of formal and including a definite interest in portraiture. Nonetheless, excavations in Petén sites have shown that Teotihuacán influence was quite pervasive. From Tikal, for example, comes Stela 31, depicting a richly garbed Maya lord, festooned with jade ornaments, standing between two warriors from Teotihuacán. These foreigners carry shields that bear the visage of the Teotihuacán rain god, Tlaloc. It is certain that there was a three-way trading relationship between Tikal, Kaminaljuyú, and Teotihuacán in Early Classic times.

Thus, the Teotihuacán involvement with Tikal and the Central Subregion may have taken, as at Kaminaljuyú, the form of *pochteca* trading colonies that exerted some control over the lowland Maya. The lord on Stela 31 may have been a puppet ruler manipulated by tough merchant-warriors. Teotihuacán as a city and capital of an empire began to weaken toward the close of the 6th century. It could therefore be expected that the disruptions that effectively ended the life of the great Mexican capital would be reflected in the Maya area. This is exactly the case. In the Guatemalan highlands, Kaminaljuyú declined rapidly after AD 600, and the entire Southern Subregion was to play little part in Maya culture until the Late Post-Classic. The lowland Maya suffered some temporary reverses; few stelae were erected between 534 and 692, and there is evidence that existing monuments were mutilated.

LATE CLASSIC MESOAMERICA (600–900)

The cultural situation in Late Classic Mesoamerica is the reverse of that prevailing in the Early Classic. Central Mexico now played only a minor role, while the lowland Maya reached their intellectual and artistic heights. In contrast to the old Teotihuacanos, however, the Maya were not expansionistic. It is true that Maya cultural influence has been detected along the Gulf coast and in the states of Morelos and Tlaxcala—as in the painted murals of Cacaxtla in the latter state—but it is unlikely that this was the result of a military takeover. The outcome of this state of affairs, with no one people powerful enough or sufficiently interested in dominating others, was a political and cultural fragmentation of Mesoamerica after 600. It was not until the great Toltec invasions of the Early Post-Classic that anything approaching an empire was to be seen again.

The decline in fortunes of the Valley of Mexico, and especially of Teotihuacán, cannot now be explained. Climatic deterioration, resulting in drier conditions and thus a diminished subsistence potential, may have been a factor. Nevertheless, Teotihuacán was never completely abandoned, even though its great palaces had been burned to the ground and its major temples abandoned. People continued to live in some sections, but their houses were mere hovels compared to the dwellings of the Early Classic. In general, the Valley of Mexico was a cultural and political vacuum in Late Classic times.

One of the very few centres of the Late Classic in central Mexico that amounted to much was Xochicalco, in Morelos. Strategically located on top of a hill that was completely reworked with artificial terraces and ramparts, Xochicalco was obviously highly defensible, an indication of the unsettled times then prevailing in central Mexico. The site shows a bewildering variety of cultural influences, particularly Maya. The principal structure of Xochicalco is a temple substructure of masonry that is completely carved in relief with undulating Feathered Serpents, indicating that it was dedicated to the cult of Quetzalcóatl. All indications are that Xochicalco was a cosmopolitan and very powerful centre, perhaps the most influential west of Veracruz and northwest of the Maya area. It was literate and civilized at a time when most other parts of central Mexico were in cultural eclipse.

The Late Classic occupation of Oaxaca, especially of the Valley of Oaxaca, is designated as Monte Albán III-B (450–700). The Mixtec invasions of the valley probably began in earnest around 900. The Mixtec occupied the hilly, northern part of Oaxaca; their records, which extend to the 7th century, show them to have been organized into a series of petty states headed by aggressive, warlike kings. By the Post-Classic, they had become the dominant force throughout Oaxaca and in part of Puebla.

The tendencies in central Veracruz art and architecture that began in the Late Formative culminated in the Late Classic at the great centre of El Tajín, placed among jungle-covered hills in a region occupied by the Totonac Indians, whose capital this may well have been. Its most imposing structure is the Pyramid of the Niches, named for the approximately 365 recesses on its four sides. In this and other buildings at El Tajín, the dominant architectural motif is the step-and-fret. There are a number of other temple pyramids at the site, as well as palacelike buildings with flat, concrete roofs, a tour de force of Mesoamerican engineering knowledge. El Tajín's three major ball courts are remarkably important for the reliefs carved on their vertical playing surfaces, for these give valuable information on the religious connotations of the sacred game. Like Xochicalco, El Tajín was in some way linked to the destiny of the lowland Maya, and the collapse of Maya civilization around 900 may have been reflected in the demise of the Veracruz centre.

Further down the Gulf coast plain, the Remojadas tradition of hollow pottery figurines continued to be active in the Late Classic, with a particularly large production of the mysterious smiling figures of dancing boys and girls, which were intended as funerary offerings. But in addition, there was a great deal of pottery and figurines that were fashioned under very strong Maya influence. In fact, much of southern Veracruz at this time was a cultural extension of the lowland Maya. There is no indication, however, that these peoples had any acquaintance with Maya literacy or with Maya building techniques.

LATE CLASSIC LOWLAND MAYA SETTLEMENT PATTERN

There is still controversy over whether the Late Classic sites built by the lowland Maya were actually cities or relatively empty ceremonial centres staffed only by rulers and their entourages. The common people built their simple pole-and-thatch dwellings on low earthen mounds to keep them dry during the summer rains. Thus, total mapping of a particular site should always include not only masonry structures but also house mounds as well. So far, only a few Maya sites have been so mapped. The mightiest Maya centre of all, Tikal in northern Petén, has a total of about 3,000 structures ranging from the tiny mounds up to gigantic temple pyramids. These are contained, however, within an area of six square miles (10 square km). The Tikal population has been estimated from this survey to be 10,000 to 11,000 people, but perhaps as many as 75,000 within an even wider area could have belonged to Tikal.

This sounds very much like a city, but the evidence actually can be differently interpreted. First, at the time of the conquest the Maya generally buried their dead beneath the floors of houses, which were then abandoned. Thus, an increase in number of house mounds could just as easily indicate a declining population in which the death rate exceeded the birth rate. Second, the appearance of even such a tremendous centre as Tikal is quite different from that of such true cities as Teotihuacán. An ordinary Maya family typically occupied two or three houses arranged around a rectangular open space. These were grouped into unplanned hamlets near good water and rich, well-drained soils. A survey of Petén has shown that

for every 50 to 100 dwellings there was a minor ceremonial centre; this unit has been called a zone. Several zones formed a district for which a major centre like Tikal acted as the ceremonial and political nucleus. Neither Tikal nor any other such centre shows signs of town planning or neatly laid out streets.

There are also ecological factors that must have set certain limits upon the potential for urban life in the Maya lowlands. Slash-and-burn cultivation would have made for widely settled populations and, as has been argued, the uniformity of the lowland Maya environment would have worked against the growth of strong interregional trade—always a factor in urban development. Yet these statements must be qualified. It is known that raised-field, or *chinampa*-type, farming was used in many places and at many times in the Maya lowlands. This would have allowed for greater population concentration. It is also known that there was a brisk trade in some commodities from one lowland Maya region to another.

What, then, can be concluded about lowland Maya urbanism? Clearly, the urban form, even at a metropolis such as Tikal, was not as large or as formally developed as it was at highland Teotihuacán. At the same time, a centre whose rulers could draw upon the coordinated efforts of 75,000 people must inevitably have had some of the functions of a true city— in governance, religion, and trade, as well as in the development of the arts and intellectual life.

MAJOR SITES

While there are some important differences between the architecture of the Central and Northern subregions during the Late Classic, there are many features shared between them. A major Maya site generally includes several types of masonry buildings, usually constructed by facing a cement-and-rubble core with blocks or thin slabs of limestone. Temple pyramids are the most impressive, rising in a series of great platforms to the temple superstructure above the forests. The rooms, coated with white stucco, are often little more than narrow slots because of the confining nature of the corbeled vaults, but this was probably intentional, to keep esoteric ceremonies from the public.

The so-called palaces of Maya sites differ only from the temple pyramids in that they are lower and contain a great many rooms. Their purpose still eludes discovery. Many scholars doubt that they really served as palaces, for the rooms are damp and uncomfortable, and there is little or no evidence of permanent occupation. The temples and palaces are generally arranged around courts, often with inscribed stelae and altars arranged in rows before them. Leading from the central plazas are great stone causeways, the function of which was probably largely ceremonial. Other features of lowland sites (but not universal) are sweathouses, ball courts, and probably marketplaces.

There are more than 50 known sites that deserve to be called major. Most are in the Central Subregion, with probably the greatest concentration in northern Petén, where Maya civilization had its deepest roots. Tikal is the largest and best-known Classic site of the Central Subregion. It is dominated by six lofty temple pyramids, one of which is some 230 feet (70 metres) high, the tallest structure ever raised by the Mesoamerican Indians. Lintels of sapodilla wood still span the doorways of the temple superstructures and are carved with reliefs of Maya lords enthroned amid scenes of great splendour. Some extraordinary Late Classic tombs have been discovered at Tikal, the most important of which produced a collection of bone tubes and strips delicately incised with scenes of gods and men. Ten large reservoirs, partly or entirely artificial, supplied the scarce drinking water for the residents of Tikal.

Other important sites of northern Petén include Uaxactún, Naranjo, Nakum, and Holmul, of which only the first has been adequately excavated. To the southeast of Petén are two Maya centres—Copán and Quiriguá—that show notable differences with the Petén sites. Copán is located above a tributary of the Motagua River in western Honduras in a region now rich in tobacco. Its architects and sculptors had a ready supply of a greenish volcanic tuff far superior to the Petén limestone. Thus, Copán architecture is embellished with gloriously baroque figures of gods, and its stelae and other monuments are carved with an extraordinary virtuosity. Copán also has one of the most perfectly preserved ball courts in Mesoamerica. Quiriguá is a much smaller site 30 miles (48 km) north of Copán. While its architectural remains are on a minor scale, it is noted for its gigantic stelae and altars carved from sandstone.

The principal watercourse on the western side of the Central Subregion is the Usumacinta River, originating in the Guatemalan highlands and emptying into the Gulf of Mexico. For much of its course the Usumacinta is lined with such great Maya ceremonial centres as Piedras Negras and Yaxchilán. Even more renowned is Bonampak, a satellite of Yaxchilán located on a tributary of the Usumacinta. The discovery in 1946 of the magnificent murals embellishing the rooms of an otherwise modest structure astounded the archaeological world. From floors to vault capstones, its stuccoed walls were covered with highly realistic polychrome scenes of a jungle battle, the arraignment of prisoners, and

A wall painting depicting Mayans pronouncing judgment on their captives. Bonampak, Chiapas State, Mexico/Alan Gilliam/Mexicolore/The Bridgeman Art Library

victory ceremonies. These shed an entirely new light on the nature of Maya society, which up until then had been considered peaceful.

In the hills just above the floodplain of the Usumacinta lies Palenque, the most beautiful of Maya sites. The architects of Palenque designed graceful temple pyramids and "palaces" with mansard-type roofs, embellished with delicate stucco reliefs of rulers, gods, and ceremonies. The principal structure is the Palace, a veritable labyrinth of galleries with interior courts. A four-story square tower, which may have served as both lookout and observatory, looms over it. A small stream flowing through the site was carried underneath the Palace by a long, corbel-vaulted tunnel. The temples of the Cross, Foliated Cross, and Sun were all built on the same plan, the back room of each temple having a kind of sanctuary designed like the temple of which it was a part. It can be supposed that all three temples served the same cult. The most extraordinary feature of Palenque, however, was the great funerary crypt discovered in 1952 deep within the Temple of the Inscriptions. Within a sarcophagus in the crypt were the remains of an unusually tall ruler, accompanied by the richest offering of jade ever seen in a Maya tomb. Over his face had been fitted a mask of jade mosaic, while a treasure trove of jade adorned his body.

Northward from the Central Subregion, in the drier and flatter environment of the Yucatán Peninsula, the character of lowland Maya civilization changes. Just north of Petén is the Río Bec zone, as yet little explored but noted for temple pyramids and palaces with flanking false towers fronted by unclimbable "stairways" reaching dummy "rooms" with blank entrances. Río Bec structures are carved with fantastic serpents in deep relief, a feature that becomes even more pronounced in the Chenes country to the northwest, in the modern state of Campeche. At Chenes sites, Maya architects constructed frontal portals surrounded by the jaws of sky serpents and faced entire buildings with a riot of baroquely carved grotesques and spirals.

This elaborate ornamentation of buildings is far more restrained and orderly in the style called Puuc, so named from a string of low hills extending up from western Campeche into the state of Yucatán. The Puuc sites were for the Northern Subregion what the Petén sites were for the Central, for they are very numerous and clearly were the focal point for Maya artistic and intellectual culture. Uxmal is the most important Puuc ceremonial centre and an architectural masterpiece. It has all of the characteristics of the Puuc style: facings of thin squares of limestone veneer over a cement-and-rubble core; boot-shaped vault stones; decorated cornices around columns in doorways; engaged or half-columns repeated in long rows; and lavish use of stone mosaics in upper facades, emphasizing sky-serpent faces with long, hook-shaped noses, as well as frets and latticelike designs of crisscrossed elements.

The nearby centre of Kabah, connected to Uxmal by a ceremonial causeway, has an extraordinary palace completely faced with masks of the sky serpent. Other major Puuc sites are Sayil, with a multistoried palace, and Labná. The Puuc style reaches east across the Yucatán Peninsula, for at Chichén Itzá, a great site that was to occupy centre stage during the Toltec occupation of the Northern Subregion, there are several buildings strongly Puuc in character.

Puuc sites may be said to represent a lowland Maya "New Empire" in the sense that their apogee occurred in the 9th and 10th centuries, a time during which the great Petén, or Central Subregion, centres were in decline or had collapsed. Just how late Puuc sites remained active, with major constructions being dedicated, remains something of a question.

About 1000 a major change took place in northern Yucatán. It was marked by the construction of a number of Toltec-style temples and palaces at Chichén Itzá, a site that also has many Puuc-style edifices. It is not known if Toltec Chichén Itzá existed contemporaneously with such Puuc sites as Uxmal and Labná, and if so, for how long. Eventually, Chichén Itzá appears to have dominated northern Yucatán, lasting well into the Post-Classic Period (about 1250). Questions also surround the bringers of Toltec-style architecture to Chichén Itzá. They may have been either central Mexican Toltecs or Gulf coast peoples who probably were Maya-speakers and who had adopted central-Mexican ways. In this connection, it should be noted that Puuc sites were under several influences from Gulf-coast Mexico, particularly from central Veracruz.

MAYA ART OF THE LATE CLASSIC

Maya art, at the height of its development, was fundamentally unlike any other in Mesoamerica, for it was highly narrative, baroque, and often extremely cluttered, unlike the more austere styles found elsewhere. It is essentially a painterly rather than sculptural tradition, and it is quite likely that even stone reliefs were first designed by painters. Much of this art has disappeared for all time because of the ravages of the wet, tropical environment on such perishable materials as wood, painted gourds, feathers, bark, and other substances. There must have been thousands of bark-paper codices, not one of which has survived from Classic times.

Following the downfall of Teotihuacán, Maya artists were free to go their own way. Magnificently carved stelae and accompanying altars are found at most major sites, the greatest achievement in this line being found at Copán, where something approaching three-dimensional carving was the rule. Palenque and Yaxchilán specialized in graceful bas-reliefs placed as tablets or lintels in temple pyramids and palaces. In the Northern Subregion, however, the sculptor's art was definitely inferior in

TIKAL

Tikal, a city and ceremonial centre of the ancient Maya civilization, was the largest urban centre in the southern Maya lowlands. It stood 19 miles (30 km) north of Lake Petén Itzá in what is now the northern part of the region of Petén, Guatemala, in a tropical rainforest. Uaxactún, a smaller Maya city, was located about 12 miles (20 km) to the north. The Tikal ruins are the central attraction of Tikal National Park, which was established in the 1950s and designated a UNESCO World Heritage site in 1979.

Like many Maya centres of the southern lowlands, Tikal was first occupied as a small village in the Middle Formative Period (900–300 BC); subsequently, in the Late Formative Period (300 BC–AD 100), it became an important ceremonial centre with the construction of major pyramids and temples. Its heyday, however, came in the Late Classic Period (AD 600–900), with the planning and construction of its great plazas, pyramids, and palaces, the appearance of Maya hieroglyphic writing and complex systems of time-counting, and the flowering of Maya art as seen in monumental sculpture and vase painting. The numerous dedicatory stelae at the site date from the 3rd century AD until the close of the 9th century. Such stelae, usually bearing the carved features of a priest or other important person, are inscribed with hieroglyphs and dates.

In the Early Classic Period (AD 100–600), Tikal was an important post in the great trading network that the contemporaneous central Mexican city of Teotihuacán had established in southern Mesoamerica. Tikal continued to flourish after the decline of Teotihuacán and probably extended its hegemony over a large part of the southern lowlands in the Late Classic Period. Between 600 and 800, Tikal reached its architectural and artistic peak, after which a decline set in, with depopulation and a general artistic deterioration. The last dated stela at the site is placed at 889. Small groups continued to live at the site for another century or so, but Tikal, along with the other Maya centres of the southern lowlands, was abandoned by the 10th century.

The Great Plaza at Tikal, Guatemala, with stelae (foreground), the Temple of the Jaguar (left), and the Palace of the Nobles (right). Josef Muench

The main structures of Tikal cover approximately 1 square mile (2.5 square km). Surveys in a larger area, encompassing at least 6 square miles (15.5 square km), have revealed outlying smaller structures that were residences. These, however, were not arranged in streets or in close-packed formation, as in the case of Teotihuacán, but were rather widely separated. It is estimated that at its height (c. 700) the core of Tikal had a population of about 10,000 persons but that the centre drew upon an outlying population of approximately 50,000.

The site's major structures include five pyramidal temples and three large complexes, often called acropoles; these presumably were temples and palaces for the upper class. One such complex is composed of numerous buildings beneath which have been found richly prepared burial chambers. Pyramid I is topped by the Temple of the Jaguar and rises to 148 feet (45 metres). Just west of Pyramid I and facing it is Pyramid II, standing 138 feet (42 metres) above the jungle floor and supporting the Temple of the Masks. Pyramid III is 180 feet (55 metres) high. Near the Plaza of the Seven Temples stands Pyramid V (187 feet [57 metres]). The highest of the Tikal monuments is Pyramid IV (213 feet [65 metres]), which is the westernmost of the major ruins and also the site of the Temple of the Two-Headed Serpent. Pyramid IV is one of the tallest pre-Columbian structures in the Western Hemisphere.

scope and quality and shows strong influence from alien, non-Maya cultures.

A few wooden objects have somehow survived. Particularly noteworthy are the massive wooden lintels of Tikal, with scenes of lords and their guardian deities, accompanied by lengthy hieroglyphic texts. In ancient times, wood carvings must have been vastly more common than sculptures. The wet climate has also destroyed innumerable examples of mural art.

Maya pottery can be divided into two groups: the pots and pans of everyday life, usually undecorated but sometimes with geometric designs, and grave offerings. Vessels meant to accompany the honoured dead were usually painted or carved with naturalistic and often macabre scenes. To achieve polychrome effects of great brilliance, the Maya potters painted in semitranslucent slips over a light background, then fired the vessels at a very low temperature. Relief carving was carried out when the vessels were leather-hard, just before firing.

The most precious substance of all to the Maya was jade, to which their craftsmen devoted great artistry. Jade was mainly fashioned into thin plaques, carved in relief, or into beads. In the absence of metal tools, jade was worked by applying abrasives and water with cane or perhaps other pieces of jade.

MAYAN HIEROGLYPHIC WRITING

The Mayan hieroglyphic system of writing was used by the Maya people of Mesoamerica until about the end of the 17th century, 200 years after the Spanish conquest of Mexico. (With the 21st-century discovery of the Mayan site of San Bartolo in Guatemala came evidence of Mayan writing that pushed back its date of origin to at least 300 or 200 BC.) It was the only true writing system developed in the pre-Columbian Americas. Mayan inscriptions are found on stelae, stone lintels, sculpture, and pottery, as well as on the few surviving Mayan books, or codices. The Mayan system of writing contains more than 800 characters, including some that are hieroglyphic and other phonetic signs representing syllables. The hieroglyphic signs are pictorial—i.e., they are recognizable pictures of real objects—representing animals, people, and objects of daily life.

Until the mid-20th century, very little Mayan writing could be deciphered except for the symbols representing numbers, dates, and rulers' names and denoting such events as birth, death, and capture. Most scholars accepted the theory that the Mayan writing system was entirely logographic—that is, that each glyph, or sign, represented an entire word. In addition, it was widely believed that the Mayan inscriptions were largely religious in character.

During the 1950s the linguist Yury Knorozov demonstrated that Mayan writing was phonetic as well as hieroglyphic. In 1958 Heinrich Berlin established that a certain category of glyphs referred either to places or to the ruling families associated with those places. Two years later Tatiana Proskouriakoff established that the inscriptions were primarily historical;

they recorded events in the lives of Mayan rulers and their families. The work of these three scholars constituted a revolution in Mayan studies, and in succeeding decades the decipherment of the writing proceeded at an accelerating rate.

The Mayan writing system is complex. A single sign may function as a logogram and also have one or more syllabic values. Similarly, a single logographic sign may be used to represent several words that are pronounced in the same way. In addition, different signs may share phonetic or logographic values. In some cases scholars understand the meaning of a logographic sign but have not determined its reading—i.e., what word it stands for—while other signs can be deciphered phonetically, but their meanings are not known. Nevertheless, by the early 21st century scholars had read a substantial number of inscriptions, affording much new information about Mayan language, history, social and political organization, and ritual life, as well as a completely different picture of Mayan civilization than had been previously proposed.

Books in Mayan hieroglyphs, called codices, existed before the Spanish conquest of Yucatán about 1540, but most works written in the script were destroyed as pagan by Spanish priests. Only four Mayan codices are known to survive: the Dresden Codex, probably dating from the 11th or 12th century, a copy of earlier texts of the 5th to 9th centuries AD; the Grolier Codex, discovered in 1965 and dating to the 13th century;

A page from the Dresden Codex, a pre-Columbian book of astronomical data written in Mayan glyphs; in the Saxon State Library, Dresden, Ger. Courtesy, Department Library Services, American Museum of Natural History, New York City (Neg. no. 101539); photograph, Kirschner

the Madrid Codex, dating from the 15th century; and the Paris Codex, probably slightly older than the Madrid Codex. The codices were made of fig-bark paper folded like an accordion; their covers were of jaguar skin.

Most Maya inscriptions that have been interpreted are calendrical inscriptions. Since the late 1950s it has been learned that the content of Classic Maya inscriptions was far more secular than had been supposed. For many years specialists believed that the inscriptions

recorded little more than the passage of time and that, in fact, the Maya were time worshipers. But it has been shown that certain inscriptions recorded the birth, accession, marriage, and military victories of ruling dynasties. One very significant advance in following dynastic histories and plotting political territoriality was the discovery in 1958 of "emblem glyphs," symbols standing for royal lineages and their domains.

Yet it would be misleading to contend that the hurly-burly of Maya court affairs and conquests was all that mattered, for some texts must have been sacred and god-oriented. At Palenque, in the similar temples of the Cross, Foliated Cross, and Sun, the dates inscribed on the tablets in the sanctuaries fall into three groups. The very latest seem to refer to events in the lives of reigning monarchs. An earlier group must deal with distant but real ancestors of those kings, while the very earliest fall in the 4th millennium BC and apparently describe the birth of important gods to whom the respective temples were dedicated and who may have been regarded as the progenitors of Palenque's royal house.

The meaning of many non-calendrical signs and even of complete clauses is not known, but there is a difference between this and assigning an actual Maya word to an ancient glyph or a sentence to a glyphic clause. While it is certain that the language of the Classic inscriptions was Mayan, it is also certain that it was more archaic than any of the

Mayan languages spoken at the time of the conquest, six centuries after the Classic downfall. The four extant Maya codices, none dating earlier than 1100, contain a strong phonetic component, in fact a kind of syllabary, which can be successfully read as Yucatec Maya, but the Classic peoples of the Central Subregion more likely spoke an ancestor of the Cholan branch of Maya. Furthermore, Maya hieroglyphic writing covers the entire span from about AD 250 to the conquest, during which time both the language or languages and the writing system itself must have undergone extensive evolution.

In writing systems in general, there is usually a development from pictographic signs, in which a picture stands for a word or concept, through logographic systems, in which words are still the basic unit but phoneticism is employed to reduce ambiguities (as in Chinese), to phonetic syllabaries, and finally to alphabets. Probably most Classic Maya hieroglyphs are logograms with a mainly ideographic orientation, and it seems that there was a considerable degree of flexibility in how the words and sentences could be written. By the Post-Classic, this had been codified into a much more rigid system closely resembling that of Japanese, in which a well-defined syllabary can supplement or even replace logograms. There are approximately 300 to 500 logograms in Classic Maya (the number varies according to how one separates affixes from so-called main signs), but it will probably be many years before the

majority of these are satisfactorily deciphered. Great progress, however, may be expected in unraveling their meaning in specific contexts.

THE MAYA CALENDAR

It is their intellectual life that established the cultural superiority of the Maya over all other American Indians. Much of this was based upon a calendrical system that was partly shared with other Mesoamerican groups but that they perfected into a tool capable of recording important historical and astronomical information.

Maya mathematics included two outstanding developments: positional numeration and a zero. These may rightly be deemed among the most brilliant achievements of the human mind. The same may also be said of ancient Maya astronomy. The duration of the solar year had been calculated with amazing accuracy, as well as the synodical revolution of Venus. The Dresden Codex contains very precise Venusian and lunar tables and a method of predicting solar eclipses.

Maya chronology consisted of three main elements: a 260-day sacred year (*tzolkin*) formed by the combination of 13 numbers (1 to 13) and 20 day names; a solar year (*haab*), divided into 18 months of 20 days numbered from 0 to 19, followed by a five-day unlucky period (Uayeb); and a series of cycles—*uinal* (20 *kins*, or days), *tun* (360 days), *katun* (7,200 days), *baktun* (144,000 days), with the highest cycle being the *alautun* of

THE MAYA CODICES

The Madrid Codex, the Paris Codex, the Dresden Codex, and the Grolier Codex together provide a richly illustrated glyphic text of the preconquest Mayan period. They are among the few known survivors of the mass book-burnings by the Spanish clergy during the 16th century.

The Dresden Codex (Latin: Codex Dresdensis) contains astronomical calculations—eclipse-prediction tables, the synodical period of Venus—of exceptional accuracy. These figures have given the Maya a strong reputation as astronomers. The codex was acquired by the Saxon State Library, Dresden, Saxony, and was published by Edward King, Viscount Kingsborough, in Antiquities of Mexico (1830–48). King erroneously attributed the codex to the Aztecs. The first scientific edition of the codex was made by E. Förstemann (Leipzig, 1880).

Also called (Latin) Codex Tro-Cortesianus, the Madrid Codex is believed to be a product of the late Mayan period (c. AD 1400) and is possibly a Post-Classic copy of Classic Mayan scholarship. The figures and glyphs of this codex are poorly drawn and not equal in quality to those of the other surviving codices.

The variant name Tro-Cortesianus is a result of the early separation of the manuscript into two parts, the first part (pages 22–56 and 78–112) being known as Troano for its first owner, Juan Tro y Ortolano, and the second (pages 1–21 and 57–77) being known as Cortesianus. Containing a wealth of information on astrology and divinatory practices, this codice has been of particular value to historians and anthropologists interested in identifying the various Mayan gods and reconstructing the rites that ushered in new years. Also illustrated are Mayan crafts such as pottery and weaving and activities such as hunting.

The pages of the Madrid Codex are inscribed on both sides. They were formed by folding and doubling a sheet manufactured from the bark of a fig tree. The two sections of the codex were brought together again in 1888, and the resulting document is now housed in the Museum of America in Madrid.

The Paris Codex is also called by the Latin name Codex Peresianus, derived from the name Perez, which was written on the torn wrappings of the manuscript when it was discovered in 1859 in an obscure corner of the Bibliothèque Nationale in Paris. The codex is devoted almost entirely to Mayan ritual and ceremony. The codex is fragmentary and is composed of paper made from tree bark, fashioned in a long strip and folded like a screen. The 11 individual leaves provide 22 pages of columns of glyphs and pictures of the gods. The set of year-bearers appearing in the codex offers a clue to the date of its production, placing it midway between the Classic and Conquest periods of Mayan history.

The so-called Grolier Codex, which is discussed in Michael D. Coe's The Maya Scribe and His World (1973), turned up in Mexico in 1965 and is housed in Mexico City. It was named for the Grolier Club (founded 1884) of New York City, an association of bibliophiles who first photographed, published, and presented the codex, with analysis by Coe.

The Grolier Codex consists of 11 damaged pages from a presumed 20-page book and 5 single pages that have since been photographed but are themselves unavailable to the public. Coe's analysis revealed that the Grolier Codex is related to the Dresden Codex, and like it, concerns the Venus calendar. The style of the codex is hybrid, showing Toltec and Mixtec influence.

23,040,000,000 days. All Middle American civilizations used the two first counts, which permitted officials accurately to determine a date within a period defined as the least common multiple of 260 and 365: 18,980 days, or 52 years.

The Classic Maya Long Count inscriptions enumerate the cycles that have elapsed since a zero date in 3114 BC. Thus, "9.6.0.0.0," a *katun*-ending date, means that nine *baktuns* and six *katuns* have elapsed from the zero date to the day 2 Ahau 13 Tzec (May 9, AD 751). To those Initial Series were added the Supplementary Series (information about the lunar month) and the Secondary Series, a calendar-correction formula that brought the conventional date in harmony with the true position of the day in the solar year.

The end of the Maya Long Count cycle on Dec. 21, 2012, represents the closing of a 5,126-year period. On that day, the centre of the Milky Way will be aligned with the Sun for the first time in some 26,000 years. Many interpretations of this circumstance have been posited, including most dramatically an inevitable apocalypse, as seen in the motion picture *2012*. This cataclysmic version of events is considered ludicrous at best by scholars of Maya history and astronomers alike.

Both Classic and recent Maya held the *tzolkin* as the most sacred means of divination, enabling the priests to detect the favourable or evil influences attached to every day according to the esoteric significance of the numbers and the day-signs.

CLASSIC MAYA RELIGION

It has been denied that there was any such thing as a pantheon of deities in Classic times, the idea being that the worship of images was introduced by the Toltec or Itzá invaders, or both, in the Post-Classic. Several gods who played significant roles in the Post-Classic codices, however, can be identified on earlier Maya monuments. The most important of these is Itzamná, the supreme Maya deity, who functioned as the original creator god, as well as lord of the fire and therefore of the hearth. In his serpent form he appears on the ceremonial bar held in the arms of Maya rulers on Classic stelae. Another ophidian deity recognizable in Classic reliefs is the Feathered Serpent, known to the Maya as Kukulcán (and to the Toltecs and Aztecs as Quetzalcóatl). Probably the most ubiquitous of all is the being known as Bolon Tzacab (first called God K by archaeologists), a deity with a baroquely branching nose who is thought to have functioned as a god of royal descent; he is often held as a kind of sceptre in rulers' hands.

The Classic Maya lavished great attention on their royal dead, who almost surely were thought of as descended from the gods and partaking of their divine essence. Many reliefs and all of the pictorial pottery found in tombs deal with the underworld and the dangerous voyage of the soul through that land. Classic Maya funerary ceramics show that this dark land was ruled by a number of gods, including several sinister old men often embellished with jaguar emblems, the jaguar being associated with the night and the nether regions.

The Classic, as well as the Post-Classic, Maya practiced human sacrifice, although not on the scale of the Aztecs. The victims were probably captives, including defeated rulers and nobles. Self-sacrifice or self-mutilation was also common. Blood drawn by jabbing spines through the ear or penis, or by drawing a thorn-studded cord through the tongue, was spattered on paper or otherwise collected as an offering to the gods.

The four main categories of documents that provide knowledge of the Maya civilization and its religion are archaeological remains, native books in hieroglyphic writing, books in native languages written in Latin script by learned Indians, and early accounts written in Spanish by conquerors or priests.

From surviving temples, tombs, sculpture, wall paintings, pottery, and carved jades, shells, and bone, a significant amount of valuable information can be gained—e.g., representations of god-heads and ritual scenes. Perhaps the most important archaeological source, however, is the hieroglyphic texts carved on stone monuments or stone or bone artifacts and painted on pottery. These, insofar as they can be translated, provide descriptions of ceremonies and beliefs.

Also in this category are the aforementioned native hieroglyphic books of pre-Columbian date that survived the Spanish conquest. Written on bark paper, these codices deal with astronomical calculations, divination, and ritual. They appear to be Post-Classic copies of earlier Classic originals.

After the Spanish conquest, books were written by learned Indians who transcribed or summarized hieroglyphic records. Such is the case of the *Books of Chilam Balam*, in Yucatec Maya, and of the *Popol Vuh*, in Quiché, a highland Maya language. The former consist of historical chronicles mixed with myth, divination, and prophecy, and the latter (which shows definite central Mexican influences) embodies the mythology and cosmology of the Post-Classic Guatemalan Maya. The *Ritual of the Bacabs* covers religious symbolism, medical incantations, and similar matters.

The most important of the early accounts written by the Spanish themselves is Diego de Landa's *Relación de las cosas de Yucatán* ("On the Things of Yucatán"), which dates to about 1566. It describes Post-Classic rather than Classic religion, but given the deeply conservative nature of Maya religion, it is highly probable that much of this description is pertinent for the earlier period. Landa's account is also an excellent description of other aspects of Maya life in 16th-century Yucatán.

To these archaeological, ethnohistorical, and historical sources may be added the observations of modern ethnologists about the present-day Maya. Thus, in the Guatemalan highlands, the 260-day calendar still survives, as do ancient prayers to and information about Maya gods.

It is likely that a simpler religion of nature worship prevailed in Early Formative times. This probably began to undergo modification during the Middle Formative, as astronomical knowledge became more precise. Certainly by the Late Formative (300 BC, if not earlier), with the appearance of major centres and pyramid and temple constructions, an elaborate worldview had evolved. Deified heavenly bodies and time periods were added to the earlier-conceived corn and rain gods. Concepts derived from priestly speculation were imposed upon the simpler religious beginnings. Religion became increasingly esoteric, with a complex mythology interpreted by a closely organized priesthood.

CREATION

The Maya, like other Middle American Indians, believed that several worlds had been successively created and destroyed before the present universe had come into being. The Dresden Codex holds that the end of a world will come about by deluge: although the evidence derived from Landa's *Relación* and from the Quiché *Popol Vuh* is not clear, it is likely that four worlds preceded the present one. People were made successively of earth (who, being mindless, were destroyed), then of wood (who, lacking souls and intelligence and being ungrateful to the gods, were punished by being drowned in a flood or devoured by demons), and finally of a corn gruel (the ancestors of the Maya). The Yucatec Maya worshiped a creator deity called Hunab Ku, "One-God." Itzamná ("Iguana House"), head of the Maya pantheon of the ruling class, was his son, whose wife was Ix Chebel Yax, patroness of weaving.

Four Itzamnas, one assigned to each direction of the universe, were represented by celestial monsters or two-headed, dragonlike iguanas. Four gods, the Bacabs, sustained the sky. Each world direction was associated with a Bacab, a sacred ceiba, or silk cotton tree, a bird, and a colour according to the following scheme: east–red, north–white, west–black, and south–yellow. Green was the colour of the centre.

The main act of creation, as stated in the *Popol Vuh*, was the dawn: the world and humanity were in darkness, but the gods created the Sun and the Moon. According to other traditions, the Sun (male) was the patron of hunting and music, and the Moon (female) was the goddess of weaving and childbirth. Both the Sun and the Moon inhabited the earth originally, but they were translated to the heaven as a result of the Moon's sexual license. Lunar light is less bright than that of the Sun because, it was said, one of her eyes was pulled out by the Sun in punishment for her infidelity.

Because the Maya priests had reached advanced knowledge of astronomical phenomena and a sophisticated concept of time, it appears that their esoteric doctrines differed widely from the popular myths.

POPOL VUH

The Popol Vuh is an invaluable source of knowledge about ancient Maya mythology and culture. Written in Quiché (a Guatemalan Maya language) with Spanish letters by a Maya author or authors between 1554 and 1558, it chronicles the creation of man, the actions of the gods, the origin and history of the Quiché people, and the chronology of their kings down to 1550.

The original book was discovered at the beginning of the 18th century by Francisco Jiménez (or Ximénez), parish priest of Chichicastenango in highland Guatemala. He both copied the original Quiché text (now lost) and translated it into Spanish. His work is now in the Newberry Library, Chicago.

COSMOLOGY

The Maya believed that 13 heavens were arranged in layers above the earth, which itself rested on the back of a huge crocodile or reptilian monster floating on the ocean. Under the earth were nine underworlds, also arranged in layers. Thirteen gods, the Oxlahuntiku, presided over the heavens; nine gods, the Bolontiku, ruled the subterranean worlds. These concepts are closely akin to those of the Post-Classic Aztec, but archaeological evidence, such as the nine deities sculptured on the walls of a 7th-century crypt at Palenque, shows that they were part of the Classic Maya cosmology.

Time was an all-important element of Maya cosmology. The priest-astronomers viewed time as a majestic succession of cycles without beginning or end. All the time periods were considered as gods; time itself was believed to be divine.

THE GODS

Among the several deities represented by statues and sculptured panels of the Classic Period are such gods as the young corn god, whose gracious statue is to be seen at Copán; the sun god shown at Palenque under the form of the solar disk engraved with anthropomorphic features; the nine gods of darkness (also at Palenque); and a snake god especially prominent at Yaxchilán. Another symbol of the corn god is a foliated cross or life tree represented in two Palenque sanctuaries. The rain god (Chac) has a mask with characteristic protruding fangs, large round eyes, and a proboscis-like nose. Such masks are a common element in Puuc architecture.

The three hieroglyphic manuscripts, especially the Dresden Codex, depict a number of deities whose names are known only through Post-Classic

The corn god (left) and the rain god, Chac. Drawing from the Madrid Codex (Codex Tro-Cortesianus), one of the sacred Maya books. In the Museo de América, Madrid. Courtesy of the Museo de América, Madrid

documents. Itzamná, lord of the heavens, who ruled over the pantheon, was closely associated with Kinich Ahau, the sun god, and with the moon goddess Ixchel. Though Itzamná was considered an entirely benevolent god, Ixchel, often depicted as an evil old woman, had definitely unfavourable aspects.

The Chacs, the rain gods of the peasants, were believed to pour rain by emptying their gourds and to hurl stone axes upon the earth (the lightning). Their companions were frogs (*uo*), whose croakings announced the rains. Earth gods were worshiped in the highlands, and wind gods were of minor importance in Maya territory.

The corn god, a youthful deity with an ear of corn in his headdress, also ruled over vegetation in general. His name is Ah Mun, and he is sometimes shown in combat with the death god, Ah Puch, a skeleton-like being, patron of the sixth day-sign Cimi ("Death") and lord of the ninth hell. Several other deities were associated with death—e.g., Ek Chuah, a war god and god of merchants and cacao growers, and Ixtab, patron goddess of the suicides.

In Post-Classic times, central Mexican influences were introduced—e.g., the Toltec Feathered Serpent (Quetzalcóatl), called Kukulcán in Yucatán and Gucumatz in the Guatemalan highlands.

The ancient Maya's attitude toward the gods was one of humble supplication, since the gods could bestow health, good crops, and plentiful game or send illness and hunger. Prayers and offerings of food, drink, and incense (*pom*) were used to placate the gods. A strong sense of sin and a belief in predestination pervaded the Maya consciousness. Man had to submit to the forces of the universe. The priests, because of their astronomical and divinatory knowledge, determined favourable days for such undertakings as building houses and hunting.

DEATH

As was noted above, the Classic Maya buried the dead under the floors of their houses. High priests or powerful lords were laid to rest in elaborate underground vaults. The dead were believed to descend to the nine underworlds, called Mitnal in Yucatán and Xibalba by the Quiché. There is no evidence of a belief among the Maya in a heavenly paradise, such as that which prevailed in central Mexico.

The modern Lacandón, however, believe that the dead live forever without work or worry in a land of plenty located somewhere above the earth.

ESCHATOLOGY

The present world, the Maya believed, is doomed to end in cataclysms as the other worlds have done previously. According to the priestly concept of time, cycles repeat themselves. Therefore, prediction was made possible by probing first into the past and then into the future; hence the calculations, bearing on many millennia, carved on temples and stelae. Evil influences were held to mark most of the *katun* endings. The *Chilam Balam* books are full of predictions of a markedly direful character. The priests probably believed that the present world would come to a sudden end, but that a new world would be created so that the eternal succession of cycles should remain unbroken.

SACRIFICE

Sacrifices made in return for divine favour were numerous: animals, birds, insects, fish, agricultural products, flowers, rubber, jade, and blood drawn from the tongue, ears, arms, legs, and genitals. Evidence of human sacrifice in Classic times includes two Piedras Negras stelae, an incised drawing at Tikal, the murals at Bonampak, various painted ceramic vessels, and some scenes in native manuscripts. Only in the Post-Classic era

Cenote

The cenote (from Maya dz'onot) is a natural well or reservoir, common in the Yucatán Peninsula. It was formed when a limestone surface collapsed, exposing water underneath. The major source of water in modern and ancient Yucatán, cenotes are also associated with the cult of the rain gods, or Chacs. In ancient times, notably at Chichén Itzá, precious objects, such as jade, gold, copper, and incense and also human beings, usually children, were thrown into the cenotes as offerings. A survivor was believed to bring a message from the gods about the year's crops.

did this practice become as frequent as in central Mexico. Toltec-Maya art shows many instances of human sacrifice: removal of the heart, arrow shooting, or beheading. At Chichén Itzá, in order to obtain rain, victims were hurled into a deep natural well (cenote) together with copper, gold, and jade offerings. Prayers for material benefits (which were usually recited in a squatting or standing position), fasting and continence (often for 260 days), and the drawing of blood from one's body often preceded important ceremonies and sacrifices.

These practices had become so deeply rooted that, even after the Spanish conquest, Christian-pagan ceremonies occasionally took place in which humans were sacrificed by heart removal or crucifixion. The last recorded case occurred in 1868 among the Chamula of Chiapas.

The Priesthood

Bejeweled, feather-adorned priests are often represented in Classic sculpture. The high priests of each province taught in priestly schools such subjects as history, divination, and glyph writing. The priesthood, as described by Landa, was hereditary. *Ahkin*, "he of the sun," was the priests' general title. Specialized functions were performed by the *nacoms*, who split open the victims' breasts, the *chacs* who held their arms and legs, the *chilans* who interpreted the sacred books and predicted the future. Some priests used hallucinatory drugs in their roles as prophets and diviners.

Rites

Ritual activities, held on selected favourable days, were complex and intense. Performers submitted to preliminary fasting and sexual abstinence. Features common to most rites were offerings of incense (*pom*), of balche (an intoxicating drink brewed from honey and a tree bark), bloodletting from ears and tongues, sacrifices of animals (human sacrifices in later times), and dances. Special ceremonies took place on New Year's Day, known as 0 Pop, in honour of the

"Year-Bearer"—i.e., the *tzolkin* sign of that day. Pottery, clothes, and other belongings were renewed. The second month, Uo, was devoted to Itzamná, Tzec (fifth month) to the Bacabs, Xul (sixth) to Kukulcán, Yax (10th) to the planet Venus, Mac (13th) to the rain gods, and Muan (15th) to the cocoa-tree god. New idols were made during the eighth and ninth months, Mol and Ch'en, respectively.

Both the Classic and Post-Classic Maya practiced a typically Middle American ritual ball game, as evidenced by numerous grandiose ball courts at Tikal, Copán, and Chichén Itzá. No court, however, has been found at Mayapán, and Landa does not mention that game. It appears, therefore, that the Yucatec had ceased to play it, while it remained of the utmost importance in central Mexico.

Archaeological remains at Uxmal and Chichén Itzá point to phallic rites, doubtless imported into the Yucatán from the Gulf coast. The *Chilam Balam* books strongly condemn the Mexican immigrants' sexual practices, which were quite alien to Maya tradition.

SORCERY

Ahmen, "he who knows," was the name given to sorcerers and medicine men, who were both prophets and inflicters or healers of disease. They made use of a mixture of magic formulas, chants, and prayers and of traditional healing methods, such as administering medicinal herbs or bleeding. Belief in witchcraft is widespread among present-day Maya Indians, as it most probably was in pre-Columbian times.

The evolution of Maya religion parallels that of Mexican religions from the Classic to the Post-Classic era, with the sun worship and human sacrifice complex gaining importance as it did in Mexico proper.

The profoundly original feature of Maya religious thought, in comparison with that of other pre-Columbian civilizations, is the extraordinary refinement of mathematical and astronomical knowledge, inextricably mixed with mythological concepts. Even the most learned Aztec priests never reached the intellectual level of their Maya counterparts of the 1st millennium, nor did they conceive of the eternity of time and of its "bearers," the divinized time periods. The ancient Maya may be said to have been among the very few people in history (along with the Zurvanites of Iran) who worshiped time.

The simple, naturalistic religion of the corn-growing peasants, however, subsisted apart from the priesthood's abstract speculations and has partly survived to this day among the Christianized Maya Indians or the unevangelized Lacandón.

SOCIETY AND POLITICAL LIFE

There is a vast gap between the lavishly stocked tombs of the Maya elite who ran the ceremonial centres and the simple graves of the peasantry. Careful measurements of the skeletons found in tombs and graves have also revealed that persons of the Maya ruling class were much taller than the tillers of the soil who provided them tribute. It is likely that this gulf was unspannable, for throughout Mesoamerica the rulers and nobility were believed to have been created separately from commoners.

The most revealing testimony to this royal cult is the temple pyramid itself, for almost every one explored has a great tomb hidden in its base. On death, each ruler might have been the object of ancestor worship by members of his lineage, the departed leader having become one with the god from whom he claimed descent. Ancestor worship, in fact, seems to be at the heart of ancient and modern society and religion among the Maya.

The ordinary folk may have participated in the ceremonies of even the greatest Maya centres. The modern highland Maya have a complex ceremonial life in which a man advances through a series of *cargos*, or "burdens," each one of which brings him greater prestige, costs him a great deal of money, and requires that he reside in the otherwise nearly empty centre for a year at a time carrying out his religious duties. The same may have prevailed in Classic times, though all activities were then under the direction of a hereditary and divine elite class, long since destroyed by the Spaniards.

Warfare apparently was a continuing preoccupation of the Maya lords.

Translations of hieroglyphic inscriptions show that in some cases such warfare led to territorial aggrandizement and the domination of one centre or polity by another; however, the principal purpose of war appears to have been to gain captives for slavery and sacrifice.

It has often been said that the Maya realm was a theocracy, with all power in the hands of the priests. That this is a misconception is apparent from the monuments themselves, which show kings, queens, heirs, and war prisoners, but no figures surely identifiable as priests. In 16th-century Yucatán, the priesthood was hereditary, and it is reported that younger sons of lords often took on that vocation. Quite probably such a class was also to be found among the Late Classic Maya, but neither for the Maya nor for any other Classic civilization of Mesoamerica can the term theocracy be justified.

THE COLLAPSE OF CLASSIC MAYA CIVILIZATION

In the last century of the Classic Period, Maya civilization went into a decline from which it never recovered. Beginning about 790 in the western edge of the Central Subregion, such ceremonial activity as the erection of stelae virtually came to a standstill. During the next 40 years this cultural paralysis spread gradually eastward, by which time the great Classic civilization of the Maya had all but atrophied. A date in the Maya calendar corresponding to 889 is inscribed on the last dated monuments in the Central Subregion; soon after the close of the 9th century it is clear that almost all of this region was abandoned.

For this event, which must have been one of the greatest human tragedies of all time, there are few convincing explanations. It now seems that the Classic Maya civilization in the region of its greatest development went out "not with a bang but a whimper." Massive foreign invasions can be discounted as a factor, but non-Maya elements did appear in the west at the same time as ceremonial activity terminated. These became the inheritors of whatever was left of the old civilization of the Central Subregion after AD 900, having established trading colonies and even a few minor ceremonial centres on its peripheries.

Whatever incursions did take place from the west were piecemeal and probably the result of the general decline, rather than its cause. Similarly, there is little reason to believe that there were peasant revolts on a general scale. The only real fact is that most of the inhabitants of the Central Subregion went elsewhere. Probably some were absorbed by such still flourishing ceremonial centres of the Northern Subregion as Uxmal and Kabah, while others might have migrated up into the congenial highlands of Chiapas and Guatemala. Although a population explosion and severe ecological abuse of the land must have played their role in the tragedy, the full story of the decline and fall of this brilliant aboriginal civilization remains to be told.

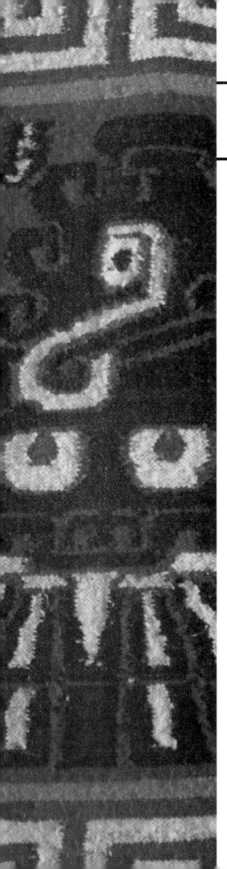

CHAPTER 3

THE TOLTEC AND THE AZTEC, POST-CLASSIC PERIOD (900–1519)

The final period of pre-Columbian Mesoamerican history is referred to as the Post-Classic. Its beginning is usually placed at 900, and it terminates with the arrival of the Spanish conquistador Hernán Cortés in 1519 or with his conquest of the Aztec in 1521. The 900 date is based on two considerations. First, the 10th century was the period of the catastrophic collapse of the lowland Maya civilization and the cessation of the custom of erecting monuments dated by the Long Count. Second, 900 was also the approximate date of the founding of the city of Tula in central Mexico and the rise of a people called the Toltec, who, according to the historical annals, built the first great empire in Mesoamerica. At one time it was thought that the date marked the collapse of all of the regional Classic civilizations of the area as the result of massive population dislocation. But it now appears that some Classic civilizations declined as early as 750, whereas others persisted until as late as 1200.

The period is usually divided into two phases: Early Post-Classic (900–1200) and Late Post-Classic (1200–1519), the former equivalent with the period of the Toltec and the latter with that of the Aztec. The Post-Classic civilizations of Mesoamerica came to an abrupt end with the coming of the Spanish in the early 16th century.

The Post-Classic Period as a whole has also been distinguished from the Classic on the basis of assumed major changes in Mesoamerican political, economic, and social institutions. It has been asserted, for example, that the Classic Period was one of relatively peaceful contact between polities, of the absence of large imperialistic states and empires (and of the militaristic élan and organization that accompanies such states). The Classic has been further characterized by the absence of true cities, by theocratic rather than secular government, and by an overall superiority of arts and crafts, with the exception of metallurgy, which appears for the first time in the Post-Classic Period. In contrast, the Post-Classic was characterized as a period of intense warfare and highly organized military organization, of empires and cities, of secular government, and of overall artistic decline.

Subsequent research, however, has cast considerable doubt on these conclusions. Many of the contrasts were drawn from events in the lowland Maya area and applied to the entire culture area; others were concluded essentially by a comparison of the Classic Maya of the lowland tropical forest of northern Guatemala and the Yucatán Peninsula with the Post-Classic Aztec living in central Mexico in a dry mountain basin 7,000 feet (2,134 metres) above sea level. The differences, in part, are the product of separate culture evolution, conditioned by ecological factors. Cities and large states comparable to those built by the Toltec and Aztec were present in Early Classic times at Teotihuacán in central Mexico and probably at Monte Albán in Oaxaca. Militarism was at least significant enough to be a major artistic theme throughout the Classic Period, even among the lowland Maya. One could also question the criterion of artistic decline, since a number of Post-Classic crafts were highly developed, such as Aztec sculpture, Mixtec ceramics and metallurgy, and Zapotec architecture.

The separation between Post-Classic and Classic is therefore little more than a convenient way of splitting up the long chronicle of Mesoamerican cultural development into manageable units for discussion and analysis. The Post-Classic is a period also in which historical traditions combine with archaeological data, whereas the Classic either lacks a written history or, in the case of the lowland Maya, provides little more than cryptic biographies of kings. Perhaps this is the best rationale for definition of the period.

SOCIETY, CULTURE, AND TECHNOLOGY

At the time of the Spanish conquest, Mesoamerica was occupied by a number of peoples speaking languages as distinct from each other as English is from Chinese. On the central Gulf coast and adjacent escarpment were the Totonac. In Oaxaca and adjacent portions of Puebla and Guerrero, two major ethnic groups, the Mixtec and the Zapotec, shared the western and eastern portions of the area, respectively. The Tarascan lived in Michoacán. Various peoples of the Maya linguistic family occupied most of Guatemala, the Yucatán Peninsula, eastern Tabasco, and highland Chiapas; a detached group, the Huastec (Huaxtec), occupied the north Gulf coast. An equally widespread family, the Nahua (to which the Aztec belonged) occupied most of the Central Plateau, a huge area in the northwest frontier, portions of Guerrero, the Pacific coast of Chiapas and Guatemala (where they were known as the Pipil), and the Gulf coast. Some detached groups had spread beyond the frontier of Mesoamerica into Nicaragua and Panama. The linguistic family to which the Nahua belong (the Uto-Aztecan) is the only Mesoamerican family with affinities to languages north of the Rio Grande, including those of such western U.S. Indians as the Hopi, Paiute, and Shoshone.

One of the Nahua-speaking nations, the Mexica, or Tenochca (or the Aztec, as they are commonly called), were the dominant people in Mesoamerica in 1519, having created by conquest an empire estimated as covering some 80,000 square miles (207,000 square kilometres) and having a population of 5 million to 6 million people.

All of these diverse ethnic groups shared a common cultural tradition, but separate historical origins and environmental factors had also produced a substantial degree of regional differentiation. Most of the cultural characteristics of the area go back at least to the beginning of the Post-Classic, and many appeared in Classic times. The various regional cultures and languages have great time depths and undoubtedly were present during the Classic Period. Common institutional characteristics included organization into centralized polities, including populations minimally in the tens of thousands, with a formal government, supported by a highly organized taxation system; stratification into social classes (including slave and serf classes); occupational specialization—in some areas full time with a guildlike organization; highly organized local and interregional trade involving professional merchants and regularly meeting markets; and a professional priesthood.

The technological base of this elaborate institutional structure seems weak by western European standards, since the primary technology (i.e., the tools used to manufacture other technology) was based on chipped and ground stone, metal being reserved primarily for ornaments. Since draft animals were absent, all power was based on human energy. The economic base of the civilization was a highly productive agriculture, but the basic tools were primitive—stone axes for clearing vegetation and a number of wooden digging tools for working the soil. The crop complex was rich, with corn (maize) serving as the staple food and beans an important source of protein. But the list of secondary crops was large: chili peppers, tomatoes, squashes, sweet potatoes, cassava (manioc), cotton, tobacco, cacao, pineapples, papayas, maguey, nopals (prickly pears), sapotes (*zapotes*), peanuts (groundnuts), avocados, *amates* (paper figs), and many others.

Many crops were limited to particular environmental zones, thus acting as a major stimulus to trade. In many areas, particularly the tropical lowlands, the slash-and-burn, or swidden, system of farming was employed. Forests were cleared, planted for up to three years, and rested for longer periods to restore fertility and eliminate the more difficult weeds. This regular rotation of fields resulted in high production per capita but had low demographic potential because in any given year most of the land lay fallow. In some lowland areas permanent grain and orchard cropping were practiced. In the drier highlands a number of specialized techniques were used, and agriculture generally was more intensive. Particularly important were terracing, irrigation, and swamp reclamation. The per capita productivity of highland agriculture was probably less (because of the higher labour input), but the demographic capacity was considerably greater than that in the lowlands.

As a result of these highly effective approaches to farming, the population was dense when compared to western Europe in the 16th century. Population estimates for the conquest period have varied from 3 million to 30 million; a reasonable estimate is between 12 million and 15 million.

The diet of the average Mesoamerican was relatively uniform throughout the area. Dried corn was boiled in lime-impregnated water to soften the hull, ground into a dough on milling stones (manos and metates), and then either made into tortillas or mixed with water and drunk as a gruel called posol. The tortillas were eaten with sauces prepared from chili peppers and tomatoes, along with boiled beans. This was essentially the diet of the peasant, with the addition of pulque, the fermented sap of the maguey, at higher altitudes. To this were added the other crops in minor quantities and combinations depending on the specific local environment. Luxury foods included cocoa drinks, meats (from game or from the only two domestic animals of significance, the hairless dog and the turkey), and fish. The diet of the peasant, as is the case even today, was low in animal protein; but apparently the quantity of vegetable protein ingested made up for this deficiency.

Major Post-Classic Mesoamerican crafts were weaving of cotton and maguey fibre; ceramics for pottery vessels, figurines, and musical instruments; stone sculpture; featherwork used for personal and architectural ornament; lapidary work (jadeite, jade, serpentine, and turquoise); metalwork (using gold, copper, and, more rarely, silver) for ornaments and a few tools; woodworking, the products including large dugout canoes, sculpture, drums, stools, and a great variety of household items; baskets for containers and mats; painting; and, most particularly, stone and lime concrete masonry architecture.

A ceramic flute unearthed in Guatemala. In addition to musical instruments, pre-Columbian Americans used ceramics to create pottery and sculpture. Kenneth Garrett/National Geographic/Getty Images

KNOWLEDGE AND BELIEF

On the intellectual, ideological, and religious levels, although some diversity and certain elaborations occurred in some regions, there was a fundamental unity to the Mesoamerican area, the product of centuries of political and economic ties. The religion was polytheistic, with numerous gods specialized along the lines of human activities. There were gods for basic activities such as war, reproduction, and agriculture; cosmogenic gods who created the universe and invented human culture; and gods of craft groups, social classes, political systems, and their subdivisions. Gods were all-powerful and had to be constantly propitiated with offerings and sacrifices, a concept reaching its peak in personal bloodletting and human sacrifice. Certain gods, such as the god of rain (called Tlaloc in central Mexico), were found throughout the area. A fundamental concept was that of a quadripartite multilevel universe that, by 1519, had gone through five creations and four destructions. Mesoamerican religion heavily emphasized the astral bodies, particularly the Sun, the Moon, and Venus, and the observations of the movement of these bodies by the astronomer-priests were extraordinarily detailed and accurate. The major purpose of these observations was astrological, and the Mesoamerican priests had developed a number of time counts, or calendrical rounds, based in part on these observations. Two basic calendars, a 260-day divinatory calendar and one

based on the solar year of 365 days, were found throughout the area.

One of the great intellectual achievements of Mesoamerican civilization was writing; in Post-Classic times books were made from the inner bark of the paper-fig tree and used to record calendars, astronomical tables, dynastic history, taxes, and court records.

Religion was a pervasive force in Mesoamerican life, as the art demonstrates, and considerable surplus energy was devoted to it (e.g., temple construction, support of a numerous professional priesthood). Many writers have stated that the major focus of Mesoamerican culture was in this sphere. In fact, the contrast between Post-Classic and Classic was in part based on the presumed even greater emphasis on religion in the art and architecture of the latter period.

THE HISTORICAL ANNALS

A major characteristic of the Post-Classic, in contrast to the Classic, is the abundant historical documentation. The Aztec record is particularly rich, and much of it is undoubtedly genuine, although there is always the possibility that records were rewritten or tampered with for political reasons. One of the functions of Mesoamerican writing was to record the succession and achievements of dynastic lines, and consequently it served as a validation of power. Virtually all of the dynasties of the local states recorded their history. A problem in the utilization of these documents, other than the low number of survival, is the fact that many of them have strong mythological overtones.

The Rise of the Aztec

The Aztec themselves, for example, as creators of a great empire, explained their rise in part to the fact that they were the chosen people of the war god Huitzilopochtli and were the sustainers of the sun god Tonatiuh. They started their history as a poor, nomadic tribe from the north, who entered the Basin of Mexico, led by a magician-priest, and ultimately settled on the lake islands because of a series of astrological predictions and signs. They lived for a while as a subject people and then embarked on their destined role as conquerors and priests of the sun god. Virtually all historical traditions of local groups begin with a migration, a period of trials, and ultimate success—and some records even claim that the people were hunters and gatherers during the early part of their history.

On the northern frontier of Mesoamerica, in the arid Mexican Plateau, true hunters and gatherers, referred to as the Chichimeca by the civilized peoples, did actually reside in 1519. The name Chichimeca was frequently applied to the migrant groups. It is difficult to see how hunting and gathering bands could successfully invade areas of dense civilized populations, but agricultural groups, during periods of dynastic weakness, undoubtedly could. In fact, the term Chichimeca was also applied to agricultural but less civilized peoples (such as the Otomí in central Mexico) and thus connoted a lack of polish or a rustic lifestyle. Since the northwestern portion of Mesoamerica was occupied by such people and since they were Nahua in speech, the legends of periodic north-south migrations of invaders, though they may have a factual basis, probably refer to movements of agricultural rather than hunting and gathering peoples.

The histories of these invading groups take on a more convincing historical character after the legends of migration. In the Aztec case they record the founding of Tenochtitlán in 1325. By 1376 the Aztec had increased in numbers and prestige sufficiently to obtain a member of the ruling family of Culhuacan, a neighbouring state, to rule as their *tlatoani*, or king. His name was Acamapichtli. The Aztec at this time were paying tribute to another state, Azcapotzalco, on the lake shore; and they remained under this obligation through the reigns of his two successors, Huitzilhuitl (c. 1390–1415) and Chimalpopoca (1415–26). During the reign of Chimalpopoca, Maxtla, the ruler of Azcapotzalco, attempted to secure tighter control over subject states by replacing their *tlatoani*s with his own men. He succeeded in arranging the assassination of Chimalpopoca and the exile of Nezahualcóyotl, ruler of Texcoco, a state on the east shore of Lake Texcoco. In response to these acts, a coalition was formed between Nezahualcóyotl, Itzcóatl (Chimalpopoca's successor), and another small state (Tlacopan), and the power of Azcapotzalco was broken.

A triple alliance was then formed between Tenochtitlán, Texcoco, and Tlacopan, which by 1519 resulted in the dominance of Aztec Tenochtitlán. Under the Aztec rulers Itzcóatl (1428–40), Montezuma I (1440–69), Axayacatl (1469–81), Tizoc (1481–86), Ahuitzotl (1486–1502), and Montezuma II (1502–20), and the two Texcocan rulers—Nezahualcóyotl (1431–72) and Nezahualpilli (1472–1516)—the triple alliance succeeded in conquering the vast domain described above. Tlacopan seems to have been relegated to an inferior political role early in the history. The records of the Aztec and neighbouring states in the Basin of Mexico between 1300 and 1519 are relatively free from mythological tales and have sufficient cross-referencing to present a reasonably clear picture of military events, dynastic succession, institutional changes, and economic development. The period from 1200 to 1300 is essentially one of migration legends of the dynasties of the various states, the historical traditions of which are discussed below.

THE QUESTION OF THE TOLTEC

The historical traditions also state that these migrations were responsible, along with a series of natural disasters, for the collapse of a great empire ruled by a people called the Toltec from their capital of Tollan, or Tula. Many dynasties of the conquest period, not only in central Mexico but even as far afield as highland Guatemala and the Yucatán Peninsula, claimed descent from the Toltec, apparently as a result of their dispersion after the fall of Tula.

The traditions describe the Toltec as the first civilizers, the first city builders, and the originators of craft skills and astrological knowledge. The major questions are: Did the Toltec really exist as a people? Where was Tula? Did these people actually play the extraordinary political and cultural roles ascribed to them? To begin with, the annals themselves are in fundamental disagreement with respect to dates and the lists of Toltec kings. There are at least three major chronologies of the Toltec Empire. The dates by Ixtlilxóchitl, a learned mestizo of the postconquest period, place the Toltec well within the Classic Period of Mesoamerican archaeology, but the others correlate them with the early portion of the Post-Classic. Most writers favour the later dates, but this would mean that the Toltec were not the first civilized peoples in central Mexico, as they claim.

Adding further doubt to the veracity of the Toltec history is the admixture of myth and magic in the annals, not only at the beginning (which, like the histories of later dynasties, begins with a migration under a magician-priest) but throughout the narrative. The ruler Topiltzin, for example, is also called Quetzalcóatl (the Nahua name for the Feathered Serpent god); he is opposed by Tezcatlipoca (also an Aztec god) and is driven out of Tula. He flees with his followers to the Gulf of Mexico and embarks on a raft of serpents.

The story sounds like a duplicate of the cosmic myth or conflict between the two gods. Notably, the Maya in Yucatán had a tradition of a landing on the west coast made by foreigners, under a leader named Kukulcán (which is the Maya word for Feathered Serpent), who founded a city at Chichén Itzá and ruled over the Maya.

In spite of all the objections, the traditions of a great empire and of the city of Tula are so persistent that they must refer to some historical event and, indeed, have some archaeological support.

ARCHAEOLOGICAL REMAINS OF POST-CLASSIC CIVILIZATION

The early Post-Classic Period (900–1200) in central Mexico is associated with three major sites, all of which began in Classic times: Cholula in Puebla, Xochicalco in Morelos, and Tula in Hidalgo. Cholula was a major centre as far back as Early Classic times, probably as a political dependency of Teotihuacán. It reached its maximum growth in Late Classic times, following the collapse of Teotihuacán, when the largest structure ever built by Mesoamericans was erected.

In Post-Classic times Cholula continued as a major religious and cultural centre. Xochicalco probably was of minor significance in Early Classic times, but it went through a phase of explosive growth in the Late Classic and was probably abandoned by 1200, possibly earlier. Tula, on the other hand, a small centre in the Late Classic, went through a rapid growth during the period 900–1200 and then declined to a provincial centre in the Late Post-Classic. There is a strong suggestion that the demise of Classic Teotihuacán was in part related to the emergence of one or all of these major centres.

TULA

The location of the Toltec capital of Tollan, or Tula, is not certain. The archaeological site located on a low ridge near the modern town of Tula has been the persistent choice of all historians since the conquest, in part because of the coincidence of place-names. There is further support for this identification in that the annals provide a great number of place-names near the modern Tula that have persisted since the conquest. There is also support for the identification in that the glyph Ad Acatl, the birthday and birth name of the great Toltec leader Topiltzin, has been found carved on a hill near Tula. Moreover, the sculpture from the site is heavily loaded with symbolism that relates to the Quetzalcóatl cosmology and cosmogony. It clearly was the city of the god Quetzalcóatl. The confusion between the god and the ruler can be ascribed to the fact that the name Quetzalcóatl may have served as a title of office carried by all Toltec rulers. The archaeological dates are in agreement with the *Anales de Cuauhtitlán* and the Codex Ramírez.

The major factors that have made some researchers reluctant to accept this identification lie in the claim that Tula was the capital of a great pan-Mesoamerican empire and that the Toltec were the first civilizers in central Mexico. Archaeologically, it is quite clear that Tula was preceded by the great Classic centre of Teotihuacán. Tula as a site does not really approach the earlier Teotihuacán or the later Tenochtitlán in size, in the number of public buildings, or in estimated population, although studies indicate that Tula had a population of between 30,000 and 60,000. Furthermore, although some basic stylistic elements of the art and architecture of Tula are widespread, the style, in an integrated specific sense, is limited (with one notable exception) to a small area in central Mexico. These facts make it difficult to accept Tula as the capital of a great empire. But archaeological evidence of even the Aztec empire is skimpy. In both cases, this may mean that the expansion was a rapid, explosive one that failed to last long enough to register these effects. But at least in the case of Tenochtitlán it did result in the rapid growth of a truly gigantic urban centre.

Because of these objections and because Teotihuacán fits better with the description of the Toltec as the builders of the first truly civilized society in central Mexico, that site must still be considered a possible candidate.

The art and architecture of Tula shows a striking similarity to the later art and architecture of Tenochtitlán, and the themes represented in the art indicate a close approximation in religious ideology and behaviour. The symbols of sun sacrifice and the marching predators represented in sculpture both suggest that the concept the Aztec had of themselves as the warrior-priests of the sun god was directly borrowed from the people of Tula.

On the basis of the symbolism represented in the carvings on a temple pyramid at Tula called Structure B, it has been concluded that the pyramid was dedicated to the god Quetzalcóatl, lending further support to the identification of the site as the Toltec capital.

CHICHÉN ITZÁ

Also in support of the identification of Tula as the Toltec capital are the architectural characteristics and stylistic features of the sculpture of a large site in northern Yucatán called Chichén Itzá. The resemblance between the two sites is extraordinarily close. At Chichén are found flat beam and masonry roofs (contrasting sharply with the typical Maya corbeled vault); serpent columns; colonnaded halls attached to the bases of temples; altars with Atlantean figures; sculptured representations of skulls and crossbones, marching felines, canines, and raptorial birds devouring human hearts; and depictions of warriors with typical Toltec accoutrements. Furthermore, there are even scenes showing Toltec and Maya warriors in combat. The Temple of the Warriors at Chichén Itzá looks like an attempt to duplicate Structure B at Tula.

Some of the walls of Chichén Itzá are decorated with images of skulls. Other designs within the temple include scenes of animals devouring human organs and Toltec warriors mid-combat. Shutterstock.com

One of the puzzling aspects of the relationship between the two sites is that the public architecture of Chichén Itzá is actually more monumental than that at Tula, leading at least one Mesoamerican specialist to believe that Tula's style was derived from Chichén. Many of the stylistic features themselves, however, have prototypes in Classic Teotihuacán, whereas there is little in Classic Maya culture that could be considered as the source. What is more probable—and this agrees with the Toltec version of the relationship—is that the Toltec state in Yucatán was politically independent from Tula and was larger in area and population. The presence of rival states in central Mexico such as Xochicalco and Cholula may have kept the core of the Toltec polity relatively restricted in space. The much larger area and population controlled by the Toltec state at Chichén would explain the differences in the scale of architecture. The superior military organization and equipment of the Toltec perhaps explains their apparent success in Yucatán.

ARCHAEOLOGICAL UNITY OF THE POST-CLASSIC

The Post-Classic Period of Mesoamerican archaeology generally is a period characterized by considerable regionalism combined with a certain degree of uniformity. To a great extent, the latter was the product of the large states and extensive trade networks centred in the central plateau region. The Early Post-Classic in some areas may be described as a continuation of the Late Classic; on the Gulf coast, for example, sites like El Tajín continued to be occupied, while in the Valley of Oaxaca (although Monte Albán was abandoned) the Zapotec tradition continued with the new centre at Mitla. In other areas, new styles either began or reached their climactic development, such as the Mixteca–Puebla style in painting, ceramics, and metallurgy, which evolved either in western Oaxaca or, more probably, at Cholula in Puebla. On the Guatemalan Pacific piedmont and in Tabasco, two specialized ceramic traditions (both of which began in Late Classic times) evolved: (1) plumbate (so called because of its slip, which had an unusually high iron content in the natural clay that fired to a lead-colour glaze); and (2) Fine Orange (so called because of its fine-grained, temperless paste). Wares of these two styles were widely traded.

The unity of the Post-Classic consisted primarily of the diffusion of religious ideology, particularly the sun god–warfare–sacrificial complex and of the related institutional development such as the military orders (the latter probably originated at Classic Teotihuacán). This ideology clearly originated in central Mexico, at either Cholula or Tula or both. The specific artistic style of representation of the themes in painting and sculpture spread as well. Along with this was diffused a specific style of representation of the social calendar and writing generally and much greater emphasis on the 52-year cycle. The specific style most probably originated at Cholula.

In the highland areas of Mesoamerica the Late Post-Classic was a period of maximum population growth. The Early Post-Classic was, however, the period of maximum expansion of sedentary peoples on the northern frontier, probably the product of minor changes in climate as a result of increased rainfall. This frontier retracted substantially in Late Post-Classic times, possibly because the rainfall decreased. This was perhaps the major factor in the precipitate arrival of barbarous tribes into the plateau, as the annals state.

The Post-Classic, over large areas of the lowlands, on the other hand, was strikingly different. One of the most intriguing problems of Mesoamerican archaeology is the peculiar sequence of events in the lowland Maya area. At the time of European contact much of the northern portion of Yucatán was well settled. A narrow band of densely settled country also extended along the east coast south to modern Belize City and along the entire length of the west coast (where it joined another area of substantial settlement in the south Gulf coast). Most of the heart of the peninsula, the department of Petén in Guatemala, and large portions of the states of Campeche and Quintana Roo in Mexico (the most densely settled portion of the Classic Maya territory) were virtually abandoned.

One of the major problems of Mesoamerican archaeology is the explanation of this massive population decline. The immediate causes are clear: it must have been the product of migrations out of the area or a set of internal factors that caused a decline in situ, or both. Various hypotheses as to processes and causes have been suggested. These may be grouped in the following categories: natural disasters (earthquakes, famines, epidemics, and hurricanes have all been suggested); ecological processes (primarily the deterioration of the natural environment by overintensification of land use in response to population pressure); and sociopolitical processes (internal warfare, invasion from outside, peasant revolts, breakdown of critical trade networks). Some of these hypotheses are clearly derivations from others or are not explanations but rather are descriptions of events that were produced by other processes. It seems certain that the causes were multiple and in some way related. Of great interest is the fact that at least one other lowland area, the Pacific Coastal Plain of Guatemala, experienced a comparable Post-Classic decline.

AZTEC CULTURE TO THE TIME OF THE SPANISH CONQUEST

At the time of the Spanish conquest the dominant people of Mesoamerica were the Aztec. This description is based primarily on written documents from the 16th century but also includes some archaeological data. The literature, both published and unpublished, of the 16th century is enormous and takes in all aspects of Aztec culture. Much of it covers the period within a few decades after the conquest, and it is uncertain how much change had occurred because of the introduction of Spanish culture. Some Aztec institutions, such as the military orders, were immediately abolished by the Spaniards; the sources, therefore, give only the barest outline of their organization. This information, however, combined with archaeological data, gives a fairly detailed picture of Aztec culture at the time of the Spanish conquest.

ACCOUNTS WRITTEN BY THE CONQUISTADORES

Eyewitness accounts of Aztec culture on the eve of the conquest are, of course, the most directly pertinent sources because they describe Aztec culture before it became transformed by the Spanish conquest. Important among these are the *Cartas de Relación* ("Letters of Information"), sent by Hernán Cortés to the Holy Roman emperor Charles V, and the *Historia verdadera de la conquista de*

Key information about Aztec culture before the European invasion can be found in accounts written by Spanish conquistador Hernán Cortés and other explorers. Hulton Archive/ Getty Images

la Nueva España (1632; "The True History of the Conquest of New Spain") by Bernal Díaz del Castillo. Religious rites and ceremonies, temples, and paraphernalia of the cults are often described in these accounts. Their value, however, is lessened by the writers' ignorance of Nahuatl (the Aztec language at the time of the conquest), their lack of understanding of the Indian way of thinking, and their deep hostility to the native religion, which they considered to be inspired by the devil. These documents, therefore, have been interpreted with utmost caution.

Roman Catholic missionaries also wrote accounts of the Aztec. Paradoxically, the priests generally showed more understanding and tolerance than did the laymen. Thanks to their training and theological knowledge, they were able to analyze the Indian mind and to gain insight into the meaning of the myths and ritual. The missionaries, as a rule, learned the native languages, especially Nahuatl.

POSTCONQUEST HISTORIES

Within a few decades of the conquest, a series of histories had been written in the Spanish language, based in part on Aztec books and in part on information supplied by the upper class. Among the most detailed of these is the three-part *Historia de las Indias de la Nueva España e Islas de Tierra Firma* ("History of the Indies of New Spain"), written about 1580 by the Dominican friar Diego Durán.

These works are comparable in methodology and subject matter to the kinds of studies of native peoples conducted by present-day anthropologists. Probably the finest of them was written by Bernardino de Sahagún. Sahagún was a Franciscan priest who arrived in Mexico very early (1529), learned the Nahuatl tongue, and spent his life building a wonderful monument, a real encyclopaedia called the *Historia general de las cosas de Nueva España* ("General History of the Things of New Spain"). His work covers virtually all aspects of Aztec culture. It contains particularly detailed accounts of religion, ethnobotany, folk medicine, and economics, dictated to him in Nahuatl by Aztec noblemen and priests. As a source, it has the added value of being written in both Nahuatl and Spanish. One of the most complete versions of this work, written in Nahuatl, is called the Florentine Codex.

THE CODICES

Aztec sacred books and works, which were kept in the temples, and other native books have become known in Western scholarship as codices. Sacred books were written (or rather, painted) on deerskin or agave-fibre paper by scribes (*tlacuiloanime*), who used a combination of pictography, ideograms, and phonetic symbols and dealt with the ritual calendar, divination, ceremonies, and speculations on the gods and the universe. Because of their religious content

An illustration from a reproduction of the Codex Magliabecchi depicting an Aztec priest performing a sacrificial offering of a living human heart to the war god Huitzilopochtli. Library of Congress, Washington, D.C. (neg. no. LC-USZC4-743)

only a small fraction of these escaped destruction by the Spaniards; the few specimens that have survived—such as the Codex Borbonicus, the Codex Borgia, the Codex Fejérváry-Mayer, and the Codex Cospi—usually come accompanied by Spanish notations. These sources are limited in scope and subject matter but nevertheless are valuable documents. Their interpretation is far from easy. Only a few of them, such as the Borbonicus, are truly Aztec, while others, such as

the Borgia, seem to emanate from the priestly colleges of the "Mexica-Puebla" area, between the central highlands and the Oaxaca Mountains.

Other native books, either pre-Cortesian or post-Cortesian, also afford valuable material. Examples include such manuscripts as the Codex Telleriano-Remensis, the Azcatitlan, and the Codex of 1576, which describe the history of the Aztec tribe and state and occasionally depict religious scenes and events; the

NAHUATL LANGUAGE

Nahuatl was the language of the Aztec and Toltec civilizations of what is now Mexico. It belongs to the Uto-Aztecan family of American Indian languages. A large body of literature in Nahuatl, produced by the Aztecs, survives from the 16th century, recorded in an orthography that was introduced by Spanish priests and based on that of Spanish.

The phonology of Classical Nahuatl, the language of the Aztecs, was notable for its use of a tl *sound produced as a single consonant and for the use of the glottal stop. The glottal stop has been lost in some modern dialects—replaced by* h—*and retained in others. The* tl *sound, however, serves to distinguish the three major modern dialects: central and northern Aztec dialects retain the* tl *sound, as can be seen in their name, Nahuatl. Eastern Aztec dialects, around Veracruz, Mex., have replaced the* tl *with* t *and are called Nahuat. Western dialects, spoken primarily in the Mexican states of Michoacán and México, replace the* tl *with* l *and are called Nahual.*

Classical (i.e., 16th-century) Nahuatl used a set of 15 consonants and four long and short vowels. Its grammar was basically agglutinative, making much use of prefixes and suffixes, reduplication (doubling) of syllables, and compound words.

Codex Badianus, an herbal with magnificent drawings of medicinal plants; and the Codex Mendoza and the *Matrícula de tributos,* both tax documents of the Aztec empire. A number of books were written in the Latin alphabet—either in Nahuatl or in Spanish—by learned Aztec chroniclers, who used ancient pictographic manuscripts as their basis. Among those that were prepared in central Mexico are the Codex Chimalpopoca (also called the *Anales de Cuauhtitlán;* "Annals of Cuauhtitlán"), in Nahuatl, and the Codex Ramírez (also called the *Historia de los mexicanos por sus pinturas;* "History of the Mexicans Through Their Paintings"), in Spanish; both are anonymous compilations.

OFFICIAL ECCLESIASTICAL AND GOVERNMENT RECORDS

Much of this literature is unpublished. Its purpose was administrative rather than intellectual, but it has provided an extraordinarily rich source of information for all 16th-century ethnic groups. The documents vary from tax lists, censuses, and marriage and baptismal records to broad geographic-economic surveys. Among the most valuable of the last type are the *Relaciones geográficas* of 1579–85, a series of surveys ordered by Philip II of his overseas possessions. Formal questionnaires were drawn up that demanded information from each town in the empire on virtually all aspects of Mesoamerican life: questions on the natural environment and resources, crops, population history, settlement patterns, taxes paid, markets and trade, the language, native history and customs, and progress of the missionization program.

AGRICULTURE

The homeland of the Aztec, from which they ruled their vast domain, was a large (about 3,000 square miles [4,828 sq km]), mountain-rimmed basin with a floor at approximately 7,000 feet (2,164 metres) above sea level. The surrounding ranges reached a maximum elevation of 18,000 feet (5,486 metres) in the volcano of Popocatépetl. The annual rainfall varied from 20 to 35 inches (50 to 89 centimetres) in the valley floor to a maximum of 50 inches (127 cm) on the southern escarpment. Approximately 80 percent of the rain fell between May 1 and October 1. Because of the high elevation, the area suffered from severe winter frosts that normally began in mid-October and lasted until the end of March. Normally, the rainfall was adequate for corn, even in the drier portions of the basin, but a major problem was the timing of the rains and the frosts. A delay of the rainfall to mid- or late June, accompanied by early autumn frosts, could produce crop disasters.

Another major problem for the pre-Hispanic cultivator was the paucity of level land. Much of the land surface is sloping, and the problem of soil erosion was acute. Furthermore, of the 1,600 square miles (2,575 sq km) of relatively level land, 400 square miles (644 sq km) were occupied by a chain of lakes; and much of the immediate lakeshore plain was waterlogged.

Because of the effect of elevation on the growing season, the areas above 8,300 feet (2,530 metres) were also unsuitable for cultivation, removing an additional 400 square miles (644 sq km) from the agricultural resource. Even within zones of cultivation, the presence of steep slopes and thin soil further reduced the area of cultivation. It is doubtful that more than 50 percent of the basin was suitable for labour-intensive methods of cultivation. Yet in 1519 it supported a population of 1 million to 1.5 million; i.e., a density of 500 people per square mile (200 per square kilometre), the densest population in Mesoamerican history. This was achieved by an extraordinarily intensive system of farming that involved a number of specialized techniques. Soil fertility was maintained by plant and animal fertilizers, by short-cycle fallowing, and by irrigation. In gently sloping terrain, erosion was controlled by earth and maguey terraces, in steeper areas by stone terracing. The problem of humidity was solved by canal irrigation of both the floodwater and permanent type. Much of the irrigation was done just before planting in April and May in order to give crops a head start and hence avoid the autumn frosts. Terracing functioned also as a method of conserving moisture. There is also evidence that dry-farming techniques were applied to store moisture in the soil.

OBSIDIAN

A natural glass of volcanic origin, obsidian is formed by the rapid cooling of viscous lava. It is extremely rich in silica (about 65 to 80 percent), is low in water, and has a chemical composition similar to rhyolite (the lava form of granite). Obsidian has a glassy lustre and is slightly harder than window glass. Though obsidian is typically jet-black in colour, the presence of hematite (iron oxide) produces red and brown varieties, and the inclusion of tiny gas bubbles may create a golden sheen. Other types with dark bands or mottling in gray, green, or yellow are also known.

Obsidian generally contains less than 1 percent water by weight. Under high pressure at depth, rhyolitic lavas may contain up to 10 percent water, which helps to keep them fluid even at a low temperature. Eruption to the surface, where pressure is low, permits rapid escape of this volatile water and increases the viscosity of the melt. Increased viscosity impedes crystallization, and the lava solidifies as a glass.

Different obsidians are composed of a variety of crystalline materials. Their abundant, closely spaced crystallites (microscopic embryonic crystal growths) are so numerous that the glass is opaque except on thin edges. Many samples of obsidian contain spherical clusters of radially arranged, needlelike crystals called spherulites. Microlites (tiny polarizing crystals) of feldspar and phenocrysts (large, well-formed crystals) of quartz may also be present.

Most obsidian is associated with volcanic rocks and forms the upper portion of rhyolitic lava flows. It occurs less abundantly as thin edges of dikes and sills. The obsidians of Mount Hekla in Iceland, the Eolie Islands off the coast of Italy, and Obsidian Cliff in Yellowstone National Park, Wyoming, U.S., are all well-known occurrences.

Obsidian was used by American Indians and many other aboriginal peoples for weapons, implements, tools, and ornaments and by the ancient Aztecs and Greeks for mirrors. Because of its conchoidal fracture (smooth curved surfaces and sharp edges), the sharpest stone artifacts were fashioned from obsidian; some of these, mostly arrowheads, have been dated by means of the hydration rinds that form on their exposed surfaces through time. Obsidian in attractive and variegated colours is sometimes used as a semiprecious stone.

The most significant achievement of Aztec agriculture, however, was that of swamp reclamation, even including colonization of the lakes. This system of farming, called *chinampa*, was first applied to Lake Chalco. The lake covered approximately 60 square miles (96.5 sq km) and apparently varied in its character from swamps to ponds of fairly deep, open water. By a process varying from digging drainage ditches to artificial construction of land from lake mud and vegetation, most of the lake was converted to highly productive agricultural land. A series of masonry causeway dikes were constructed across the lake to control flooding. By a system of dikes and sluice gates the Aztec even managed to convert a portion of saline Lake Texcoco, the largest and lowest lake in the basin, to a freshwater bay for further chinampa colonization.

The total area colonized was probably in the neighbourhood of 30,000 acres, and Tenochtitlán, the Aztec capital, depended on these lands for much of its food. By a comparable method, much of the waterlogged lakeshore plain was also converted into agricultural land. Particularly notable is the fact that all of these techniques of food production were achieved by human power and simple hand tools.

Aside from agriculture, the basin had a number of major resources, some of which were exploited not only for local consumption but also to supply other areas of Mesoamerica. Obsidian, natural glass of volcanic origin, was a superb material for a great variety of stone tools. The northeastern ranges of the basin contained one of Mesoamerica's major deposits. Basalt for manos and metates (milling stones) was also abundant. Lake Texcoco was a major source of salt, and the lakes generally provided waterfowl, fish, and other aquatic foodstuffs. The great pine forests above the limits of agriculture were a major source of lumber. On the other hand, the basin, because of its high elevation, was unsuitable for a great variety of tropical products, including cotton, paper, tropical roots and fruits, tobacco, copal incense, rubber, cacao, honey, precious feathers and skins, and such prized goods as metal, jade, and turquoise. The major motivation of Aztec conquest was to obtain control of these resources.

SOCIAL AND POLITICAL ORGANIZATION

Aztec technology differed little from that of other Mesoamerican groups. One of its distinctive aspects was differentiation by status levels. The use of most of the extra-local resources noted above was limited to a small upper and middle class; and there were striking differences in dress, housing, and diet by social class. Commoners, for example, wore clothing woven from maguey fibre, while the upper classes wore cotton garments. The use of imported foods, at least on a regular basis, was limited to the upper and middle classes. Commoners lived in small adobe or stone and mud huts, while the upper and middle class inhabited large multiroomed palatial houses of cut stone, lime plaster, and concrete.

Aztec social and political organization can be divided into a number of levels of increasing size and complexity of organization. The nuclear family—that is, a pair of cohabiting adults and their unmarried children—formed the lowest level of organization. The nuclear family functioned in procreation, education of children, and as a unit of food preparation and consumption, with a well-defined division of labour between husband and wife. Among the Aztec, however, a number of nuclear families usually resided together in a single cooperating household, or extended family. Such a family usually consisted of a man, his married sons or brothers, and their families.

The average peasant household of this type was small. Up to three nuclear families occupied a small multiroom house divided into apartments for each family. The houses were usually placed within a courtyard fenced with organ cactus or adobe walls, forming a compound. The extended family household probably functioned as a unit of land use and food production. In the towns, however, some households could be considerably larger, and the household of Montezuma II included several thousand people.

A number of households, varying from a few score to several hundred, were organized into an internally complex corporate group referred to as a *calpulli* by the Aztec and translated as *barrio* ("ward") by the Spaniards. Questions about the structure and function of this level of Aztec organization have caused a great deal of debate among Mesoamerican specialists. It is clear, however, that it was a physical and territorial unit as well as a socially organized one. It was a unit of land tenure. *Calpulli* lands were owned communally but were distributed among various households. The household retained the right of usufruct, but only the *calpulli* as a whole could sell or rent lands.

The *calpulli* rural communities varied considerably in physical appearance. Some were isolated, tightly nucleated physical settlements surrounded by their agricultural land, whereas in others houses were dispersed through the land holdings. In a few cases, they were physically attached as wards to one or more other *calpulli*. These differences corresponded to ecological, economic, and political factors. Rural, dispersed settlements were found on terraced hillsides in which houses were tightly integrated with the terrace; in the chinampa area, each house was placed on its chinampa holding. On the other hand, nucleated, isolated *calpulli* were found in areas of level land, and the ward type was usually found in the towns and cities. In the latter case, many lost their agricultural character and became units of craft specialization. The *calpulli* was a unit of political administration within the larger unit that will be referred to here as the state. It was ruled by a council of household heads presided over by a chief selected by the council from within a particular lineage. The *calpulli* functioned as a unit of taxation to the central government, as a unit of corvée labour, and as a military regiment.

The structure of the *calpulli* is open to question. Some sources call it a kin group, "a lineage" with a common ancestor; and as a result some anthropologists have referred to it as a clan, or sib. There is no evidence, however, of either exogamy or unilineal descent; in fact, marriage records from the postconquest period show a strong tendency toward endogamy. There is some evidence of internal ranking and significant status differentiation, another non-clanlike feature. The sources also mention smaller territorial subdivisions, referred to as *barrios* pequeños, or "little wards." If these are descent lines, then the *calpulli* resembled quite closely a type of kin group called by anthropologists a ramage, or a conical clan. This is a group with a myth of common descent, divided into ranked senior and junior lineages based on the seniority of older versus younger brother in the group genealogy. In support of this reconstruction is the statement that the *calpulli* god was a deified ancestor. The *calpulli* also functioned as a unit of education, for each possessed a school for young men—the telpuchcalli—primarily for military and moral instruction.

Above the level of the *calpulli* was the state. With the exception of those historical periods when larger polities, such as the Aztec empire, emerged, such states in Mesoamerica, including the Basin of Mexico, were small. Just prior to the Aztec expansion there were 50 or 60 such states in the basin, with an average size of about 50 to 60 square miles (80 to 96.5 sq km). In 1519 these once independent domains had an average population of 25,000 to 30,000 people. In less densely settled areas, the territories were larger and populations smaller. The range of size was from a few thousand up to 100,000.

The average small state included a central town with a population of several thousand, the balance of the population consisting of the rural *calpulli*. The central town was divided into wards that corresponded in size and to a certain degree in structure to the rural *calpulli* but were clearly different in function; they in turn were divided into *barrios pequeños*.

At the head of the state was an official called the *tlatoani,* to whom all household heads owed allegiance, respect, and tax obligations. The *tlatoani*'s position was fixed within a particular lineage, the particular choice varying from state to state. In some areas, succession passed from father to son; in others, the succession went through a series of brothers and then passed to the eldest son of the eldest brother.

In still other states, the office was elective, but the choice was limited to sons or brothers of the deceased ruler. The office was accompanied by all of the trappings and sumptuary behaviour typical of despotic states. The ruler resided in a large, multiroom masonry palace inhabited by a great number of wives, servants, and professional craftsmen. He was carried in a sedan chair in public and treated with exaggerated respect by his subordinates. The *tlatoani* held considerable power. He appointed all lesser bureaucrats, promoted men to higher military status, organized military campaigns, and was the distributor of booty and tribute. He also collected taxes in labour, military service, and goods from his supporters; owned private estates manned by serfs; was the final court of appeal in judicial cases; and was titular head of the religious cult and head of the town market.

Many of these functions were delegated to a large staff of professional administrators, including priests, market supervisors, military leaders, judges, tax collectors, and accountants. The tax collectors, or *calpixque,* were especially important administrators because they acted as the rulers' agents in collecting goods and services from the *calpulli* chiefs.

Most of these positions were appointed and selected from two classes—the *pipiltin* (plural of *pilli*), and the professional warriors. Society was divided into three well-defined castes. At the top were the *pipiltin,* nobles by birth and members of the royal lineage. Below them was the *macehual* class, the commoners who made up the bulk of the population. At the base of the social structure were the *mayeques,* or serfs, attached to private or state-owned rural estates. Within these three castes, a number of social classes could be differentiated, according to wealth, occupation, and political office. The Aztec system made a distinction between ascribed and achieved status.

By a system of promotions, usually as a reward for military deeds, commoners were appointed to such political offices as *calpixque* and judges. Many *pipiltin* held no political office and, unless they had inherited private estates, were forced to live off the largess of the ruler. Commoners who had captured four enemy warriors in combat were promoted to the rank of *tecuhtli,* entered one of the military orders, were assigned a private estate with serfs for their maintenance, and acted as an elite professional army. The children of both *pipiltin* and *tecuhtli* could enroll in the religious college, or *calmecac,* where they could be trained as priests or political administrators. The calmecac apparently was also open to certain other commoners, such as wealthy and influential merchants and craftsmen.

Aside from the commoner-warriors, the *macehual* class was further differentiated into class levels. Certain occupations were accorded higher prestige than others (merchants, lapidarians, goldsmiths, and featherworkers are mentioned, and the list probably included stone sculptors), and all urban occupations were assigned higher status as compared with rural farming. Since occupations were restricted to *calpulli* membership and since the *calpulli* were kin groups, it follows that crafts tended to be hereditary. In small towns the craft specializing group would have to be the *barrio pequeño.* In the cities it was definitely the larger unit, but in either case crafts would be found within hereditary corporate groups.

The system of social stratification emphasized ascribed status but also permitted considerable vertical mobility. The land-tenure system was an important aspect in maintaining both processes, as could be expected in a basically agrarian society. Although most of the land was held in common by the *calpulli,* private estates with serfs helped to maintain the prestige of the *pilli* class and similar estates assigned to political office; and *tecuhtli* positions freed able commoners from the necessity of subsistence procurement.

The taxation system also helped to maintain the social system. All heads of households owed military service to the

tlatoani. For the *pipiltin* and *tecuhtli,* this was the only tribute demanded. Urban craftsmen also paid tribute in their craft products but were exempt from corvée labour. That obligation, plus taxes in agricultural products, were the burdens of the rural peasants, and the *mayeques* owed their labour and agricultural produce to their overlord.

Two other elements in the Aztec social system were pawns and slaves. The former were poor men who could sell themselves or members of their household for a specified period of time. Their rights were carefully defended by Aztec law, and they were not slaves but more like indentured servants. True slaves did exist and in some parts of Mesoamerica were used as workers or servants. Among the Aztec, the *mayeques* were their counterpart. Slaves were bought in lowland markets and used primarily for human sacrifice.

The high development of craft specialization—much of it full-time—in Aztec towns has been noted above. But many rural communities also had part-time specialities, a feature due in part to the heterogeneity of the highland environment, with its highly local distribution of resources. Foreign goods were brought into the Aztec homeland by great caravans of professional merchants called *pochteca,* who frequently undertook journeys exceeding a year in length. As a group the merchants enjoyed very high prestige and even had their own tribunals. Various merchant wards of a great number of towns and cities in central Mexico were organized into one great trading guild that had its centre at Tenochtitlán. They also organized and administered the town markets, another highly evolved aspect of Aztec institutions. These markets were held in great open plazas—in smaller towns every fifth day, in larger towns and cities daily, although in the latter case the market population reached a peak every fifth day.

The centres and the political organization of large states such as the Aztec empire were fundamentally similar in character to small ones; but the vast differences in size (Tenochtitlán, the Aztec capital, may have had 140,000 to 200,000 inhabitants in 1519) demanded some changes. Generally, when one central Mexican state conquered another, the ruler of the conquering town extorted an annual tribute, but there was little attempt at political integration. In the case of the Aztec, this policy was generally maintained, but many conquered states were given Aztec governors. Furthermore, conquest was usually accompanied by an exchange of women from the two ruling lineages (conqueror and conquered), and successors to the throne of the conquered states were through these women, from the royal lineage of Tenochtitlán. As a result, the ruling class gradually tended toward a single kin group.

Because of the great number of states conquered by the Aztec (400 to 500), some form of intermediate-level territorial and administrative organization became imperative. The states conquered by the Aztec were grouped into 38 provinces. One town in each province served as capital, and an Aztec tax collector-governor was placed there to supervise the collection, storage, and disposition of the tribute. In many provinces, the Aztec established garrisons. These consisted of warriors and their families culled from all of the towns of the Valley of Mexico, and they were assigned lands in the conquered province. Since they supported themselves, they were colonists as well as troops. The planting of colonists, combined with such factors as the merchant guild and royal family intermarriage, suggests that the Aztec elite were attempting to integrate more closely the population of the Valley of Mexico as a kind of core nationality for the empire.

Other indications that the Aztec were in the process of achieving further political integration are statements in several *relaciones* that the tax collectors served as courts of appeals in serious judicial cases and also that the Aztec introduced the cult of their national god Huitzilopochtli to conquered provinces.

THE AZTEC CAPITAL: TENOCHTITLÁN

Tenochtitlán itself was a huge metropolis covering more than 5 square miles (8 sq km). It was originally located on two small islands in Lake Texcoco, but it gradually spread into the surrounding lake by a process, first of chinampa construction, then of consolidation. It was connected to the mainland by several causeway dikes that terminated in smaller lakeside urban communities. The lake around the city was also partly covered with chinampas with numerous rural settlements. Together, the complex of settlements—the city, the chinampa villages, and the settlements along the lakeshore plain—must have appeared from the air as one gigantic settlement. The population in 1519 was about 400,000 people, the largest and densest concentration in Mesoamerican history.

The majority of people in the city were non-food-producing specialists; i.e., craftsmen, merchants, priests, warriors, and administrators. In Tenochtitlán, as in other larger towns, the larger *calpulli* formed craft guilds. Guild organization was internally complex, an economic development related to the higher level of political integration and the greatly expanded trade and tax base that accrued from it. The great market in the barrio of Tlatelolco was reported by the Spaniards to have had 60,000 buyers and sellers on the main market day. The Spaniards also described the enormous canoe traffic on the lake moving goods to the market. There is even evidence that many chinampa cultivators, in response to the expanded market, were shifting from the production of staple crops to truck gardening.

The Aztec capital was originally two separate cities, Tlatelolco and Tenochtitlán, which merged into one through the conquest of Tlatelolco. The division was maintained for administrative purposes, however, and with further growth it became necessary to divide Tenochtitlán into four great wards (also referred to as *calpulli*). Each ward contained 12 to 15 *calpulli*, some 50 to 60 in all. Tlatelolco must have had 10 to 20 *calpulli* as well, bringing the total up to perhaps 80.

With this enormously expanded tax base, the central government became internally complex. The Spaniards described the palace of Montezuma II as containing 300 rooms grouped around three courts. Land titles dating from after the conquest give it an area of 10 acres. Aside from the private apartments of the king, the palace included libraries, storehouses, workshops for royal craftsmen, great halls for justice and other councils, and offices for an army of accountants. The sources even describe a royal zoo and aviary and a number of country retreats. The internal organization of the taxation, military, and judicial departments must have been far more complex than in small states, but precise data is lacking.

Within the city there were literally hundreds of temples and related religious structures. There were at least two large complexes, religious centres of the dual cities of Tenochtitlán and Tlatelolco. Each of the four great wards of Tenochtitlán, as well as each *calpulli*, had smaller temple complexes, so that the total number must have run into the hundreds. The great temple complex of Tenochtitlán consisted of three large pyramid temples (the principal temple platform, dedicated to Huitzilopochtli and Tlaloc, was 100 feet

(30 metres) high and measured 300 feet (91 metres) on a side at its base). There were also six small pyramid temples, three calmecac buildings (dormitories and colleges for priests), a ball court, a great wooden rack for the skulls of sacrificed victims, a sacred pool, a sacred grove, and several large open courts. All of these structures were placed within a vast walled enclosure, 1,200 feet (366 metres)on a side. The temple complex at Tlatelolco was at least half as large.

AZTEC RELIGION

Perhaps the most highly elaborated aspect of Aztec culture was the religious system. The Aztec derived much of their religious ideology from the earlier cultures of Mesoamerica or from their contemporaries. This was particularly true during the final phase of their history, when their foreign contacts broadened. Indeed, much confusion about Aztec religious ideology stems, in part, from the fact that Aztec civilization was still in a process of assimilation and reorganization of these varied religious traditions. Moreover, as the empire expanded and Tenochtitlán evolved into a heterogeneous community, the religious needs correspondingly changed from those of a simple agrarian society. The ruling class, particularly, demanded a more intellectual and philosophical ideology.

The Aztec approach to contact with the supernatural was through a complex calendar of great ceremonies, which were

BALL COURT

Hacha, carved stone, c. AD 300–900, found in Veracruz, Mex. Height 16 inches (40 cm). Courtesy of the Asian Art Museum of San Francisco, the Avery Brundage Collection, Adriani Bequest to the California Palace of the Legion of Honor.

The ball court was used for the ritual ball game (ollama) played throughout pre-Columbian Mesoamerica. Possibly originating among the Olmecs (La Venta culture, c. 800–c. 400 BC) or even earlier, the game spread to subsequent cultures, among them those of Monte Albán and El Tajín; the Maya (as pok-ta-pok); and the Toltec, Mixtec, and Aztec. In Aztec times, ollama was a nobles' game and was often accompanied by heavy betting. Various myths mention the ball game, sometimes as a contest between day and night deities. It is still played in isolated regions. Tlachtli and ollama are Nahuatl words.

The ball court, shaped like a capital I with serifs and oriented north–south or east–west, represented the heavens. The game itself was not unlike modern football (soccer). Players, wearing heavy padding, used elbows, knees, and hips—no hands—to knock a gutta-percha ball into the opponent's end of the court; in Post-Classic times (after c. AD 900), the object was to hit the ball through one of two vertical stone rings (placed on each side of the court). The ball represented the sun (or moon or stars), and the rings represented the sunrise and sunset or the equinoxes. If the ball went through a small hole in the carved stone disk or hit the circular goal, the game was won. Tremendous exchanges of personal property resulted from such a victory—indeed, often life itself was forfeited in important contests.

The culture of the ball court is also thought to be the source of some unusual stone carvings discovered in Veracruz. Although these objects have been found throughout Central America from central Mexico to El Salvador, their centre seems to have been in the coastal Veracruz area. One of the objects, the palma, or palmate stone (shaped like a hand with extended fingers), was initially thought to have had some religious significance. Experts now consider the palma a ritual object or trophy representing a protective device—worn together with the yugo, or yoke, and the hacha, or axe—used in the ceremonial ball game.

held at the temples and were performed by a professional priesthood that acted as the intermediary between the gods and human beings. Many of these were public in the sense that the populace played the role of spectators. Elements in all the ceremonies were very similar and included ritual ablutions to prepare the priests for the contact; offerings and sacrifices to gain the gods' favour; and theatrical dramas of myths by masked performers in the form of dances, songs, and processionals. Each god had his special ceremony that, considering the richness of the pantheon, must have filled the calendar. These ceremonies must have played a significant recreative function, as do ceremonies held in honour of patron saints in present-day Mexico.

Aztec religion heavily emphasized sacrifice and ascetic behaviour as the necessary preconditions for approaching the supernatural. Priests were celibate and were required to live a simple, spartan life. They performed constant self-sacrifice in the form of bloodletting as penitence (by passing barbed cords through the tongue and ears). This pattern of worship reached its climax in the practice of human sacrifice; it was in this aspect of Aztec culture that religion, war, and politics became closely related. Ideologically at least, Aztec warfare was waged for the purpose of obtaining sacrificial victims. The tribute lists, of course, demonstrate that there was a more mundane purpose as well, and it would be a serious mistake to think of Aztec warfare as functioning primarily in the religious sphere.

The cult of the gods required a large professional priesthood. Spanish documents indicate that the priesthood was one of the most elaborate of Aztec institutions. Each temple and god had its attendant priestly order. At Tenochtitlán the high priests of Tlaloc and Huitzilopochtli served as heads of the entire priestly organization. Within the orders were priests in charge of ceremonies, of the education of novices, of astrology, and of the temple lands. (These consisted of specific rural communities assigned by the state to particular temples.) Furthermore, there were several grades of priests. As noted above, the priests maintained a number of schools, or *calmecacs*, where sons of the nobility and certain commoners were given instruction. Most of the novices ultimately left the priesthood and carried out economic and political functions; others remained, joined the priesthood on a permanent basis, and lived at the *calmecac*.

Much of Aztec religion probably was practiced at home at special household altars. Common archaeological artefacts are small baked-clay idols or figurines, representing specific gods apparently used in these household ceremonies, along with incense burners.

COSMOGONY AND ESCHATOLOGY

The Aztec believed that four worlds had existed before the present universe.

Those worlds, or "suns," had been destroyed by catastrophes. Humankind had been entirely wiped out at the end of each sun. The present world was the fifth sun, and the Aztec thought of themselves as "the People of the Sun." Their divine duty was to wage cosmic war in order to provide the sun with his *tlaxcaltiliztli* ("nourishment"). Without it the sun would disappear from the heavens. Thus the welfare and the very survival of the universe depended upon the offerings of blood and hearts to the sun, a notion that the Aztec extended to all the deities of their pantheon.

The first sun was called Nahui-Ocelotl, "Four-Jaguar," a date of the ritual calendar. Humankind was first destroyed by jaguars. The animal was considered by the Aztec as the *nahualli* ("animal disguise") of the creator god Tezcatlipoca.

At the end of the second sun, Nahui-Ehécatl, "Four-Wind," a magical hurricane transformed all people into monkeys. That disaster was caused by Quetzalcóatl (the Feathered Serpent) in the form of Ehécatl, the wind god.

A rain of fire had put an end to the third sun, Nahuiquiahuitl, "Four-Rain." Tlaloc as the god of thunder and lightning presided over that period.

The fourth sun, Nahui-Atl, "Four-Water," ended in a gigantic flood that lasted for 52 years. Only one man and one woman survived, sheltered in a huge cypress. But they were changed into dogs by Tezcatlipoca, whose orders they had disobeyed.

Present humanity was created by Quetzalcóatl. The Feathered Serpent, with the help of his twin, Xólotl, the dog-headed god, succeeded in reviving the dried bones of the old dead by sprinkling them with his own blood. The present sun was called Nahui-Ollin, "Four-Earthquake," and was doomed to disappear in a tremendous earthquake. The skeleton-like monsters of the west, the *tzitzimime,* would then appear and kill all people.

Two deeply rooted concepts are revealed by these myths. One was the belief that the universe was unstable, that death and destruction continually threatened it. The other emphasized the necessity of the sacrifice of the gods. Thanks to Quetzalcóatl's self-sacrifice, the ancient bones of Mictlan, "the Place of Death," gave birth to men.

In the same way, the sun and moon were created. The gods, assembled in the darkness at Teotihuacán, built a huge fire. Two of them, Nanahuatzin, a small deity covered with ulcers, and Tecciztécatl, a richly bejeweled god, threw themselves into the flames, from which the former emerged as the sun and the latter as the moon. Then the sun refused to move unless the other gods gave him their blood. They were compelled to sacrifice themselves to feed the sun.

COSMOLOGY

According to the Aztec cosmological ideas, the earth had the general shape of

Xiuhtecuhtli (Huehuetéotl), seated stone figure, c. AD 1400–1500. A. De Gregorio/DeA Picture Library

a great disk divided into four sections oriented to the four cardinal directions. To each of the four world directions were attached five of the 20 day-signs, one of them being a Year-Bearer (east, *acatl*, "reed"; west, *calli*, "house"; north, *tecpatl*, "flint knife"; south, *tochtli*, "rabbit"), a colour (east, red or green; west, white; north, black; south, blue), and certain gods. The fifth cardinal point, the centre, was attributed to the fire god Huehuetéotl, because the hearth stood at the centre of the house.

Above earth, which was surrounded by the "heavenly water" (*ilhuicáatl*) of the ocean, were 13 heavens, the uppermost of which, "where the air is delicate and frozen," was the abode of the supreme couple. Under the "divine earth," *teotlalli*, were the nine hells of Mictlan, with nine rivers that the souls of the dead had to cross. Thirteen was considered a favourable number, nine extremely unlucky.

All of the heavenly bodies and constellations were divinized, such as the Great Bear (Tezcatlipoca), Venus (Quetzalcóatl), the stars of the north (Centzon Mimixcoa, "the 400 Cloud-Serpents"), the stars of the south (Centzon Huitznáua, "the 400 Southerners"). The solar disk, Tonatiuh, was supposed to be borne on a litter from the east to the zenith, surrounded by the souls of dead warriors, and from the zenith to the west among a retinue of divinized women, the Cihuateteo. When the night began on the earth, day dawned in Mictlan, the abode of the dead.

DEITIES

The ancient tribes of central Mexico had worshiped fertility gods for many centuries when the Aztec invaded the valley. The cult of these gods remained extremely important in Aztec religion. Tlaloc, the giver of rain but also the wrathful deity of lightning, was the leader of a group of rain gods, the Tlaloques, who dwelt on mountaintops. Chalchiuhtlicue ("One Who Wears a Jade Skirt") presided over fresh waters, Huixtocíhuatl over salt waters and the sea. Numerous earth goddesses were associated with the fertility of the soil and with the fecundity of women, as Teteoinnan ("Mother of the Gods"), Coatlicue ("One Who Wears a Snake Skirt"), Cihuacóatl ("Serpent-Woman"), and Itzpapálotl ("Obsidian-Butterfly"). Their significance was twofold. As fertility deities, they gave birth to the young gods of corn, Centéotl, and of flowers, Xochipilli. As symbols of the earth that devoured the bodies and drank the blood, they appeared as warlike godheads. Tlazoltéotl, a Huastec goddess, presided over carnal love and over the confession of sins.

Xipe Totec, borrowed from the faraway Yopi people, was a god of the spring, of the renewal of vegetation, and at the same time the god of the corporation of goldsmiths. Human victims were killed and flayed to honour him.

The concept of a supreme couple played an important role in the religion

Mask of Xipe Totec, gold, cast by the lost-wax method, Mixtec culture, c. 900–1494; in the Museo Regionale, Oaxaca, Mex. Ferdinand Anton

NAGUAL

The nagual (nahual) was a personal guardian spirit believed by some Mesoamerican Indians to reside in an animal, such as a deer, jaguar, or bird. In some areas the nagual is the animal into which certain powerful men can transform themselves to do evil; thus, the word derives from the Nahuatl word nahualli *("disguise"), applied to the animal forms magically assumed by sorcerers.*

The person who is to receive his nagual traditionally goes to an isolated spot and sleeps. The animal that appears in his dreams or that confronts him when he awakens will thereafter be his particular nagual. Among many modern Mesoamerican Indians, it is believed that the first creature to cross over the ashes spread before a newborn baby becomes that child's nagual. The belief in nagualism varies from region to region. In some areas it is believed that only the most powerful leaders (usually men) possess naguals. In others, all or most people have personal animal guardian spirits.

of the old sedentary peoples such as the Otomí. Among the Aztec it took the form of Intonan, Intota ("Our Mother, Our Father"), the earth and the sun. But the fire god Huehuetéotl was also associated with the earth. In addition, Ometecuhtli ("Lord of the Duality") and Omecihuatl ("Lady of the Duality") were held to abide in the 13th heaven. They decided on which date a human being would be born, thus determining his destiny.

Among the fertility gods are to be counted the "400 Rabbits" (Centzon Totochtin), little gods of the crops, among which are Ometochtli, the god of *octli* (a fermented drink), and Tepoztécatl, the god of drunkenness.

The Aztec brought with them the cult of their sun and war god, Huitzilopochtli, "the Hummingbird of the Left," who was considered "the reincarnated Warrior of the South," the conquering sun of midday. According to a legend probably borrowed from the Toltec, he was born near Tula. His mother, the earth goddess Coatlicue, had already given birth to the 400 Southerners and to the night goddess Coyolxauhqui, whom the newborn god exterminated with his *xiuhcoatl* ("turquoise serpent").

Tezcatlipoca, god of the night sky, was the protector of the young warriors. Quetzalcóatl, the ancient Teotihuacán deity of vegetation and fertility, had been "astralized" and transformed into a god of the morning star. He was also revered as a wind god and as the ancient priest-king of the Toltec golden age: the discoveries of writing, the calendar, and the arts were attributed to him.

MYTHOLOGY OF DEATH AND AFTERLIFE

The beliefs of the Aztec concerning the other world and life after death showed the same syncretism. The old paradise of the rain god Tlaloc, depicted in the Teotihuacán frescoes, opened its gardens to those who died by drowning, lightning, or as a result of leprosy, dropsy, gout, or lung diseases. He was supposed to have caused their death and to have sent their souls to paradise.

Two categories of dead persons went up to the heavens as companions of the sun: the Quauhteca ("Eagle People"), composed of warriors who had died in service and merchants killed while traveling in faraway places, and women who died while giving birth to their first child and thus became Cihuateteo, "Divine Women." All the other dead went down to Mictlan, under the northern deserts, the abode of Mictlantecuhtli, the skeleton-masked god of death. There they traveled for four years until they arrived at the ninth hell, where they disappeared altogether.

Ancient Aztec calendars were used as a means of divination. As such, they contained symbols to mark auspicious days and also factored in a handful of "unlucky" days. AFP/ Getty Images

Offerings were made to the dead 80 days after the funeral, then one year, two, three, and four years later. Then all links between the dead and the living were severed. But the warriors who crossed the heavens in the retinue of the sun were thought to come back to earth after four years as hummingbirds. The Cihuateteo were said to appear at night at the crossroads and strike passersby with palsy.

Worldview

The world vision of the Aztec conceded only a small part to man in the scheme of things. His destiny was submitted to the all-powerful *tonalpohualli* (the calendrical round); his life in the other world did not result from any moral judgment. His duty was to fight and die for the gods and for the preservation of the world order. Moreover, witchcraft, omens, and portents dominated everyday life. That such a pessimistic outlook should have coexisted with the wonderful dynamism of Aztec civilization is in itself a remarkable achievement.

Aztec Ritual Calendar

Tonalpohualli, an Aztec term meaning "the count of days," was the name of the ritual calendar of 260 days. It ran parallel to the solar calendar of 365 days, which was divided into 18 months of 20 days and five supplementary unlucky days. The word *tonalli* means both "day" and "destiny": the 260-day calendar was mainly used for purposes of divination. The days were named by the combination of 20 signs—natural phenomena such as wind and earthquake, animals like rabbit and jaguar, plants such as reeds, and objects like flint knife and house—with the numbers 1 to 13. Thus the calendrical round included 20 series of 13 days.

Specialized priests called *tonalpouhque* interpreted the signs and numbers on such occasions as birth, marriage, departure of traders to faraway lands, and election of rulers. Each day and each 13-day series were deemed lucky, unlucky, or indifferent according to the deities presiding over them. Thus Ad-Coatl ("One-Snake") was held as favourable to the traders, Chicome-Xochitl ("Seven-Flower") to the scribes and the weavers, and Nahui-Ehécatl ("Four-Wind") to the magicians. The men who were born during the Ad-Ocelotl ("One-Jaguar") series would die on the sacrificial stone, those whose birth took place on the day Ometochtli ("Two-Rabbit") would be drunkards, and so on. The *tonalpohualli* dominated every aspect of public and private life.

CHAPTER 4

ANDEAN CIVILIZATION

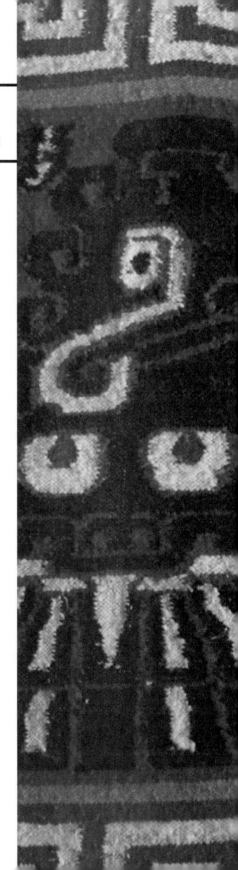

For several thousand years before the Spanish invasion of Peru in 1532, a wide variety of high mountain and desert coastal kingdoms developed in western South America. The extraordinary artistic and technological achievements of these people, along with their historical continuity across centuries, have encouraged modern observers to refer to them as a single Andean civilization.

A look at a modern map reveals that no single South American state encompasses all of the territories controlled by the Inca before the coming of the Spanish; rather these territories were spread over parts of Ecuador, Peru, Bolivia, Chile, and Argentina, and in 1532 they were all part of a single Inca state called Tawantinsuyu, the "Realm of the Four Parts." Earlier, local hegemonies—some coastal, others centred in the mountains, and still others bridging these geographic barriers—had risen, expanded, and eventually collapsed.

The Inca of Cuzco (Cusco) were themselves newcomers to most of the regions that they came to dominate. Such rapid expansion did not allow for complete consolidation, and the Spanish were able to take advantage of what had been a recent incorporation of numerous regional ethnic groups and the resentments that the Inca victory had created among the ethnic lords. Some of these, like Don Francisco Cusichaq, lord of Xauxa, the earliest colonial capital, lived long enough after 1532 to testify before a Spanish court of inquiry that he regretted having opened the country to the Europeans. For 30 years his book-keepers had recorded on their knotted quipu (*khipu*) accounts not only every-thing the Spanish had received from Xauxa warehouses but also, on separate knot-strings, everything that had been considered stolen.

The outsider visiting the Andes per-ceives two overwhelming geographic realities: the Pacific coastal desert stretching for thousands of miles and the high Andes rising parallel to the coast. These contrasting regions—utter desert on the coast and high, looming moun-tains to the east (where the bulk of the pre-Columbian population lived above 10,000 feet [3,000 metres])—could, and at several times in Andean history did, coalesce into a single political entity. Thus, it is possible to speak of a single Andean civilization, even if at times, early and late, there was no political integration. One indicator of this social unity is extant even now: Quechua, one of the Andean languages, is still spoken by some 10 million people from northern Ecuador to northern Argentina, a dis-tance of thousands of miles.

THE NATURE OF ANDEAN CIVILIZATION

The coastal desert was inhabited for mil-lennia by fishermen, and many of their settlements have been studied by archaeologists. The people in these com-munities were familiar with the sea and depended heavily on its products, but from very early times they also used and possibly cultivated native varieties of cotton. Textiles have been the major art form in the Andes for thousands of years. It is known that these textiles—found preserved in the coastal sands—have woven into them a wealth of information on Andean peoples; and, while the infor-mation in the textiles still cannot be read, it is believed that they will eventually be as revealing as have been the Mesoamerican codices.

In modern Peru irrigation eventually may permit the cultivation of the lower reaches of most rivers. Still, it is useful to note that of some 50 rivers descending from the Andean glaciers to the Peruvian coast, only three have water flowing through them year-round. Such an ambi-tious irrigation scheme would be most productive only if the waters were tapped quite high on the western slope and if several rivers were connected through canals high in the Andes, thus allowing the scarce waters of three or four valleys to be pooled into a single one as needed. Rumours of such a project reached the first Spaniards in Peru: in the final decade before the invasion, the Inca were said to be planning to bore through a mountain in what today is northern Chile, so that water from the Amazonic watershed would flow westward to the deserts and thus alter the continental divide.

Archaeologists, particularly non-Peruvian scholars, have concentrated on the study of coastal peoples: they have found that sites are more accessible along the Pan-American Highway; that

The tomb of a Moche leader, discovered in the 1980s, has revealed much about the lives, livelihoods, and social hierarchy of ancient coastal Peruvian civilizations. Bill Ballenberg/Time & Life Pictures/Getty Images

the hot and dry climate presents none of the challenges of the high altitudes; and that the remains, mummified in the desert sands, are immediately rewarding. Pottery finds have portrayed such things as fishing or warfare, diseases, weapons, cultivated plants, and differences in rank and in sexual habits among the Andeans. Usually this evidence has been recovered by professional grave looters but sometimes also by archaeologists themselves. One of the most remarkable of the latter type of finds is the grave of a Moche leader that was discovered near the village of Sipan on the northern coast of Peru in the mid-1980s. Since the mid-20th century architectural studies of ceremonial and political centres have allowed researchers to follow changes in the location and the architectural features of important Andean cities. Distance from the sea and the degree of dependence on maritime products, the proximity to irrigation waters from the highlands, and the repeated efforts to control militarily more than a single irrigated valley have all received attention from archaeologists.

A major question remains: did these coastal polities extend upward to the Andean highlands to control areas beyond the slopes where the irrigation works tapped the rivers? The Peruvian historian María Rostworowski has pointed to similarities, found in colonial administrative papers, between coastal places-names and personal names in the Cajamarca Highlands, an area due east and above the coastal political entities. The colonial papers have not explained the presence of such distant colonies, but they have introduced a topic fundamental to understanding Andean success: given the apparently inhospitable environments of both the desert coast and the nearby high Andes, how could so many separate societies have fed such enormous populations and constructed highways, palaces, and temples in what were clearly urban centres for so many centuries?

AGRICULTURAL ADAPTATION

One answer to this question was suggested in the 1930s by the German geographer Carl Troll. His solution took into account a unique aspect of Andean ecology: the greatest population concentration (more than 1 million people) and the highest agricultural productivity occurred around Lake Titicaca, which is some 12,500 feet (3,810 metres) above sea level. Nowhere else in the world—not even in Tibet or Nepal—has cultivation been so successful at such a high altitude. The effort to understand the ramifications of this paradox is far from complete, but Troll's insights have proved fertile: (1) The fields and terraces clustered around the lake were located just a few degrees south of the equator, where daytime temperatures are truly tropical. (2) At this altitude climatic contrasts are not so much seasonal as diurnal, i.e., summer by day and winter by night. Contrasts of 55 to 70 °F (30 to 40 °C) within a single 24-hour period are not uncommon, and nearly 300 nights of frost per year have been recorded on the high, windy plateau (puna) surrounding the lake. (3) Populations settled in such circumstances seem to have endured as others have survived in the Arctic, the Kalahari, and the Gobi, but it is clear that in the Andes a far denser population fared much better than have groups in other environmentally harsh regions, acquiring with time an intimate familiarity with the agricultural and pastoral possibilities of high altitude.

These peoples cultivated many varieties of tubers, of which only the potato has achieved widespread use in the world. But since the soils at this altitude were easily exhausted, "second- and third-year" tubers had to be domesticated to take advantage of the nutrients left unused in the soil. Then, as now, it was usual to allow the ground to rest—for 6, 8, or even 10 years—after which some of the "rested" acreage was returned to cultivation annually, a rotation pattern that is still familiar to the local people.

The upper elevation limit of cultivation has varied throughout the centuries, as the climate has fluctuated. Thus, considerable effort was invested in the development of ever more frost-resistant varieties of tubers. Modern observers have noted that tubers grown close to and above about 13,000 feet (3,962 metres) were mostly of the pentaploid varieties (i.e., those having five times the basic number of chromosomes), bitter hybrids resulting from selection and crossing by the grower. Although they usually required additional nurture and processing that were beyond the procedures

familiar today, the bitter varieties represented a gain in total productivity.

A significant improvement in agriculture was the construction of massive terraces, which not only extended the cultivated area but also created protected microclimates where particular varieties could flourish. It has been suggested that an "amphitheatre" found in the Cuzco region was actually an experimental field where the concentric terraces reproduced tiny variations in the upland environment. When the use of highland irrigation and raised-ridged fields are taken into account, it becomes clear that these upland populations were highly familiar with, and respectful of, the potential for high-altitude agriculture and were intent on gaining additional acreage in circumstances that elsewhere would not have seemed worth the effort.

Another incentive for settlement at high altitudes was the presence of glacier-fed pastures for alpaca herds. The llama—it and the alpaca were the two camelids domesticated by the Andean peoples—could live at altitudes ranging from sea level to those in the high mountains. The alpaca's habitat, however, was much narrower; it did best above 13,000 feet (3,962 metres), and its preference for a swampy range was catered to by pastoralists. It has been found that even today alpaca herding is a full-time occupation, almost impossible to combine with agriculture. While Andean herders did belong to wider ethnic groups, they tended to be specialists, relying for their food staples on their kinsmen closer to Lake Titicaca.

Llamas and alpacas grazing in the Bolivian foothills. Herding these creatures is an occupation that Andean communities have engaged in from pre-Columbian times to the present day. Aizar Raldes/AFP/Getty Images

Present-day distribution and use of these animals (known collectively as camelids) tends to mask their importance in pre-Columbian times. A European inspector, reporting in the 1560s on the camelid wealth of a single Aymara chiefdom near Lake Titicaca, claimed, "I have heard of an Indian who is not even a lord, one don Juan Alanoca of Chucuito, who has more than 50,000 head." Such control of vast herds, combined with the hundreds of varieties of high-altitude tubers and grains, helps to explain the density of Andean populations.

THE COLD AS A RESOURCE

Beyond such skilled manipulation of the natural geography there lay an awareness of frost. As noted above, in the high Andes frost can occur almost every night of the year. Elsewhere people have endured the cold; in the Andes the cold was transformed into a positive and even creative factor.

It is not known when this step was taken. For at least 1,000 years people in the Andes have been aware that the sharp alternation between tropical noon and

QUECHUAN LANGUAGES

Quechuan languages were spoken in the former Inca Empire in South America, and they are the principal native languages of the central Andes today. According to archaeological and historical evidence, the original languages were probably spoken in a small area in the southern Peruvian highlands until about 1450; after that their geographical range was rapidly enlarged by the Inca conquests. When the Spanish conquered the empire in 1532, Quechuan languages were spoken in western South America from what is now southern Colombia to central Chile and from the Pacific coast to the borders of the Amazon Basin.

Although the languages are still spoken by a large population of Indians, many of whom are monolingual, they are slowly losing ground to the Spanish language, which is the language of government and education.

arctic midnight can be utilized. Any animal or vegetable tissue exposed to this daily contrast can be processed into nutritive products that keep for decades, and the process can be achieved either at the household or the state level.

Chuño is the name popularly used for processed tubers, but a rich vocabulary for tubers exists in the Quechuan (Andean) languages: there is a separate term for each plant and for each mode of preparation. Chuño cannot be made where a diurnal temperature extreme is absent; thus, north of modern Cajamarca in northern Peru no chuño is prepared, since nocturnal frosts are rare or absent. Animal tissues also can be handled in this manner. After 1532 European meats were added to those of local birds, fish, and camelids. The name for these preserved meats is *charqui,* or jerky (*ch'arki* in Quechua), the one Andean word that has made its way into common English usage.

Such food reserves allowed both the peasants and the state to compensate for natural and man-made calamities. They filled thousands of warehouses—many of which are still extant—that were built in ways and places so as to use the tiny differences of exposure to the sun, winds, and humidity. Those built by the state or by the ethnic lords along the more than 15,500 miles (24,945 km) of roads provided food for both human and camelid porters, for the armies, and for priests traveling to the many shrines.

The presence of such large stores made possible the incredible forays of Spaniards like Diego de Almagro, who reached Chile from Cuzco across thousands of miles of deserts and snow-covered mountains. As late as 1547, 15 years after the Spanish invasion, one Spaniard, Polo de Ondegardo, reported that he had fed 2,000 soldiers for seven weeks with the food still stored above Xauxa, which had been the first European capital. A detailed archaeological study of an Inca storage system was made by the American anthropologist Craig Morris, who found almost 500 warehouses at Huánuco Pampa. There were some 1,000 warehouses at Xauxa and many more near Cuzco, the Inca capital.

The Highlands and the Low Countries

The cultivators of high-altitude tubers and lowland crops—the plants of which seem botanically far apart at first glance—were actually in continuous contact. This point was stressed by the pioneer Peruvian archaeologist Julio C. Tello and was later verified by foreign scholars. The inhabitants all along the Andean highlands were aware of the diverse populations and climates of the Pacific coastal deserts to the west and of the Amazon lowlands to the east. The Chilean researcher Lautaro Núñez has traced the several societies who inhabited a single valley. Products and settlement patterns changed through the centuries, but at all times each successive ethnic group accumulated resources from diverse ecological niches into a single system.

By adding written Spanish sources to the information provided by archaeologists, it is possible to explain further the density of the Andean population and its great productivity. Throughout the Andes, south of Cajamarca, political units large and small were characterized by a dispersed settlement pattern. The preferred location of the seat of power frequently was at very high altitudes, almost at the upper limit of cultivation, and kinsmen of these highlanders were settled permanently at 3, 5, or even 10 days' walk from the political centres. The German anthropologist Jürgen Golte has stressed that the agricultural calendar permitted such absences, since crops matured at different dates according to altitude, but many outliers were too far away from the political and demographic nucleus to permit seasonal migrations. The outlier communities could be large or small and could be established on the dry Pacific shore or in wet Amazonic enclaves. The Lupaca (Lupaqa), an Aymara-speaking polity whose political centre was located on the puna on the shores of Lake Titicaca, controlled outliers on both slopes.

Other ethnic groups reached in only one direction. For example, the two lords of the Karanga (Caranga), on what today is the highest part of the Bolivian High Plateau, do not seem to have controlled any outliers of their own on the Amazonic slope. Their main puna farms and most of their subjects lived above 12,000 feet (3,659 metres), and their camelid herds were pastured even higher. The Karanga also controlled corn (maize) fields at less lofty altitudes in what today is Chilean territory, several days' walk away. Farther west and closer to the coast were their fruit and coca-leaf gardens. Finally, even farther north, across the Atacama

Desert near the modern city of Arica, the Karanga had their "own" fishers.

One unexpected feature of such outliers is that they were usually multiethnic: several political centres shared settlements of salt miners, fishers and seaweed gatherers, cultivators of hot peppers and coca leaves, and timber cutters and honey gatherers. The political mechanisms by which conflicting groups could reach truces, even if temporary, or the means by which caravans moved with safety when connecting the central settlements with their multiple outliers are still not known.

This diverse pattern of settlement and political control and of pooling dispersed resources and populations has been named "Andean ecological complementarity" or the "vertical archipelago." Such complementarity went beyond the efficient control of the nocturnal cold and of the high altitude. Even if many details of how it worked still escape understanding, it is obvious that each ethnic group was able to diversify the risks that would have existed if each had been concentrated in any of the separate Andean ecological tiers. Beyond defensive strategies, in ecological complementarity it is possible to detect new opportunities that would permit massive storage of a wide range of foods going beyond those grown locally. Eventually there emerged dense populations and large polities like the Inca. It is notable that the foci of Andean civilizations across the centuries—Chavín, Huari (Wari), Tiwanaku (Tiahuanaco), Cuzco—were all located on the high puna.

THE PRE-INCA PERIODS

The names the several prehistoric populations called themselves are not known, and archaeologists have come to distinguish the various peoples and civilizations by descriptive terms—the Late Preceramic, the Initial (or Lower Formative) Period, the Early Horizon, the Early Intermediate Period, the Middle Horizon, the Late Intermediate Period, and the Late Horizon (also called the Upper Formative, or Inca, Period). Each of the periods lasted for centuries, some for millennia. These designations stress the differences between the peoples who inhabited the coast and those who lived in the highlands, although contacts between the two areas were frequent at all times in prehistory. What have been termed "horizons" in Andean studies were much shorter periods of time when wide areas of the central Andes were united culturally and politically with one another and with sections of the Pacific coast.

THE LATE PRECERAMIC

There is ample evidence of human occupation by 3500 BC, at which time there was already considerable diversity along the Pacific. In the central and northern coastal areas lived people who cultivated beans, squash, cotton, and chili peppers and who exploited the sea, catching fish with cotton nets and shell or composite hooks, collecting shellfish, and hunting sea mammals. One group at Chilca, south of modern Lima, built conical huts of cane thatched with sedge. The dead were buried wrapped in twined-sedge mats and the skins of the guanaco, a wild camelid. Some people camped in winter on the *lomas*, patches of vegetation outside the valleys that were watered at that season by fogs. In summer, when the lomas dried up, they built camps along the shore. The lomas provided wild seeds, tubers, and large snails; deer, camelids (probably guanaco), owls, and foxes were hunted. The lomas had long been shrinking, and the winter camps were abandoned (*c.* 2500 BC) in favour of permanent fishing villages. Nowhere are the deposits thick enough to show stratification, but they have been arranged in chronological order by comparing the implement types and noting their distribution within the shrinking patches of vegetation. Some small patches still survive.

In the far south, the lomas were and still are more extensive than in the centre, and projectile points are abundant in them and in caves in the valleys. Deer can still be seen on the lomas, and it appears that hunting of them and of guanaco was the main activity in Late Preceramic times.

In the far north, in the Talara region and extending north into Ecuador, are stone tools and mangrove-dwelling mollusks, left by people who enjoyed a wetter climate than that now prevailing, and one inland site at El Estero, provisionally dated somewhat earlier (*c.* 5000 BC), has well-made polished stone axes and mortars that indicate the exploitation of forests and grasslands yielding seeds.

Much longer periods of occupation have been postulated for the highlands: the American scholar Richard S. MacNeish has suggested a human presence as early as 15,000 BC in the Ayacucho Basin, which would correspond to the traditional "first wave" of immigrants into the New World. Since there has been much less research in the highlands than on the coast, little is known of the highland Late Preceramic. The caves at Lauricocha at about 13,000 feet (3,962 metres) in the central Andes, which had been occupied by deer and camelid hunters since nearly 8000 BC, were still used, at least as summer camps, by hunters who employed small leaf-shaped points. Gourds, squash, cotton, and *lucuma*, with seed plants such as quinoa and amaranth, were cultivated in the Ayacucho Basin before 3000 BC; corn and beans came within the next millennium. There were also ground stone implements for milling seeds. It has been claimed that llamas and guinea pigs long had been domesticated.

After about 2500 BC came a great increase in the speed of development, which is best known on the coast. Population increased, and stable settlements were established in many places. By 2000 BC there were perhaps 100 villages on the coast with populations of 50 to 500 people, with a few of up to 1,000, indicating a total population of about 50,000. This was a far cry from the thinly scattered bands and occasional villages of about 1,000 years before. Considerable variation has been observed from place to place, but most sites have shown a predominance of seafood, including fish, shellfish, sea lions, and sea birds.

On the north central coast, the stretch between the Casma and Huarmey rivers was heavily populated. One site, at Culebras, was a large village on a terraced hillside, with semi-subterranean houses whose underground parts were lined with basalt blocks and whose upper parts were built of lighter materials such as adobe blocks. They originally had hard clay floors, and some had guinea-pig hutches consisting of stone-lined tunnels connecting two rooms at floor level. The guinea pig, normally vegetarian, appears to have been taught to feed on small fish. A site at Huarmey has provided the earliest known instance of corn on the coast, and corn also occurred in the top Preceramic levels at Culebras.

Burials at Culebras were tightly flexed, wrapped in twined mats and cotton cloth, and accompanied by gourd vessels and beads and pendants of stone, shell, or bone. The skulls of these people were deformed by having been bound to cradleboards in infancy. There was a cemetery, but many burials were under house floors. No ceremonial buildings are known in this area.

Farther north, at the mouth of the Chicama River, is Huaca Prieta, which was the first Preceramic site to be excavated. A thick midden, it contains some subterranean houses lined with cobblestones and roofed with earth supported by whalebones and wooden beams. The twined textiles found there were the vehicle for a peculiar art style, showing highly stylized crabs, double-headed snakes, birds, and human beings, expressed by warp manipulation designed to bring groups of warps of one colour to one face. The dyes have faded, and the only way to recover the designs is by examination under a microscope. Such textiles were not confined to this area, but they have been more fully studied there. Woven textiles were rare, and weaving was combined with twining in a way that shows that a loom was not used.

Unlike the area farther north, sites along the central coast had ceremonial buildings, of which the most remarkable is El Paraíso in the Chillón Valley. This is an imposing stone-built structure on an artificial mound, with a central stairway leading up to a group of rectangular rooms. The central block, which occupied a commanding position in a side valley, has been partly reconstructed, but there were extensive wings that may have been residential, though they now appear as little more than piles of stones. Floodwater farming may have been practiced there, but definite signs of it have been obliterated by modern cultivation. At Río Seco, a few miles to the north, are two pyramids, constructed by filling a group of preexisting rooms with boulders, building adobe-walled rooms on top of them, and finally filling these up also.

Apart from one site, Kotosh, near modern Huánuco in the central Andes, little is known of the highland final Preceramic. A Japanese research team has found structures of undressed stone chosen to present flat wall surfaces, set in mud, covering an area of at least 200 by 100 yards (180 by 90 metres), in some parts of which was a succession of buildings piled up to a considerable height. Among these were two superimposed temples, the lower being a rectangular structure on a stepped platform about 26 feet (8 metres) high. The floor was surrounded by a broad, low bench, and each outside wall had two or three rectangular niches. The walls and floor were covered with two coats of mud plaster, and beneath the central niche at one end was a pair of crossed forearms modeled in the same material. This temple was later buried in boulders surrounded by a retaining wall and covered by a new floor on which a second temple was built, of which little remains. The burial of the first temple to act as a raised foundation for the second recalls the construction at Río Seco.

THE INITIAL PERIOD

The next epoch, called the Initial Period by the American scholar John H. Rowe, and the Lower Formative by the Peruvian archaeologist Luis G. Lumbreras, began with the introduction of pottery. The earliest ceramics have yielded radiocarbon dates of about 1800 BC, although Rowe has suggested that even a date of 2100 BC is plausible. Ceramics from this period have been found on the central coast between Las Haldas, in the Casma-Huarmey region, and Lima. These are considerably later than the earliest

pottery finds at Puerto Hormiga on the northern coast of Colombia near Panama (before 3000 BC) and Valdivia in Ecuador (c. 2700 BC). The period ends with the spread of the Chavín cult (also called the Early Horizon).

Lumbreras has stressed agriculture as a more telling indicator: while no single starting date has been cited for this achievement, beans may have been cultivated for centuries; if not millennia; before the date of the earliest pottery. Bottle gourds and squashes were other cultivated species. Potatoes and other tubers, so important in later times, did not keep well in highland circumstances; but some researchers believe that Andean peoples were reliant on wild tubers and rhizomes 10,000 years ago, although these groups had not yet domesticated them. It has been demonstrated that on the coast virtually all the crops that were important in 1532 (with the notable exception of corn) were already known and in daily use during the Initial Period.

The introduction of pottery at first made little difference to the general pattern of life; cooking continued to be done by roasting on hot stones. On the coast, there was a gradual increase in the consumption of cultivated plants, grown mainly in the lower reaches of the valleys, but the basic reliance on seafood continued. An important innovation was the development, or possibly the introduction, of the heddle loom, but, if it was introduced, its origin is not known. At first it seems only to have been used for making plain-weave cotton cloth. Village life and temple buildings spread over the country, except to the far south, where conditions favoured the continuance of hunting and gathering. Corn spread from the centre over most of the coast, and cassava, or manioc (an edible root), and peanuts (groundnuts) appeared there for the first time, their ultimate source being the Amazonian lowlands.

New ceremonial centres showed considerable diversity. Examples include La Florida, a huge pyramid in Lima that formed the nucleus of a yet-unmapped building complex. The Tank site at Ancón consists of a series of stone-faced platforms on a hill. Las Haldas has a platform and three plazas; two smaller similar sites are also known. The old centres at El Paraíso and Río Seco had been abandoned, but, in the highlands, Kotosh continued to be occupied. Any constructions at Yarinacocha in a wet, stoneless area would have been of wood or other perishable materials.

The variety of the pottery suggests that it was derived from several different sources. In the Lima area, the earliest examples are neckless jars and incurved bowls with thickened rims and rounded bottoms, very uneven in shape. Some later types are pebble polished and the jars thinner. Other later types include bottles with straight spouts, which may have simple incised or applied decoration, and open bowls. Finally, as the period drew to a close, tan-coloured decorated wares, with punctate or red-painted areas outlined by incised lines, as well as orange ware with black stripes, were produced. A type found on the south coast is a small, double-spouted bottle with simple negative-painted decoration, the first appearance of a form long-lived in that area and of a decorative technique that later spread widely over the country.

In the highlands, the earliest pottery at Kotosh consists predominantly of simple bowls with somewhat constricted mouths, and bowls with gently rounded bases meeting the vertical to outsloping concave walls at a sharp angle. There are rare double-spout-and-bridge bottles, closed vessels with two tubular spouts connected by a solid bridge. The ware is mainly dark grey, black, or dark brown to sombre red, and it may have a red slip. The decoration—which was either applied to a broad zone covering most of the walls or, on the neckless jars, formed a ring around the mouth— consists of linear incision, hatching, stamped circles, punctation, or excision. Postfired painting in red, yellow, and white frequently covers excised, hatched, and stamped areas. Despite the fact that Kotosh was on the eastern side of the Andean watershed, its pottery had little in common with that of Yarinacocha, save some similar decorations and the double-spout-and-bridge bottle.

The first known pottery of Yarinacocha is far from primitive. It consists mainly of bowls, mostly with complex outlines. Large open bowls with a broad labial flange, concave sides, and in some cases a second flange where side meets base, could have been cooking pots. Small bowls with inward-sloping sides meeting the rounded base at a sharp angle could have served for drinking; and a shallow bowl, with rounded base meeting the low, slightly outsloping concave sides at a lesser angle, may have been a plate for solid food. There are shards from large urns that may have served for brewing cassava beer. Decoration of finely hatched or cross-hatched geometrical areas, outlined by broad incised lines, occurs on most vessels, and one has a similarly executed feline face. In spite of severe weathering, postfired red paint, later so characteristic of the south coast, is found on some vessels.

The Early Horizon

The Early Horizon emerged after the appearance and rapid spread of the Chavín art style, ending the regional isolation of the Initial Period. The Chavín art style derives its name from the ruined temple complex of Chavín de Huántar in the Andean highlands of central Peru. The dates suggested for the emergence of the style beyond the environs of the temple, however, vary among scholars. Rowe dated it from 1400 BC, while Lumbreras suggested 850 BC; and the very designation of Chavín as a horizon has been challenged. But even those who have most favoured dropping the concept of horizon for this period have noted that in about 1000 BC there was an invasion of highlanders into the coastal Casma Valley who brought with them radically different architectural styles, ceramics, and food plants and animals that supplanted those in the valley; such a penetration was clearly a unification of the coast and the highlands into a single polity.

Chavín came to cover most of the north and centre of Peru, and its influence affected a good part of the south coast, excluding only the southern highlands. The art style, which is regarded as the expression of a cult, is expressed in painted textiles (of which few have survived), in pottery, and chiefly in stone carvings. Archaeologists at one time generally agreed that the chief object of worship was a cat, probably the jaguar, but this has been questioned, although many natural bird, animal, and human forms had feline mouths and other attributes. Feline representations were widespread, whereas some unquestioned deities were confined to the immediate neighbourhood of Chavín.

Chavín Monuments and Temples

Most Chavín temples seem to have been ceremonial centres without people living around them, although the complex at Chavín itself seems to have been accompanied by a considerable town. The remainder appear to have been foci for scattered settlements. The most elaborate temple known is that at Chavín, which lies at an elevation of 10,530 feet (3,210 metres) on a tributary of the Marañón River, east of the Callejón de Huaylas district of the Santa River. The temple consists of a group of stone platforms formed of rubble

The main feature of temple remains at Chavín is a tall shaft of white granite, into which has been carved the smiling likeness of a god known as El Lanzón. Herman du Plessis/Gallo Images/Getty Images

faced by walls of coursed masonry in which two thin courses alternate with one thick one. They are honeycombed with galleries running parallel to the walls at different levels and ventilated by shafts. The oldest part of the temple is a U-shaped structure, with the open top of the U facing east; the rectangular central arm contains a cruciform gallery, at the crossing of which stands a remarkable prismatic shaft of white granite, some 15 feet (4.5 metres) high, carved in low relief to represent a standing human figure with snakes typifying the hair and a pair of great fangs in the upper jaw. This figure, which has variously been called El Lanzón, the Great Image, and the Smiling God, is thought to have been the chief object of worship in the original temple.

The southern arm of the temple was subsequently twice widened by rectangular additions, into which some of the original galleries were prolonged. After the second addition, the two were joined by a freestanding facade having a central portal with a lintel supported on two cylindrical columns. The lintel bears 14 eagles in low relief, supplied with feline jaws with prominent fangs behind the beak, and each column is entirely covered by a mythical bird bristling with feline fangs and faces. These have been interpreted as attendants of the god worshiped in that part of the temple, who had perhaps superseded the Smiling God and could have been the god shown on the Raimondi Stone, now in Lima. The stone shows the Staff God, a standing semi human figure having claws, a feline face with crossed fangs, and a staff in each hand. Above his head, occupying two-thirds of the stone, is a towering, pillarlike structure fringed with snakes and emerging from a double-fanged face, which Rowe interpreted as a symbolic treatment of the Staff God's hair as a tongue coming out of a mouth. Unlike the Smiling God, this figure has been found in areas as far from Chavín as the northern and southern coasts of Peru.

Except for the columns, which are of black slate, the stones of the facade are light in colour on the south side and dark on the north. East of the facade is a small sunken court of the same period, which contained a number of slabs with carvings in low relief, and to the east of this is a much larger court surrounded by platforms. Within this court is a square, slightly sunken area, in which was found the Tello obelisk, a rectangular pillar carved in low relief to represent a caiman and covered with Chavín symbolic carvings, such as bands of teeth and animal heads. This is considered to be an object of worship like the Smiling God and Staff God. Carvings found on and around the temple include a cornice of projecting slabs, on the underside of which are carved jaguars, eagles, and snakes, and a number of tenoned heads of men and the Smiling God; they are thought to be decorations or the attendants of gods rather than objects of worship.

On the coast, the temples were built mostly of adobe. In the Nepeña Valley, two temples—Cerro Blanco and Punkurí—differ so much that they must also differ

Carved animals and faces sprout from the walls of the Chavín temple. Archaeologists suspect that these carvings are purely decorative, not objects of worship. Herman du Plessis/ Gallo Images/Getty Images

in age, but it is not known which is the earlier. Cerro Blanco is a massive platform of conical adobes and stones, supporting rooms with walls bearing Chavín decoration, including eyes and feline fangs, modeled in mud plaster in low relief and painted red and greenish yellow. Punkurí has a low, terraced platform with a wide stairway on which stands a feline head and paws, modeled from stone and mud, and painted. By the paws was buried a woman, believed to have been sacrificed. At Moxeke and Pallca in the Casma Valley to the south, there are terraced, stone-faced pyramids with stone stairways. The first has niches containing clay-plastered reliefs of mud, stone, and conical adobes showing felines, snakes, and human beings of Chavinoid character painted in polychrome. Also in Casma is a temple at Cerro Sechín, consisting of a series of superimposed platforms with a central stair, on either side of which, at the bottom level, stands a row of irregularly shaped flat stones with incised designs

CHAVÍN

The Chavín were the earliest highly developed culture in pre-Columbian Peru, which flourished between about 900 and 200 BC. During this time Chavín artistic influence spread throughout the northern and central parts of what is now Peru. The name given to this early civilization derives from the great ruin of Chavín de Huántar in the northern highlands of the Peruvian Andes, but that site may not have been the actual centre of origin of the culture and artistic style. Important regional manifestations are also found at Kotosh and Kuntur Wasi, in the highlands, and at sites in the Casma, Nepeña, and Chicama valleys of the northern coast. One of the best-known coastal phases is the Cupisnique of the Chicama valley.

The central building at Chavín de Huántar is a massive temple complex constructed of dressed rectangular stone blocks and containing interior galleries and incorporating bas-relief carvings on pillars and lintels. The principal motifs of the Chavín style are human, avian, feline, and crocodilian or serpentine figures; these are often combined in highly complex and fantastic images. Chavín de Huántar was designated a UNESCO World Heritage Site in 1985.

Chavín culture undoubtedly had earlier prototypes in the Initial Period (c. 1800–900 BC). During this period a sedentary agricultural way of life became fully established in Peru, with the development of such crafts as weaving, pottery making, and stone carving. The significance of Chavín is that for the first time many of the local or regional cultures of the area were unified by a common ideology or religion. The extent of political unification remains uncertain.

showing standing men carrying clubs, severed heads, and other designs. Lacking Chavín characteristics, these have been interpreted variously as ancestral Chavín or derived from it, the latter being the more plausible. There is a Chavín ceremonial centre at Garagay in the Chillón Valley but none to the south.

THE POTTERY OF
CHAVÍN AND PARACAS

Chavín pottery is best known from the decorated types found in the galleries in the temple at Chavín and in graves on the northern coast, where it is called Cupisnique. Until the end of the period, the ware was monochrome—dull red, brown, or gray—and hard and stonelike. Vessels were massive and heavy, especially in the early part of the period. The main forms are open bowls with vertical or slightly expanding sides and flat or gently rounded bases, flasks, and stirrup-spouted bottles. The surface may be modeled in relief or decorated by incision, stamping, brushing, rouletting, or dentate rocker-stamping, all of which may be applied to particular zones in contrast with other smooth ones. Some bowls have deeply incised designs on both the inside and outside faces. Many of the forms and decorative features, apart from specifically Chavinoid designs (particularly feline fangs), were already present at Kotosh in the previous phase.

Considerable time changes are represented in Chavín pottery; for example, the earliest stirrup spouts were relatively small, very thick, and heavy, and the spout had a thick flange. As time went on, the stirrups became lighter and the spouts longer; the flange was reduced and finally disappeared. The necks of the flasks underwent similar changes. The decoration on some of these is extremely striking; one has incised flower designs, and another has a roughened surface in which there are a number of concave circular depressions with a notably high polish. The Cupisnique stirrup-spouted vessels, some of which were modeled in the form of human beings, animals, or fruits, were the beginning of a north-coast tradition of naturalistic modeling, which persisted throughout its history. Toward the end of the period, a bichrome (dark red on cream) pottery came into use.

There is a considerable area on the south Peruvian coast with its focus in the Ica Valley, where strong influences from Chavín have been found in the Paracas pottery style, and two painted textiles in pure Chavín style have survived from the same valley. Paracas pottery was very different from that of Chavín, but various motifs have enabled the two to be correlated closely. Paracas began at practically the same time as Chavín, about 1000 BC, and lasted throughout its span and beyond it, perhaps to about 200 BC. The most characteristic form of Paracas pottery was a closed globular vessel with a somewhat flattened base, which had two narrow spouts connected by a flat bridge, or more frequently, with one spout replaced by a human or bird head. Simple round-based bowls were very common. The ware was most commonly black or very dark brownish, and much of the surface was covered with decoration outlined by incision and painted in polychrome with hard, shiny, resinous colours after firing. A panel bearing a feline face on one end of a spout-and-bridge vessel was one of the most frequent forms of decoration. Paracas is also distinguished for its gorgeous embroidered textiles, generally found in the mummy bundles of the important dead. Embroidery had a popularity at this time that it afterward lost, but a surprisingly wide range of weaving techniques were also used in various parts of the coast.

THE EARLY INTERMEDIATE PERIOD

The Early Horizon was succeeded by what has been termed the Early Intermediate Period. The onset of the Early Intermediate marked the decline of Chavín's cultural influence and the attainment of artistic and technological peaks in a number of centres, both on the coast and in the highlands.

THE SOUTHERN COAST

The beginning of the period is best determined by the evolution of the Paracas pottery style into that of the Nazca

THE THREE MAIN ARTS OF SOUTH AMERICA

Hammered gold crown from Chongoyape (Peru), Chavín era, 900 BC–500 BC; in the George Gustav Heye Center of the National Museum of the American Indian, New York City. 5.5 inches × 9.5 inches (14 cm × 24 cm). Courtesy of the Museum of the American Indian, Heye Foundation, New York

Weaving was one of the three arts that were South American strengths, the two others being metalwork and pottery. No other peoples in the Western Hemisphere—and less than a handful elsewhere in the world—came close to equaling the aesthetic and technical accomplishment of the Peruvian weaver. One can imagine the astonishment of the early Spanish explorers when they saw this radiant clothing for the first time, even though they very soon passed it over for the gold they coveted.

Metalwork was at its zenith in Peru, Colombia, and Ecuador, each of which developed major cultures whose arts were equal to the demands of the raw material. Tairona gold, in Colombia, rates very high in design and craftsmanship, as does the work of the Quimbaya, whose skill in creating polished metal flasks is remarkable. Notable also is Sinú casting, which could execute works weighing several pounds. In Ecuador the goldwork found at La Tolita is legendary and shows a skill in casting and overlay that did not seem to exist elsewhere in the region. In Peru most surviving goldwork was created by the Chimú and Nazca peoples. Yet, that this was a well-advanced art as early as the Chavín era is demonstrated by major discoveries at Chongoyape; indeed, these pieces seem to be the earliest gold products in America, having been created about 900 BC–500 BC.

Perhaps the art that was most widespread and had the greatest variety of form is pottery. In the exciting range of imaginative forms, exuberant vessels are found side by side with sombre, formal works. The use of brilliant colour is common, and the degree of careful modeling makes many of these pottery containers veritable sculptural masterpieces.

(Nasca) area on the southern coast; this is traditionally estimated to have occurred about 200 BC, but Rowe's date of 400 BC is probably more reliable, since this is the area where his detailed succession was worked out.

Nazca ware is marked by the introduction of slip painting applied before firing, which took the place of the resin painting applied afterward. The style evolved continuously, and the polychrome tradition continued. The most common forms were bowls and beakers, all with rounded bases, but double-spout or head-and-spout jars were also characteristic. In contrast to the Moche area on the northern coast, figure modeling played a very minor role. Designs were painted in up to eight colours and fell into two main groups, one characterized by stylized but recognizable life forms such as birds, fish, or fruits, with some humans, and the other depicting mythical subjects such as complex demons. Between approximately middle and late Nazca, mythical figures became increasingly angular and elongated and developed a tangled mass of appendages. Trophy-head representations, which were modeled as complete vessels as well as painted in profile on simple vessels, increased greatly at the same time. Because Nazca art was less realistic than that of Moche, little can be learned of the appearance and life of the people.

In the time of the Nazca style what has been described as a small city was located in each of the south-coast valleys of Pisco, Ica, Nazca, and Acarí. At Cahuachi, in Nazca, this included a ceremonial centre consisting of six pyramids, which were terraced and adobe-faced natural hills associated with courts. Tambo Viejo in Acarí was fortified, which supports inferences drawn with some difficulty from late Nazca art that a concern with warfare developed at that time.

THE NORTHERN COAST

A cultural peak was reached in the valleys of Pacasmayo, Chicama, and Moche on the northern Peruvian coast. A large proportion of this area has been grouped by archaeologists into a Moche culture, although some of the territory encompassed by these valleys was not part of the polity called Moche. The Japanese archaeologist Izumi Shimada has referred to this kind of control as "horizontally discontinuous territoriality." The coast–highland "vertical" type of polity described above appears to have emerged later in coastal history. Thus, this "horizontal discontinuity" may have been related to coastal trade, as products were sought north of the desert coast, while at a later time it may have coexisted with "verticality."

The Moche culture is distinguished by a ceremonial pottery style, commonly covered with a white or red-and-white slip, which may have had decoration painted on it, chiefly in red on the white parts. Some pots are molded in forms that include figures, animals, plants, and weapons; and some have molded designs in low relief. Molding and painting both convey highly realistic impressions of the people, things, and scenes they represent and are a vivid source of information about the life and activities of the people, though some important aspects, such as agricultural processes, are not represented. Moche pottery has been divided into five phases that were originally defined mainly by differences in the stirrup-spouted jars, but this has been extended to other forms—for example, bell-shaped bowls, double vessels, and jars with collars. The prevalence of stirrup spouts and the quality of the modeling connect Moche much more closely with Chavín–Cupisnique than with the intermediate styles, in which features such as the spout-and-bridge vessels suggest intrusive influences from the south. Among Moche buildings are adobe pyramids, like the enormous Huaca del Sol in the Moche Valley, palaces with large rooms (on terraces in the case of the Huaca de la Luna near the Sol), and fortified structures perched on the sides of valleys. These structures reinforce the evidence, provided by warriors and enthroned dignitaries depicted on pots, for the existence of an aggressive hierarchical state, and it may be inferred that this grew up as the result of dependence on highly developed irrigation systems in the restricted areas available in the valleys.

There were no towns in the northern valleys. Dispersed communities, built in places where they would not use the valuable irrigated agricultural lands, seem to have been situated in ways suggesting dependence on one of the ceremonial centres.

THE NORTH HIGHLANDS

In the north highlands, the remarkable pottery style of Recuay has been found in the Callejón de Huaylas region. This pottery is related to the negative-painted representative of Gallinazo in the Santa Valley and is painted with black negative designs over white and red, one of the most characteristic being a feline in profile with a comb on the head. There is a good deal of lively modeling, but it is much less naturalistic than that of Moche. A typical feature is a broad, nearly horizontal flange surrounding the mouth of a jar, and many jars also have a horizontal spout below the flange. Most of this pottery has come from stone-lined graves, and some stone buildings of two or three stories may have belonged to the people who made it.

The Cajamarca Basin is the site of a pottery style (called cursive) that was entirely independent of known outside influences and that spanned at least the Early Intermediate Period and the Middle Horizon. It has lightly painted running-scroll designs, which vaguely recall writing (whence the name cursive), as well as small animals and faces, in brownish black or red on a cream background, mostly on open bowls with ring bases. It was traded widely in the north, and south as far as Huari, during the Middle Horizon.

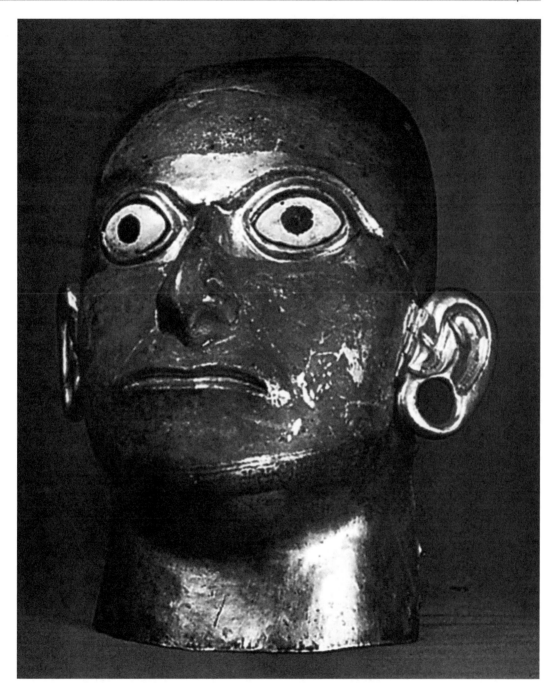

Mask of copper and gold alloy with eyes of shell, found in the Huaca de la Luna, Moche River valley, c. 400 BC–AD 600; in the Linden-Museum, Stuttgart, Germany. Ferdinand Anton

The South Highlands

Large urban and ceremonial centres emerged at this time near the shores of Lake Titicaca. One site, Pucará, includes a well-built, horseshoe-shaped sanctuary of concentric walls of red sandstone enclosing a slightly sunken terrace lined with white-sandstone slabs. Within the terrace is a sunken court some 50 feet (15 metres) square and seven feet (2 metres) below the surface, also lined with white sandstone and reached by a stairway. This court contains two stone-lined grave chambers, and the outer horseshoe wall has small chambers, each containing one or two altarlike slabs in its thickness. There are also squat stone statues of men carrying trophy heads and stelae bearing recessed geometrical carvings and snakes. The pottery includes a reddish-buff micaceous ware painted in red, black, and yellow; cats, human or bird heads, and geometrical figures are all outlined by incision. The faces have the eyes divided vertically, one half of each eye black, the other half the natural colour of the ware. Pucará occurred early in the period, before the main development of Tiwanaku, and it may have taken shape about 400 BC. It appears to have controlled an area between the site and Lake Titicaca or farther.

Tiwanaku is a well-known ceremonial centre whose stone remains are now a tourist attraction in the Andes second in popularity only to the ruins of Machu Picchu. The occupation of the ceremonial centre is believed to have begun very early in the period, since some of the earliest pottery shows similarity to that found at Pucará.

The ceremonial buildings—whose exact age is uncertain—include a large stepped pyramid or platform called Acapana (Akapana), with foundations of buildings on the top; a semi-subterranean temple with stone heads tenoned into the walls; and a low rectangular platform called Calasasaya (Kalasasaya), enclosed by a retaining wall of upright stones alternating with smaller rectangular blocks. In one corner of the platform stands a great monolithic doorway, not in its original position, cut from a large block of lava. At the top of the doorway is carved a central low-relief figure attended by three rows of smaller winged figures that appear to run inward toward him. The central figure, carrying staves that may represent a spear thrower and darts, has been likened to the Chavín Staff God and for convenience may be called the Doorway, or Gateway, God. Versions of the Doorway God and his attendants are found almost everywhere within the range of Tiwanaku influence in the subsequent Middle Horizon. Another feature of the site is a number of large and finely finished stone blocks with niches, doorways, and recessed geometric decorations. Tiwanaku masonry is sometimes held together by accurately cut notches, sometimes by copper clamps set in either straight or T-shaped grooves. Several massive monolithic statues have been found in and around Tiwanaku, the largest being 24 feet (7 metres) high. They resemble pillars bearing relief designs, and some carry beakers.

Decorated Tiwanaku pottery is a finely polished polychrome, which commonly has a red slip with designs painted in various colours. Felines and hawks in profile, with eyes divided vertically into black and white halves, are common designs, as are geometric figures such as triangles and steps. Like all Tiwanaku art, the designs are stiff and formal. The shapes include a tall, graceful, hollow-sided beaker and various types of bottles and hollow-sided bowls with flat bases, including a form bearing a jaguar head and tail on the rim.

THE MIDDLE HORIZON

Both Pucará and Tiwanaku were early forms of what became known as the Middle Horizon, an expansion of multiple-valley political rule that had two centres: one in the southern Altiplano, the other centred on Huari (Wari), near the modern Peruvian city of Ayacucho. This development is usually dated about AD 600. Some Tiwanaku effigy vessels have been discovered at Huari, but otherwise they seem to have been independent entities. Subsequent research has located parallel occupations near each other in the vicinity of the modern city of Moquegua.

The American archaeologist William H. Isbell has argued that Huari was a true state which displayed archaeological manifestations of administrative recording, had storage facilities on a scale suggesting major revenues, contained status tombs and palaces, and had other symbols and ornaments of a ruling class. Huari colonies and control also have been detected in the evidence. Attempts to explain what Huari and Tiwanaku were doing outside the areas of their immediate control have pointed toward religious proselytism, as well as to trade. It has also been suggested that, although these polities employed an extensive form of control, they did not attempt to rule all of the intervening territories.

After a period of consolidation, the expansion was intensified, eventually reaching Cajamarca and the Chicama Valley in the north and the Ocoña Valley on the far southern coast, by about 800. The growth of the empire and its nature is shown by a number of features. One was the spread of Huari pottery styles and local copies of them, some bearing the Doorway God and other religious figures but many with neutral or secular motifs such as bands of chevrons. These generally were polychrome wares, and figures appearing on them—mythological, human, or animal—may have the eyes divided vertically into black and white halves, as at Tiwanaku. A result of the increasing dominance of Huari styles was the obliteration of the old pottery styles over the whole coast from Nazca to Moche. The southern burial custom of huddled, cloth-wrapped mummies spread northward along the coast, displacing the older fashion of extended burial. The presence of large groups of

MACHU PICCHU

Machu Picchu is the site of ancient Inca ruins located about 50 miles (80 km) northwest of Cuzco, Peru, in the Cordillera de Vilcabamba of the Andes Mountains. It is perched above the Urubamba River Valley in a narrow saddle between two sharp peaks—Machu Picchu ("Old Peak") and Huayna Picchu ("New Peak")—at an elevation of 7,710 feet (2,350 metres). One of the few major pre-Columbian ruins found nearly intact, Machu Picchu was designated a UNESCO World Heritage site in 1983.

Although the site escaped detection by the Spaniards, it may have been visited by the German adventurer Augusto Berns in 1867. However, Machu Picchu's existence was not widely known in the West until it was "discovered" in 1911 by Yale University professor Hiram Bingham, who was led to the site by Melchor Arteaga, a local Quechua-speaking resident. Bingham had been seeking Vilcabamba (Vilcapampa), the "lost city of the Incas," from which the last Inca rulers led a rebellion against Spanish rule until 1572. He cited evidence from his 1912 excavations at Machu Picchu, which were sponsored by Yale University and the National Geographic Society, in his labeling of the site as Vilcabamba; however, that interpretation is no longer widely accepted. (Nevertheless, many sources still follow Bingham's precedent and erroneously label Machu Picchu as the "lost city of the Incas.") Evidence later associated Vilcabamba with another ruin, Espíritu Pampa, which was also discovered by Bingham. In 1964 Espíritu Pampa was extensively excavated under the direction of the American explorer Gene Savoy. The site was much deteriorated and overgrown with forest, but Savoy uncovered remains there of some 300 Inca houses and 50 or more other buildings, as well as extensive terraces, proving that Espíritu Pampa was a much larger settlement.

Machu Picchu was further excavated in 1915 by Bingham, in 1934 by the Peruvian archaeologist Luis E. Valcarcel, and in 1940–41 by Hungarian-born film director and anthropologist Paul Fejos. Additional discoveries throughout the Cordillera de Vilcabamba have shown that Machu Picchu was one of a series of pucaras (fortified sites), tambos (travelers' barracks, or inns), and signal towers along the extensive Inca foot highway.

The dwellings at Machu Picchu were probably built and occupied from the mid-15th to the early or mid-16th century. Machu Picchu's construction style and other evidence suggest that it was a palace complex of the ruler Pachacuti Inca Yupanqui (reigned c. 1438–71). Several dozen skeletons were excavated there in 1912, and, because most of those were initially identified as female, Bingham suggested that Machu Picchu was a sanctuary for the Virgins of the Sun (the Chosen Women), an elite Inca group. Technology at the turn of the 21st century, however, identified a significant proportion of males and a great diversity in physical types. Both skeletal and material remains now suggest to scholars that Machu Picchu served as a royal retreat. The reason for the site's abandonment is also unknown, but lack of water may have been a factor.

The high level of preservation and the general layout of the ruin are remarkable. Its southern, eastern, and western portions are surrounded by dozens of stepped agricultural terraces formerly watered by an aqueduct system. Some of those terraces were still being used by local

Machu Picchu. © Digital Vision/Getty Images

Indians when Bingham arrived in 1911. Walkways and thousands of steps, consisting of stone blocks as well as footholds carved into underlying rock, connect the plazas, the residential areas, the terraces, the cemetery, and the major buildings. The Main Plaza, partly divided by wide terraces, is at the north-central end of the site. At the southeastern end is the only formal entrance, which leads to the Inca Trail.

Few of Machu Picchu's white granite structures have stonework as highly refined as that found in Cuzco, but several are worthy of note. In the southern part of the ruin is the Sacred Rock, also known as the Temple of the Sun (it was called the Mausoleum by Bingham). It centres on an inclined rock mass with a small grotto; walls of cut stone fill in some of its irregular features. Rising above the rock is the horseshoe-shaped enclosure known as the Military Tower. In the western part of Machu Picchu is the temple district, also known as the Acropolis. The Temple of the Three Windows is a hall 35 feet (10.6 metres) long and 14 feet (4.2 metres) wide with three trapezoidal windows (the largest known in Inca architecture) on one wall, which is built of polygonal stones. It stands near the southwestern corner of the Main Plaza. Also near the Main Plaza is the Intihuatana (Hitching Post of the Sun), a uniquely preserved ceremonial sundial consisting of a wide pillar and pedestal that were carved as a single unit and stand six feet (1.8

metres) tall. In 2000 this feature was damaged during the filming of a beer commercial. The Princess's Palace is a bi-level structure of highly crafted stonework that probably housed a member of the Inca nobility. The Palace of the Inca is a complex of rooms with niched walls and a courtyard. At the other end of Machu Picchu, another path leads to the famous Inca Bridge, a rope structure that crosses the Urubamba River. Many other ruined cities—like that atop the dark peak of Huayna Picchu, which is accessible by a lengthy, precipitous stairway and trail— were built in the region; Machu Picchu is only the most extensively excavated of these.

Machu Picchu is the most economically important tourist attraction in Peru, bringing in visitors from around the world. For this reason the Peruvian government wishes to repatriate the materials taken by Bingham to Yale. The ruins are commonly reached in a day trip from Cuzco by first taking a narrow-gauge railway and then ascending nearly 1,640 feet (500 metres) from the Urubamba River valley on a serpentine road. Smaller numbers of visitors arrive by hiking the Inca Trail. The portion of the trail from the "km 88" train stop to Machu Picchu is normally hiked in three to six days. It is composed of several thousand stone-cut steps, numerous high retaining walls, tunnels, and other feats of classical engineering; the route traverses a wide range of elevations between about 8,530 and 13,780 feet (2,600 and 4,200 metres), and it is lined with Inca ruins of various types and sizes. At Machu Picchu there is a hotel with a restaurant, and thermal baths are at the nearby village of Aguas Calientes. The Inca Bridge and other parts of Machu Picchu were damaged by a forest fire in August 1997, but restoration was begun immediately afterward. Concern for the damage caused by tourism was heightened by discussion of the building of a cable-car link to the site.

storage buildings at Piquillacta in the Cuzco Valley and at Viracochapampa, near Huamachuco far to the north, suggests military activity like that of the later Incas. On the coast, some great cities in the north—of which Chan Chan, near modern Trujillo, is the best-known—originated at this time, apparently under southern influence, and the rectangular Great Enclosure Compounds in the Virú Valley may be an expression of the same phenomenon. All these changes, taken together, point strongly to military conquest.

Tiwanaku designs, derived through Huari, are seen on coastal textiles as well as on pottery, and they are found particularly on tapestry. Besides recognizable figures like the Doorway God and his attendants, there are many examples, perhaps somewhat later in date, on which only the divided eyes—in black and white or other combinations of colours—can be inferred to belong to human or animal figures.

Pachacamac, on the central coast, which survived until Inca times as a great temple and oracle, was established as a ceremonial centre by the beginning of the Middle Horizon. At that time it also became a considerable town, with a degree of independence in the Huari empire, as is demonstrated by the presence of its own local variety of coastal Huari pottery—distinguished by the frequent depiction of a creature, sometimes called a griffin, with a winged feline body, human hands, and an eagle head, or sometimes the head alone—from Pachacamac north to Chicama, south to Nazca, and inland to Huancayo. Its influence may have been more religious than political, as in Inca times.

The Moche pottery style disappeared from the Chicama and neighbouring valleys under Huari pressure, but it is unlikely to have become entirely extinct because many features of it reappeared later on Chimú pottery. It probably survived, along with a remnant of the Moche state, in some valleys farther north (including perhaps Lambayeque), but the succession there has not been sufficiently worked out to demonstrate this.

When the Huari empire reached its maximum extent, about 800, it collapsed at the centre. Huari was abandoned, as it appears was Cajamarquilla, a large urban centre near Lima. Also at this time, it appears that construction peaked at Tiwanaku—which is estimated to have had 5,000 to 10,000 inhabitants—although the city's influence on the region continued. Thereafter, few signs of urban life occur in the south, except at Pachacamac, until Inca times. Curiously, the decline of the cities in the south appears to have coincided with the beginnings of urban settlement on the northern coast at Chan Chan, Pacatnamú, and other places.

After Huari fell, signs of new influences from there disappeared in the provinces, but various changes evolved in local pottery styles. Among these was the development of a new style on the north-central coast. One of the most distinctive products of this style was a face-collar jar, in many cases oval, decorated in pressed relief with cats and other Huari-derived designs and painted in washy black, white, and orange on a buff ground (Huari Norteño B). Other examples are the Epigonal styles of Nazca and Ica, characterized by bowls and flasks with occasional Huari motifs, such as animal heads, carried out in what has been described as "a slovenly, rounded; and hasty" manner.

THE LATE INTERMEDIATE PERIOD

The Late Intermediate Period began about 1000 (Rowe has said 900) with the dying out of the signs of unity imposed by Huari. The seeds of the Chimú state were probably sown at the same time, but they are not recognizable until considerably later. Elsewhere there were small independent states, which on the central and southern coasts were in most cases no bigger than a single valley, to judge from the distribution of the distinct pottery styles.

There were few new advances in techniques, and perhaps the most notable was the spread of bronze to the Peruvian coast from northwest Argentina and Bolivia, where tin ore was found and where the manufacture of bronze appears

Arts of Tiwanaku

The origin and the whole story of the development of Tiwanaku are not yet fully understood, but experts do know that it came to exert a tremendous influence over a wide area of South America from AD 250 to 750. One of its most characteristic qualities was the use of stone—in walled cities, huge doorways with intricately carved paneling, and great paved roads. In general Tiwanaku art has a rather angular expression, with repetitive motifs. The pottery from this site is strong in colour, but it does not show the variety and technical perfection seen in the wares of the nearby Inca and Nazca. The great art here, as elsewhere in South America, was weaving. The Tiwanaku produced ponchos, caps, pouches, and other costume pieces that are instantly recognizable wherever seen and challenge the contemporary weaver with their variety, fantastically tight weave, and remarkable richness of colour.

to have originated during the Middle Horizon. A hard alloy of copper and arsenic had been used previously in the centre and north. Pottery improved in quality in most areas, though its artistic character was not equal, for instance, to the earlier products of Moche and Nazca. There was a tendency toward standardization and toward reduction in the number of colours, which went with a degree of mass production. The modeling tradition of the north coast revived, but it was dull and lifeless by comparison with that of Moche times and was generally executed in black ware.

In other parts, entirely new styles evolved. That of Chancay, on the central coast, was thin, dull red or cream in colour, with rather a dusty-looking cream slip and painted decoration in black. A common style was an egg-shaped jar with a flaring collar and a pair of small loop handles, which were sometimes turned into a figure by modeling a face on the collar and adding ill-shaped limbs. Bowls and beakers with slightly bowed, almost vertical sides, were other common shapes. The porosity of the ware and the flaky nature of the slip made this pottery inferior in quality to that of other coastal areas. In the south, pottery of an attractive style was made in the Ica Valley. It was hard, well-burnished buff or red ware, covered with painted, textile-derived patterns in black, white, and red, although some vessels also depicted small birds and fish. Highly characteristic are bowls with a rounded base meeting the inward-sloping sides at a sharp angle and a thickened rim of triangular section.

It is difficult to determine whether any new textile techniques were adopted, but it is unlikely since the extreme versatility of the Peruvian weavers appears already to have covered most of the imaginable varieties at one time or another. On the other hand, fashions varied, and a relevant instance is the use of tapestry.

Tapestry was known in the Early Horizon, suffered something of an eclipse in the Early Intermediate Period, and grew greatly in popularity in the Middle Horizon, when notable examples were produced. During the Late Intermediate Period its popularity waned again, although it was used for the finest garments on into the Inca Period. But in Chimú textiles it was generally confined to borders and other small areas. Textiles were similar over the whole coast, and to distinguish between those of different areas is a task for specialists. Some of the most characteristic types were garments adorned with regular rows, horizontal or diagonal, of stylized birds or fish, executed in brocade or double cloth.

In most of the northern valleys; irrigation systems reached their maximum extent; the Virú Valley—which has been the most thoroughly studied—is deceptive in this respect, because much of the land went out of cultivation, possibly owing to removal of part of the population to other valleys by the Chimú rulers. In some cases, the systems of more than one river were connected, and water was taken, for instance, from the Chicama Valley to that of Moche, where Chan Chan was situated.

THE CHIMÚ STATE

The legendary Chimú ruler Ñançen Pinco, who began to expand the state, is thought to have begun his reign about 1370, and the names of two predecessors are known; so it is a fair guess that the state was taking shape in the first half of the 14th century, when distinctively Chimú pottery forms appeared. Various rather exotic pottery styles dating before this time have been found in the northern area, but insufficient work has been done on their distribution in time and space.

An early type consisted of bottles on a ring base with a loop handle and a narrow, tapering spout, decorated with geometric designs and cursive scrolls in black on a red-and-white ground. There were double whistling vessels, with modeled figures on one vessel connected to a tapering spout on the other by a flat, arched bridge; some early examples were of orange ware with a few dark-red stripes on the spout and bridge, but later ones were black. Carinated whistling vessels of black ware with hornlike projections above the ears on a ring base, with a tapering spout connected to a figure by a bridge, also have been found at an early stage. Similar vessels with two spouts connected by a bridge had a considerable range in time. Another form was a bottle, of black ware, with a tapering spout emerging from a modeled figure or head. These vessels had a strap handle and ring base of variable height. Many of the later blackware vessels had panels in pressed relief, a form of decoration that continued through Chimú times; these bore designs such as men holding staves, moons, or cats on a background of raised dots.

The overwhelming majority of Chimú vessels were of black ware. There was a revival of stirrup spouts, either on modeled vessels such as human figures or reed balsas, or on plain ones with or without pressed relief panels, and these normally had a monkey sitting on the stirrup at the base of the spout. Double vessels, often with a bird head to balance the spout and pressed relief panels on the bodies, continued. Many vessels were lentil-shaped. Jugs with strap handles and pressed relief panels sometimes took on a flattened section to become canteens. These are only a few of the forms that have been found, some resembling immediate predecessors, some new, and some, especially the stirrup spout, revivals of earlier types.

Ñançen Pinco is believed to have conquered the coast from the Saña River, just south of Lambayeque, south to Santa. After him came six rulers before Minchançaman, who conquered the remainder of the coast from at least as far north as Piura and possibly to Tumbes, south almost to Lima. His triumph was short-lived since he himself was conquered by the Inca in the early 1460s.

The Chimú state originated in the Moche Valley, where its capital, Chan Chan, lay. There were other cities at Farfán and Pacatnamú in the Pacasmayo Valley and at Purgatorio and Apurlé in the Leche and Motupe valleys, respectively, which shared some features with Chan Chan. All included large walled compounds. Apart from the cities, there were defensive settlements, such as one in the narrow part of the Moche Valley, up which it straggled for five miles (8 km), occupying terraced hillsides and side valleys and commanding three of the main canals. A third type of settlement consisted of scattered compounds in the midst of large irrigated areas, one example of which was found in the Chicama Valley alongside an irrigation canal that took water to Chan Chan. The capital covered an area of about 14 square miles (36 sq km), with a central area of about 2.5 square miles (4 sq km) containing 10 or more large rectangular enclosures sometimes called *ciudadelas* ("citadels"). These were surrounded by tapering adobe walls, 10 feet (3 metres) thick at the base and about 30 feet (9 metres) high. They ranged in size from about 400 by 200 yards (365 metres by 182 metres to 650 by 400 yards (594 metres by 365 metres).

At least six of these citadels have similar plans, and one has been studied in detail. It has a narrow opening at the north end and is divided into three parts by high walls. The northern part contains a large entry court, flanked by a kitchen area and several smaller courts, leading to a densely built area of small courts, some of which have a U-shaped structure at one end, while others are filled with small rooms. The U-shaped structures, which do not appear to have been roofed, may have been shrines, and the courts that contain them may have had walls covered with mud-plaster reliefs, such as bands of animals, birds, or fish, scrolls, or step frets, arranged in a manner reminiscent of Chimú textiles. The central part has a somewhat smaller entrance court leading to several courts occupied by rooms, perhaps storerooms, although nothing was found in them. Another feature of this area is a great burial platform with rows of chambers arranged in three levels. All these features are connected by narrow and tortuous passages. The southern part is an open area, containing one or more *pukíos* (rectangular areas where the ground has been lowered to the water table, either to supply water or to grow plants). In the spaces between the enclosures, and elsewhere in the city, are large areas of dwellings, irrigated areas, and cemeteries.

It is now thought that the *ciudadelas* may have been the dwellings of the ruling classes and their immediate retainers, and it has even been suggested that they were the palaces of successive rulers, maintained by their descendants in the way that those of deceased Inca were maintained in Cuzco. The number of recognizable *ciudadelas* agrees with the number (10) of known Chimú rulers. This intriguing suggestion is further supported by the belief that the Inca learned a great deal from the Chimú after they conquered them, for, not content with carrying Minchançaman off to Cuzco, they established a colony of north-coast workmen there, and Topa Inca Yupanqui (Thupa 'Inka Yupanki) appears to have worked out the political organization of the empire at the same time, basing it largely on the Chimú system.

Roads between the valleys were always necessary to coastal states and were vital to the Chimú, and the Inca may have learned something in this connection also. There are almost continuous traces of a road from just north of Lambayeque to the Chao Valley just south of Virú, with remains even farther south in Santa, Nepeña, and Casma. The remains differ in elaboration and tend to be wider and more imposing near the cities; in the deserts between valleys they were tracks marked by posts or bordered by low walls, but in the valleys the simplest type is a leveled surface 15 to 25 feet (4.5 metres to 8 metres) wide, with walls of stone or adobe about three feet (1 metre) high and with the surface of the road sometimes being raised.

Although the Chimú had a powerful, aggressive, organized state, their dependence on elaborate irrigation systems for the maintenance of concentrated populations rendered them vulnerable to attack, which was one of the main factors that enabled the Inca to take them over comparatively easily.

THE CHINCHA

The growth and expansion of Chimú were paralleled on the southern coast by Chincha, which was a similarly well-organized polity. Comparison between them has been difficult because of the very different evidence available. Whereas Chimú has become familiar through extensive archaeological research, data on the Chincha has come primarily from the study of historical sources.

In the first few years of Spanish rule, the Holy Roman emperor Charles V complained that he had not received any of the newly conquered lands as a personal fief. The conquistador Francisco Pizarro and his brother Gonzalo hurried to assign him three ethnic groups: (1) The Aymara kingdom of the Lupaqa, listed on the Inca *quipu* at 20,000 households, (2) the tropical island of Puná, in the Gulf of Guayaquil in modern Ecuador, with an unknown aboriginal population, and (3) the coastal Chincha polity, allegedly with 30,000 households. Unfortunately for the Chincha, their population vanished within the first three decades of the Spanish invasion; the royal affiliation and proximity to Lima did not help protect the Chincha.

Belonging to the crown, however, did promote account keeping and administrative reports to the Spanish court. The unusual feature about Chincha was its considerable orientation to the sea. Several thousand households were listed as high-seas fishers and sailors, and thousands more were engaged in long-distance trade with lands to the north. Because the waters off the Chilean and Peruvian coast were cold, there was a long-standing interest in the warm waters off the Ecuadorean coast, more than 1,000 miles (1,609 km) away, where the Antarctic current was no longer present. The details of these exchanges are not known, but one feature was paramount in Andean eyes: throughout the central and southern Andes, wherever puna dwellers were the dominant population, there was a demand for the spiny oyster (*Spondylus*), the shells of which were believed to encourage rainmaking. The one Quechua literary text available lists the spiny oyster as the favourite food of the gods, although it was inedible for humans.

While there has been a long-standing archaeological interest in the shells of this mollusk, the extent and the organization of the shell traffic has not been verified archaeologically. One of the witnesses of the invasion, Pedro Pizarro (a cousin of Francisco), reported being told that the Chincha lord had 100,000 rafts on the "Southern Sea." The number need not be accurate: even 1,000 oceangoing rafts, with keels and sails, would imply a major economic operation.

Chimú and Chincha have received considerable attention from non-Peruvian scholars; understanding of the contemporaries of these peoples in the highlands, however, has remained sketchy. The oral tradition reported by the early European observers claimed that before the expansion of Tawantinsuyu, the Inca state, there were many polities

Spiny oysters were prized among the Chincha, who ascribed special powers to their spiked shells. Mere mortals did not eat the oysters' meat, which was a delicacy allegedly favoured by the gods. Shutterstock.com

large and small, all ruled by traditional lords and frequently at war with one another. To what extent the notions of ecological complementarity or the vertical archipelago were attempts to bridge these conflicts or their consequences cannot be stated with any certainty.

The 17th-century Andean writer Felipe Guamán Poma de Ayala (Waman Puma) reported the oral tradition that he had learned from his forebears, who were minor ethnic lords in the Huánuco region. In the century before the Inca conquest, people had lived in the "epoch of the soldiers." During this period:

> they began to fight and there was much war and death...one lord against the other...bloodshed and taking of prisoners. And they also grabbed their wives and sons and took their fields and irrigation waters and pastures. And they were very cruel and stole each other's property, cloth, gold, copper, even their millstones....And so they went and settled on the heights where they built walls and houses inside...and wells to draw water.

Poma de Ayala's description of Late Intermediate settlement patterns on mountaintops, at the very edge of and even beyond puna cultivation, has been confirmed by field research undertaken near Lake Titicaca by the American archaeologist John Hyslop. He found dozens of walled-in enclosures of 50 to 100 acres (20 to 40 hectares) and larger. During the Late Horizon—which corresponds to the century of Inca rule—these populations were moved to the lakeshore, along the royal road.

CHAPTER 5

THE INCA

Forty years had elapsed since Columbu's landfall when, in 1532, fewer than 200 Spaniards brought down the Inca (Inka) state. Ever since then, historians have been pondering the reasons for this sudden collapse. The evidence seems to favour internal subversion. Don Francisco Cusichaq, lord of the Huanca in central Peru, opened the country to alien rule; he wanted to destroy his hereditary enemies, the Inca. The Andean pattern of many dispersed regional polities that frequently were at war with one another—a situation that the Inca had manipulated but had not eliminated—and the diverse archipelago-like string of the communities may also have facilitated the relatively effortless Spanish victory.

By 1532 Tawantinsuyu, the Inca state, had incorporated dozens of coastal and highland ethnic groups stretching from what is now the northern border of Ecuador to Mendoza in west-central Argentina and the Maule River in central Chile—a distance roughly equal to that between New York City and the Panama Canal. By conservative estimates the Inca ruled more than 12 million people, who spoke at least 20 different languages. A century earlier, during the wars of the Late Intermediate, they had controlled little beyond the villages of their own Cuzco Valley. While forming their state they subordinated more than 100 independent ethnic groups. How much of this achievement corresponded to political experience gained during the Middle Horizon cannot be told. It is likely that the memory of that multiethnic expansion was alive in the ruling families of the major polities.

THE ORIGINS AND EXPANSION OF THE INCA STATE

Inca origins and early history are largely shrouded in legends that may be more mythical than factual. Their later history, particularly from the reign of Pachacuti Inca Yupanqui (Pachakuti 'Inka Yupanki) onward, is largely based on fact, even though it presents what the Inca wanted people to know. Whether these historical traditions are true, in the sense that they accurately related what happened, is not so important as the fact that the Inca used them to justify their various imperial conquests.

THE NATURE OF THE SOURCES

The Inca kept detailed accounts of their dynastic history, knotted onto the quipu records kept by professional accountants. The major local ethnic lords also kept records. As mentioned, Don Francisco Cusichaq kept records of Spanish exactions, which were offered to and accepted in evidence by Spanish administrators. Through the study of Cusichaq's *quipu*, modern researchers have learned that there was both a quantitative and a historical dimension to Andean records. Cusichaq's quipu refers to more than 20 separate events—all recorded in perfect historical sequence—but the way in which these events were recorded has not been fathomed.

The quantitative record, which was easier to decipher, lists counts of men and women on the first two cords, followed by the number of domestic animals (llamas being separated from alpacas). Cloth, the most valuable commodity according to Andean reckoning, comes first among the goods listed, followed by food and household items. The quipu could incorporate strings for new, Spanish items. Thus, in Cusichaq's records Spanish sandals are itemized separately from Andean footwear, and eggs and imported hens have their own strings.

The Cuzco bookkeeping records were used by the Spanish in the early days of their rule in order to divide the country and its population among the invaders. The accuracy of the information about distant places and peoples available to the Inca rulers astonished the Spanish observers. Some among them transcribed what they were told; these accounts became the source of the fragmentary information available to modern researchers. In 1549 and again in the 1570s systematic efforts were made by the Spanish to investigate the Andean past. Some of the interviewers were excellent ethnographers who noted discrepancies between separate oral traditions and contradictions from one set of claims to another. Just as in Mexico, where there were true ethnographers like Bernardino de Sahagún, so in the Andes a young soldier, Pedro de Cieza de León, was a remarkable interviewer, who constantly checked what he had been told by the members of one royal lineage against alternate versions.

Bookkeeper (right) rendering accounts to the Inca ruler Topa Inca Yupanqui. The contents of the storehouses (foreground and background) are recorded on the bookkeeper's quipu of knotted strings. Drawing by Felipe Guamán Poma de Ayala from El primer nueva coronica y buen gobierno. *Courtesy, Library Services Department, American Museum of Natural History, New York City (Neg. No. 321546)*

Thus, the present knowledge of Inca society has been derived from a combination of archaeological studies and the written accounts sent to Spain by the early Spanish observers. Some of these accounts reached a wide public: within two years of the fall of the Inca, two quite different versions of what happened at Cajamarca (the place where Pizarro first met and kidnapped the Inca ruler Atahuallpa) were already in print in Europe. One of these was the official version of the Pizarro brothers, while the other criticized their actions. At a time when printing was still a rare skill and censorship was severe, such ample coverage of the invasion is notable.

The first serious study of the Andean peoples was written by Cieza de León, who had reached the Americas as a 14-year-old soldier and had settled in what today is Colombia. A decade or so later he drifted by horse to what is now Peru. He then rode for some 1,300 miles (2, 092 km), traveling as far south as the mines at Potosí, in present-day Bolivia. Cieza de León was encouraged by the clergy, many of them partisans and correspondents of the Dominican missionary and historian Bartolomé de Las Casas, to interview both Spanish and Andean participants of the invasion and of the wars that some Andean factions had fought against one another.

The most widely read source during the colonial period was the work of Garcilaso de la Vega, also called El Inca—the son of an Inca royal woman and a Spanish nobleman (whose name the son adopted when he "returned" to his father's estate in Spain). He lived in Spain nearly 60 years, leading the life of a gentleman, reading, translating love poetry, editing the memoirs of one of the early invaders

QUIPU

The quipu (quipo, khipu) is an Incan accounting apparatus consisting of a long rope from which hung 48 secondary cords and various tertiary cords attached to the secondary ones. Knots were made in the cords to represent units, tens, and hundreds. In imperial accounting, the cords were differently coloured to designate the different concerns of government—such as tribute, lands, economic productivity, ceremonies, and matters relating to war and peace. The quipus were created and maintained as historical records and were kept not only by high officials at the capital of Cuzco—judges, commanders, and important heads of extended families—but also by regional commanders and village headmen.

of Florida, and, finally, writing a vast account of his mother's ancestors, *The Royal Commentaries of the Inca.*

Guamán Poma de Ayala was one of the few Andean writers whose work is available. He wrote a 1,200-page "letter" to Philip III of Spain, consisting of two books combined into one. The first book was a "new chronicle," describing Andean achievements and history; the second, much larger part advised the king on how to achieve a "good government." The second included 400 pages of pen-and-ink drawings, which have remained a major contribution to the modern understanding of Andean society. The manuscript somehow reached the Danish Royal Library in Copenhagen, where it was discovered in 1908 and where it still resides.

SETTLEMENT IN THE CUZCO VALLEY

Several of the modern Andean peoples trace their ancestries to mythical figures who emerged from holes in the ground.

These places of origin, or *paqarina*, were regarded as shrines, where religious ceremonies had to be performed. The Inca *paqarina* was located at Paqari-tampu (Paccari Tampu), about 15 miles (24 km) south of Cuzco. There are three caves at Paqari-tampu, and the founders of the Inca dynasty—Manco Capac (Manqo Qhapaq), his three brothers, and his four sisters—supposedly emerged from the middle cave. They assumed leadership over 10 groups of people, or *ayllus*, that emerged from the caves on either side and led them on a journey lasting an unknown number of years.

During this period the Inca and their followers moved from village to village in search of enough fertile land to sustain themselves. Manco Capac succeeded in disposing of his three brothers. One of his sisters, Mama Ocllo, bore him a son named Sinchi Roca (Zinchi Roq'a). Eventually, the Inca arrived at the fertile area around Cuzco, where they attacked the local residents and drove them from the land. They then established themselves in Cuzco and gradually began to meddle in the affairs of their neighbours, forcing them to pay tribute in order to retain their freedom.

By this time Manco Capac was quite old and close to death. In order to ensure that all he had accomplished would be preserved for posterity, he named his eldest son, Sinchi Roca, to succeed him to the throne. He then directed his next eldest son to shelter and care for all of his other children and their descendants, who composed the Chima *panaca*. The traditions say little about Sinchi Roca, the second emperor, but apparently he was a peaceful man who made no military campaigns to add lands to the Inca domain. It is not clear whether or not Sinchi Roca married his sister, as his father had done. It is clear, however, that he did not follow his father's lead in naming his eldest son as his successor, for the third emperor, Lloque Yupanqui (Lloq'e Yupanki), had an older brother. Lloque Yupanqui, like his father, was not warlike and added no lands to the Inca domain.

The demand for additional lands and, more important, the resources they could provide first became apparent during the reign of the fourth emperor, Mayta Capac (Mayta Qhapaq). The reasons for the appearance of this need in the 14th century are undoubtedly complex, and any single-factor explanation is probably insufficient. But one possible explanation may lie in the fact that rainfall began to diminish very slightly about this time throughout the central Andes. In an area like the Cuzco Valley, this would imply that some of the marginal farmlands were either abandoned because they could not be watered adequately or were less productive than they had been earlier. Given this situation, if the Inca attempted to maintain their old standard of living, they might have placed some pressure on their food resources. One way of alleviating the problem would have been to acquire additional land and sources of water in an adjacent part of the valley. This is apparently what Mayta Capac did.

Mayta Capac is described in the chronicles as a large, aggressive youth who began fighting with boys from a neighbouring group when he was very young. Pedro de Cieza de León and Pedro Sarmiento de Gamboa (who also was one of the more reliable Spanish chroniclers) indicate that the quarrel began because the Inca were taking water from this group, although they differ on the details concerning who actually took the water. By the time Mayta Capac became emperor, this quarrel had grown into a full-scale war, which the Inca won. They looted the homes of their enemies, took some of their lands, and probably imposed some sort of tribute payment on them.

THE BEGINNINGS OF EXTERNAL EXPANSION

The fifth emperor, Capac Yupanqui (Qhapaq Yupanki), was appointed ruler by his father before he died. He was apparently not the eldest son but was named emperor because his older brother was considered ugly. Capac Yupanqui was the first Inca ruler to conquer lands outside the Cuzco Valley, although these were only about a dozen miles away. Inca Roca ('Inka Roq'a 'Inka) succeeded his father and subjugated some groups that lived about 12 miles (19 km) southeast of Cuzco. He is mostly remembered in the chronicles for the fact that he fathered a large number of sons, one of whom, Yahuar Huacac (Yawar Waqaq), was kidnapped by a neighbouring group when he was about 8 years old. The boy's mother, Mama Mikay, was a Huayllaca (Wayllaqa) woman who had been promised to the leader of another group called the Ayarmaca ('Ayarmaka). When the promise was broken and Mama Mikay married Inca Roca, the Ayarmaca went to war with the Huayllaca and were defeating them. As a peace offering, the Huayllaca agreed to deliver Mama Mikay's son to the Ayarmaca. This tale says a great deal about the way war was waged around the Cuzco Valley at this time; the fact that the Ayarmaca held the boy for several years before returning him to his father suggests that the Inca were no more powerful than several other groups in the area.

Two years before his death, Inca Roca named Yahuar Huacac as the seventh emperor, ensuring a peaceful succession to the throne. Yahuar Huacac was never very healthy and apparently spent most of his time in Cuzco. His brothers Vicaquirao (Wika-k'iraw) and Apo Mayta ('Apu Mayta) were able military leaders and incorporated lands south and east of Cuzco into the Inca domain. Yahuar

Huacac's principal wife was apparently an Ayarmaca, indicating that at that time sister marriage was not the rule. She bore him three sons, and he attempted to follow his father's example by naming their second son as the next emperor; the son was murdered through the intrigues of another of his wives, who wanted her own son named to the throne. The emperor himself was apparently killed shortly thereafter, and the elders chose Viracocha Inca (Wiraqocha 'Inka) as his successor.

The Inca conquest began during the reign of Viracocha Inca in the early part of the 15th century. Up to this time, neighbouring ethnic groups were conquered and their lands taken, but no garrisons or Inca officials were placed among them. They were left undisturbed until the Inca felt it necessary to attack them again. This pattern of raiding and plundering changed during Viracocha Inca's reign. He planned to establish permanent rule over these groups and was ably assisted by his uncles, Vicaquirao and Apo Mayta, who developed military tactics that made permanent conquest possible. Their victory over the Ayarmaca kingdom in the southern Cuzco Valley provided a model for many subsequent campaigns. They first conquered lands in the upper part of the Urubamba Valley that lay behind the Ayarmaca territory. They then successfully attacked the Ayarmaca from two directions—one force coming from Cuzco and the other from the Urubamba Valley.

This was a relatively small-scale campaign, but it made the Inca a political power in the Urubamba Valley, an

QUECHUA

The Quechua (self-name Runa) are South American Indians living in the Andean highlands from Ecuador to Bolivia. They speak many regional varieties of Quechua, which was the language of the Inca empire (though it predates the Inca) and which later became the lingua franca of the Spanish and Indians throughout the Andes.

The Quechua have formed an important part of the agricultural backbone of Andean civilization since the early 15th century, when they were conquered by the Chanca, who were themselves subjugated by the Inca in the later years of that century.

The Inca requirements of public service did not much disturb the traditional Quechua way of life. When the Spanish conquered the Inca empire in the 16th century, however, and the Quechua came under Spanish rule, Quechua society was drastically altered. The Spanish encomienda system of tribute required the Quechua to produce unfamiliar crops for the Spanish at the expense of their own food supply. The Spanish system, unlike its Inca predecessor, did not provide for the welfare of the labourer and his family during his term of forced labour. The Spanish concentrated the Quechua in larger, more populous villages than they were accustomed to, thus further straining Quechua political and social institutions. The Roman Catholic Church made additional demands on the time and resources of Christianized Quechua. A growing desire for the trappings of Spanish wealth even further alienated the Quechua from their own society. By the time Spanish rule ended in the 19th century, the Quechua had been so changed that many remained as servants on the grand haciendas and estates. Others went to the towns and cities of the lowlands to find employment, though some stayed in their mountainous homeland.

In the early 21st century the Quechua lead isolated lives as marginal farmers in the high Andes. Their religion is an amalgam of Roman Catholicism and native folk beliefs. They practice their traditional fibre handicrafts, spinning wool and weaving fabrics for both domestic use and sale to outsiders. Because of the lack of distinct anthropological identity between Quechua speakers and those of Quechua heritage, population estimates in the early 21st century range between 13 million and 16 million. The Quechua have been the subject of numerous biological and medical studies aimed at understanding physiological adaptation to high-altitude living.

important passageway between Cuzco and the Lake Titicaca Basin. As a result of their conquest, the Inca were invited to interfere in a conflict between two Aymara-speaking kingdoms, the Colla and the Lupaca, in the northern part of the Titicaca Basin. The Inca allied themselves with the Lupaca, probably because the Colla were located between themselves and the Lupaca. But before the Inca could attack, the Colla attacked the Lupaca and were defeated. The battle was over by the time the Inca arrived; they joined in a victory celebration with the Lupaca but did not share in the booty.

During the early 15th century a group called the Chanca was emerging as a political power in the area west of the Inca territory. Presumably, they, too, may have been feeling the effects of diminishing food resources and were trying to maintain their standard of living by acquiring land outside their home territory. They moved from their place of origin in Huancavelica and conquered the Quechua (K'ichuwa), a large group whose lands lay immediately west of those controlled by the Inca. In about 1438 the Chanca attacked the Inca. One of the major effects of the Chanca invasion was to foment a civil war among the Inca.

INTERNAL DIVISION AND EXTERNAL EXPANSION

For some time there had been palace intrigue in Cuzco over who would succeed Viracocha Inca to the throne.

The emperor chose Inca Urcon ('Inka 'Urqon) as his successor, but the two generals Vicaquirao and Apo Mayta preferred another son, Cusi Inca Yupanqui (Kusi 'Inka Yupanki). As the Chanca approached Cuzco, Viracocha Inca and Inca Urcon withdrew to a fort near Calca, while Cusi Inca Yupanqui, the two generals, and a few nobles remained to defend the city. They defended it successfully, and after their allies joined them they inflicted two heavy defeats on the Chanca. Cusi Inca Yupanqui then attempted to resolve the differences between his faction and that of his father, but the negotiations failed, and he set himself up as emperor, taking the title of Pachacuti (Pachakuti). At this point, there were two Inca states, one in Cuzco, headed by Pachacuti Inca Yupanqui, and the other in Calca, headed by Viracocha Inca. As the power and prestige of the Cuzco group increased, many people left the Calca faction to join Pachacuti Inca Yupanqui.

Pachacuti Inca Yupanqui had to deal simultaneously with two enemies—the Chanca and his father's forces. The Cuzco faction had made some gains during their two encounters with the Chanca; they took some Quechua lands from the Chanca and formed an alliance with the Quechua, who supported them against the Chanca. They then entered into an agreement with the Chanca that permitted either group to make independent military advances or gains as long as the other was not attacked. At this point, the Cuzco faction moved its army eastward to the edge of the tropical rain forest, thereby encircling the lands controlled by the Calca faction. By this maneuver, the Cuzco faction prevented the possibility of attack coming simultaneously from two directions. Viracocha Inca died about this time, leaving Inca Urcon as leader of the Calca faction. The latter was killed shortly thereafter in a skirmish with the Cuzco group. As a result, the differences between the two factions were resolved, and the Inca were reunited under a single leader.

The Inca forces crossed the Quechua territory and attacked the provinces of Vilcas and Soras, southwest of the area controlled by the Chanca. About 1445, Pachacuti Inca Yupanqui sent his brother Capac Yupanqui (Qhapaq Yupanki) to explore the south coast, marking the first time the Inca reached the ocean. Returning to Cuzco, Capac Yupanqui passed through Chanca territory and captured a few of their villages. The Chanca retaliated by outflanking the Inca and conquering the Colla in the Lake Titicaca Basin.

The Chanca's action increased the tension between the Inca and the Chanca, but no fighting broke out. Instead, they decided to undertake a joint invasion of the area north of Vilcas. Pachacuti Inca Yupanqui appointed Capac Yupanqui to lead the Inca contingent, warning him of Chanca treachery and instructing him to go no farther than Yanamayo. As the expedition moved northward, the Chanca distinguished themselves in battle, to the embarrassment of the Inca. When Pachacuti Inca Yupanqui heard of this, he feared that the Chanca contingent might revolt and ordered his brother to kill the Chanca leaders. The Chanca, learning of this command, fled to the tropical rain forest near the headwaters of the Huallaga River before the order could be carried out.

Capac Yupanqui pursued the Chanca well beyond the Yanamayo, the limit set by his brother, before giving up the chase. Seeing that his forces were considerably overextended, he turned northward toward the rich province of Cajamarca, which was an ally of the powerful kingdom of Chimú on the north coast. Capac Yupanqui stormed and captured Cajamarca and left a small garrison there as he set out for Cuzco.

Pachacuti Inca Yupanqui was furious at this turn of events. His orders had been blatantly disobeyed, and he was apprehensive about his brother's intentions. Perhaps fearing that Capac Yupanqui would usurp the throne, Pachacuti Inca Yupanqui had him killed before he arrived in Cuzco. The Inca still had to contend with the Chanca and with the possibility of attacks from hostile groups in the north, including the kingdom of Chimú, which had set out on a campaign of conquest.

To alleviate this situation, Pachacuti Inca Yupanqui organized two expeditions: one to conquer the peoples of the Lake Titicaca Basin and protect their exposed southern flank, and the other to subdue the area to the north. According to Sarmiento de Gamboa, the Titicaca campaign was led by two of his older sons. They had subjugated the Colla earlier and now turned their attention to the Lupaca and their allies. When the campaign was over, the Inca controlled all of the territory between Cuzco and the southern end of the lake basin.

The northern expedition was led by another son, Topa Inca Yupanqui (Thupa 'Inka Yupanki), who subjected the territories of the Quechua and the Chanca. Topa Inca Yupanqui marched north through the highlands toward Cajamarca, subduing and pacifying the country as he went. After relieving the garrison at Cajamarca, which was being threatened by the kingdom of Chimú, he conquered as far north as Quito (Ecuador) in an attempt to outflank the Chimú armies. Frustrated during this drive by his ignorance of the geography of the region, he came out of the Ecuadorian mountains near Manta, north of the Gulf of Guayaquil; the local residents told him that he could not proceed southward along the coast because the mountains came down to the sea. So he returned to the highlands and sent a small force along the shores of the Gulf of Guayaquil toward the northern border of Chimú. As a result, the Inca were still able to attack the Chimú armies simultaneously from several different directions. After a brief but bitter battle, the Inca sacked the Chimú capital at Chan Chan and then advanced southward along the coast as far as Pachacamac, bringing the area under Inca control.

ADMINISTRATION OF THE EMPIRE

Topa Inca Yupanqui returned to Cuzco, secure in the knowledge that Inca power could not be challenged. The rapid expansion of the empire, however, created a number of problems concerned with sustaining themselves and governing a large number of diverse ethnic groups. Pachacuti Inca Yupanqui and Topa Inca Yupanqui were imaginative and made several important innovations in Inca institutions.

Pachacuti Inca Yupanqui began rebuilding Cuzco, the political and religious capital of the empire. Considerable effort was put into enlarging Sacsahuamán, the huge fortress built on a hill overlooking the city. At the same time he undertook a vast agricultural project over the entire upper end of the Cuzco Valley; rivers were channeled, the valley floor was leveled, and agricultural terraces were built on the surrounding hillsides. This reclamation project undoubtedly increased the agricultural productivity of the area and involved moving many of the original inhabitants of this part of the valley to other localities for several years while the work was being completed.

Pachacuti Inca Yupanqui also turned his attention to social problems. He decreed that no ruler could inherit property from his predecessor;

The remains of Sacsahuamán, a hilltop fortress built to defend the ancient city of Cuzco.
Shutterstock.com

instead, the property of a dead ruler was to pass to his other descendants, who could then support themselves from his lands and the labour taxes owed him. Consequently, each new emperor had to acquire land and labour to support his corporation and government. Pachacuti Inca Yupanqui thus ensured that the corporations of his eight predecessors had estates in the area around Cuzco so their members could support themselves adequately, attend certain ceremonies, and perform ceremonial obligations. Pachacuti Inca Yupanqui and his successors to the Inca throne formed corporations that had lands and estates scattered throughout the empire as well as in the Cuzco Valley itself.

He probably also began the policy of forced resettlement, or *mitma*, about this time, in order to ensure both loyalty to the state and better utilization of land resources, at least from the perspective of the Inca. This practice involved moving some members of an ethnic group from their home territory to distant lands. When a new area was conquered, loyal settlers were brought in from a province that had been under Inca rule long enough so that its residents knew how the Inca system of government worked. They were replaced in their home territories by recalcitrant groups from the newly conquered province. The policy had three important consequences: first, it broke up the size and power of an ethnic group by dispersing its members throughout the empire; second, it weakened the ability of an ethnic group to be self-sufficient; and, finally, it made it more difficult for the inhabitants of an area to revolt successfully.

Pachacuti Inca Yupanqui invented a state religion based on the worship of a creator-god called Viracocha, who had been worshiped since pre-Inca times. Priests were appointed, ceremonies were planned, prayers were prepared, and temples were built throughout the empire. He also expounded the view that the Inca had a divine mission to bring this true religion to other peoples, so that the Inca armies conquered in the name of the creator god. His doctrine was a relatively tolerant one. Conquered groups did not have to give up their own religious beliefs; they merely had to worship the Inca god and provide him and his servants with food, land, and labour.

TOPA INCA YUPANQUI

About 1471, Pachacuti Inca Yupanqui abdicated in favour of his son Topa Inca Yupanqui, thereby ensuring the peaceful succession to the throne. Topa Inca Yupanqui was a great conqueror who was to bring most of the Central Andes region under Inca rule. Yet his first military campaign as emperor, an invasion of the tropical rain forest near the Tono River, was not particularly successful. The Inca were always fascinated with the rain forest and its products but never got used to military operations in this type of environment. This campaign did, however, establish trade relations with the area and secured a contingent of archers in return for a few bronze tools. The emperor soon abandoned the campaign because of a revolt that had broken out in the Lake Titicaca Basin. The rebellion was led by the Colla and Lupaca and was fanned by the rumour that Topa Inca Yupanqui had been killed during his expedition into the jungle.

The Colla's mountaintop forts around Pucará fell one by one as the Inca attacked them. After subduing the Colla, the Inca moved against the Lupaca, who had retreated to the southwest corner of the Lake Titicaca Basin, where they had allied themselves with another Aymara-speaking group, the Pacasa. The Inca armies were again victorious, and the revolt was ended. Topa Inca Yupanqui then turned southward, conquering all of highland Bolivia, northern Chile, and most of northwestern Argentina. He set the boundary markers of the Inca empire at the Maule River in central Chile.

At this point, the southern coast of Peru still had not been incorporated into the Inca state. The area, however, was now surrounded by the Inca on three sides, and about 1476 Topa Inca Yupanqui launched a campaign against this region. Each valley, beginning with those in the south, was attacked separately. Most valleys submitted peacefully or put up only minimal resistance; the inhabitants of the Cañete Valley, however, put up a stubborn fight; it took the Inca nearly three years to subdue them.

During the remainder of his reign, Topa Inca Yupanqui concerned himself with the administration of the empire. He spent much of his time traveling throughout his territories, making assignments of land and establishing local administrations. He introduced a system of classifying the adult male population into units of 100, 500, 1,000, 5,000, and 10,000, which formed a basis for labour assignments and military conscription. He also instituted a system of tribute in which each province provided Chosen Women (Aqllakuna) to serve as temple maidens in state shrines or to become the brides of soldiers who had distinguished themselves in combat.

Huayna Capac

Topa Inca Yupanqui's unexpected death about 1493 precipitated a struggle for the succession. It appears that Topa Inca Yupanqui had originally favoured the succession of Huayna Capac (Wayna Qhapaq), the youngest son of his principal wife and sister. Shortly before his death, he changed his mind and named as his successor Capac Huari (Qhapaq Wari), the son of another wife. Capac Huari, however, never became emperor. The claims of his mother and her relatives were suppressed by the supporters of Huayna Capac. This group was led by Huaman Achachi (Waman 'Achachi), the child's uncle and presumably the brother of the emperor's principal wife.

A regent named Hualpaya (Walpaya) was appointed from this group to tutor Huayna Capac in the ways of government until the child was old enough to rule in his own name. Hualpaya, however, tried to assert the claims of his own son to the throne and, as a result, was killed by Huaman Achachi. Huayna Capac's reign was mostly peaceful; he devoted much of his time to traveling, administering the empire, and suppressing small-scale revolts. He did extend the empire by conquering Chachapoyas, a mountainous country in northeastern Peru, and later northern Ecuador. After conquering Chachapoyas, he recruited part of his bodyguard from the warlike inhabitants of the area. The conquest of northern Ecuador occupied the last years of his life and took place shortly before the Spaniards arrived. During these campaigns, he pushed the frontiers of the Inca empire to the Ancasmayo River, the present-day boundary between Ecuador and Colombia.

While he was fighting in northern Ecuador, Huayna Capac received word that the Bolivian frontier had been invaded by a Guaraní-speaking group that periodically crossed the Gran Chaco from Argentina to raid Inca frontier settlements for bronze tools and ornaments made of precious metals. They were more of a nuisance than an actual threat to the empire, but Huayna Capac dispatched a general named Yasca (Yaska) to drive them from the area and to build forts along the frontier.

Meanwhile, he undertook another expedition in northern Ecuador to wipe out isolated pockets of resistance. During this campaign, he learned that an epidemic was sweeping Cuzco and the surrounding countryside. He left immediately for Quito, on the high road to Cuzco, to deal with this crisis and arrived there about the same time the epidemic did. The pestilence had spread rapidly from Bolivia and, judging by its description, was either smallpox or measles, both of which were European diseases introduced into South America by the Spanish settlers at La Plata. The disease was probably communicated to the Andean area by the Guaraní, who had been in contact with the Spanish at La Plata. Whatever the ailment was, Huayna Capac contracted it and died about 1525, without naming a successor in the appropriate manner. This set off another struggle over the throne.

CIVIL WAR ON THE EVE OF THE SPANISH CONQUEST

Huayna Capac's father had begun the custom of marrying a full sister in order to keep the royal bloodline pure and, more important, to prevent conflict over succession. According to this custom, one sister became the principal wife of the emperor, and one of their sons became the next ruler. As noted above, this system had failed at Huayna Capac's succession. Nor did it work at Huayna Capac's death because his principal wife had been childless. In this situation, the emperor could appoint any one of his sons as his successor, as long as one of them had "divine" approval registered on the lungs of a sacrificed llama. There were several candidates for the throne: Ninan Cuyuchi who was in Tumipampas with his father; Atahuallpa ('Ataw Wallpa), who was also in the north; Huascar (Washkar), who was apparently in Cuzco; Manco Inca (Manqo 'Inka), whose mother belonged to 'Iñaqa (the royal corporation of Pachacuti Inca Yupanqui); Topa Huallpa (Thupa Wallpa); and Paullu Topa (Pawllu Thupa).

Huayna Capac, aware of imminent death, asked the priest to perform the divination ceremony to determine whether or not he should name Ninan Cuyuchi as his successor; if the signs were not favourable, then Huascar was to be the next candidate to be tested. The emperor apparently died before the ceremony was performed. The priest then notified Ninan Cuyuchi that he was to be the next ruler, but the latter had contracted the same disease as his father and died shortly thereafter. The priest then named Huascar as the new emperor; this was highly irregular, because the priest apparently followed the old ruler's wishes without performing the required ceremony. The other candidates for the throne were not pleased with the situation.

The priest brought Huayna Capac's body back to Cuzco, while Atahuallpa remained in Quito. Huascar was so furious with the priest for leaving a rival for the throne in the north with a large army that he had him killed. This created animosity against Huascar among the members of the priest's royal corporation. Huascar then demanded that Atahuallpa return to Cuzco, but the latter ignored him and undertook a campaign to suppress a revolt around the Gulf of Guayaquil. While he was involved in this expedition, Huascar sent an officer to remove Atahuallpa's wives and insignias. Atahuallpa killed the officer and had a drum made out of him, which he sent to Huascar. This insult completed the breach between the two rivals, and a civil war resulted.

At this point, Huascar controlled the southern part of the empire, while Atahuallpa controlled Ecuador and parts of northern Peru. Atahuallpa won the first battle of the war, fought at Riobamba in Ecuador, and advanced to Tumipampas. There he lost to Huascar's army and was taken prisoner. He later escaped, rallied his forces, and drove his brother's army from the Cañari territory around Tumipampas. He then devastated the Cañari lands because he thought they had supported his brother's faction during his imprisonment. Apparently, the Cañari wanted little to do with either Inca faction and offered minimal support to whichever group controlled Tumipampas at the moment. After their lands were destroyed, they wanted nothing at all to do with the Inca, and later they became close allies of the Spaniards.

Atahuallpa's armies, led by the able generals Quisquis (Kizkiz) and Challcuchima (Challku-chima), marched south and won a series of decisive victories at Cajamarca, Bombon, and Ayacucho. As they moved southward, Huascar formed another army to defend Cuzco from the invaders. His forces were defeated, and he was captured a few miles from Cuzco in April 1532. The generals killed his entire family and fastened them to poles along a highway leading from the capital. They also killed a number of people in Topa Inca Yupanqui's corporation because they had supported Huascar during the civil war; and they burned the mummy of the deceased ruler, which was venerated by the members of this group. Atahuallpa was in the north, setting up his administration, when he learned of the victory. He ordered Challcuchima to bring Huascar to the north so he could insult him properly before being crowned.

THE SPANISH CONQUEST

Meanwhile, the Spaniards had landed at Tumbes on the northern coast of Peru early in 1532 and were seeking an interview with Atahuallpa so that they could kidnap him. It is clear that they understood the nature of the Inca civil war and were dealing with emissaries from both factions. Their actions, however, must have seemed puzzling to Atahuallpa. On the one hand, Pizarro and his men were deposing and executing leaders who were loyal to him, and, on the other hand, they were sending messages that recognized him as the legitimate ruler of Tawantinsuyu. As the Spaniards moved toward Cajamarca, he sent them a message indicating that he was now the sole ruler of his father's domain. Furthermore, he reminded the Spaniards that they were far from their base of supply and in a land controlled by his armies. The Spaniards replied to this veiled threat by indicating that they would come to his aid against

any group that opposed his rule. Atahuallpa clearly wanted the Spaniards as allies but continually misinterpreted their intentions and underestimated their abilities—even after he was kidnapped in Cajamarca on Nov. 16, 1532.

Atahuallpa was allowed to meet with his advisers while the Spaniards held him prisoner, and he arranged to have the ransom they demanded paid. An enormous ransom was raised, but Pizarro did not free him because it would have been too dangerous for the Spaniards. While he was in prison, Atahuallpa decided that the Spaniards were indifferent to the idea of having his brother slain and ordered Huascar's death. The Spaniards, of course, wanted all pretenders to authority removed but later used this act to justify their execution of the Inca ruler. Realizing that Atahuallpa's death was a mistake because it weakened their position, they approved the coronation of Topa Huallpa, a candidate whom they thought would be acceptable to both Inca factions. But the Spaniards miscalculated. Topa Huallpa had not supported Atahuallpa and, in fact, had been in hiding as long as the latter was alive. He was supported by Huascar's group and was opposed by Atahuallpa's following, who believed that the legitimate heir was the deceased ruler's son in Lima. With this act, the Spaniards suddenly found themselves closely allied with Huascar's faction and were so viewed by both Inca groups.

Topa Huallpa died within a few months—poisoned, according to Huascar's supporters. At this point, the

Spaniards reaffirmed their alliance with Huascar's following, placing Huascar's brother, Manco Inca, on the throne and assisting him in dispersing the remnants of Atahuallpa's army. The real Spanish conquest of Peru occurred during the next few years, when they prevented Manco Inca from reestablishing control over the coast and the north, much of which was still loyal to Atahuallpa or under no control at all. By 1535 the Inca ruler realized that the Spaniards were more dangerous than any threat posed by the remnants of Atahuallpa's followers. But it was too late. His attacks on the Spanish settlements were beaten back, and he was eventually driven into a remote mountainous area called Vitcos, where he established an independent Inca state that lasted until 1572.

INCA CULTURE AT THE TIME OF THE CONQUEST

The rapid incorporation of so many mountain and coastal desert polities before 1532 calls for explanation. It is tempting to view such expansion in the context of the instantaneous breakup in 1532, when some of the same forces were likely to have been at work, including dispersed territories, interlocked with some belonging to other powers in the region, and multiethnic and polyglot agglomerations in neighbouring valleys. Each political unit—as eventually was the case with the Inca state itself—was likely to share pastures, cultivated terraces, and beach installations. Hegemonies

shifted according to local and regional circumstances.

The Early, Middle, and Late horizons were temporary concatenations, and none lasted for very long. The Spanish invasion interrupted these alternations. A player had entered the field who ignored the local rules and who did not fathom the true sources of Andean wealth, which was not silver but an intimate familiarity with local conditions and possibilities and the ability to pool vastly different geographic and ecological tiers into single polities.

SOCIAL AND POLITICAL STRUCTURE

According to the incomplete evidence provided by the Spanish eyewitnesses, the Inca themselves considered the term Inca applicable only to the descendants of the 12 individuals who traditionally are said to have ruled from Cuzco. Of the 12, only four or five can be documented to have been actual historical personages. The others may have been products of later efforts to legitimate and enhance the royal genealogy. There is also the possibility that some of the "earlier" names were actually a parallel line of personalities, possibly with different functions that may have been considered "heathen" by the Spanish. This hypothesis cannot be verified with the sources now available.

In addition to the 12 lineages, the ranks of "Inca by decree" or "as a privilege" are also mentioned by some of the

Spanish sources. Their origins and functions were just as nebulous as those of the royals: one of the few Andean sources, Poma da Ayala, claims that some of the inhabitants of the Cuzco basin who were conquered early during the expansion of the Late Horizon were "granted" or "promoted to" Inca status. They were "improved," according to Poma da Ayala, although his own case is weakened by his claim that his ancestors, who lived many hundreds of miles north of Cuzco, had benefited from such social mobility.

The administrative organization of Tawantinsuyu is poorly understood, although its origins are known to lie in the earlier ethnic subdivisions. Claims have been made that authority was left in the hands of traditional lords who simply had to demonstrate their fealty. Other Spanish sources make reference to an administrative reorganization, in which all of the conquered groups were shoehorned into a decimal system. There is some evidence that decimal subdivisions were present in the Cajamarca region of northern Peru. At the time of the conquest, the decimal vocabulary apparently was in the process of being imposed on the rest of the country, presumably to rationalize the multiplicity of local and divided loyalties. The administrative papers available for a part of the Huánuco region allow the identification of a "hundred-households" unit with five actual hamlets, all of which were near each other. Since these records were kept house by house, it has been possible to test the significance of the decimal

vocabulary at its lowest level. What is meant when the records speak of "lords of 10,000 households," however, cannot now be fathomed.

A clearer picture has emerged of the ethnic lords incorporated by the Inca into their realm. Some had ruled only small units of a few hundred households. Others, like the Huanca or the Lupaca claimed to have had 20,000 domestic units. There is no record of the size of the coastal Chimú polity, which must have been quite large. The Chincha claimed 30,000 "fires," and the Chimú may well have been even larger before their defeat by Cuzco.

Usually, two lords ruled each ethnic group—which has been one of the arguments for considering as plausible a dual rule in Cuzco as well. The best evidence of the duties of the ethnic lords has come from the Aymara kingdom of the Lupaca. At one point in Inca history they rose in rebellion against Cuzco rule, and in the decades immediately prior to the arrival of the Europeans they were busy leading "6,000 soldiers" on faraway battlefields in what is now Ecuador. The testimony of the Lupaca, collected in 1567, claims that on such adventures they did not return to their lands for the harvest but devoted most of their energies to war, and in return they were exempted from farming, road building, and other state chores.

There was no tribute system in Inca statecraft, just as there had been no contributions in kind in earlier Andean polities. The peasantry owed only their energy, which was delivered through the well-understood *mit'a* system. Led by their traditional leaders, the people appeared for their obligations, lineage by lineage. The best quipu record of these obligations has come from a group who lived in the Huánuco area. Just as they had provided energy for their own lords, under Inca rule this group sent dozens of couples to labour on public works or to produce the grain that, as beer, was "fed" to the mummies of deceased Inca kings. Others became soldiers or helped fill the warehouses. Some carried loads along the Inca highway system, while still others were soldiers under the command of their traditional lords. Using this *quipu*, it has been possible to test the claim that there was no tribute system. Of its 26 cords only two deal with articles submitted in kind, wild honey and tropical feathers, both of which were lowland commodities that were gathered and not cultivated.

The absence of tribute was closely connected to the absence of markets. Just as all households owed some of their energies to their ethnic lords, to the shrines, and to Cuzco, so too their household needs were satisfied by the claims they could make to the reciprocal services of their kinfolk or ethnic peers or to the administrative services of their ethnic authorities. It is probable that with the growth of the Inca state over time, this formula was breached, particularly in the case of prisoners of war and other populations moved from their traditional areas for state purposes.

The most elaborate example of the structural changes that emerged from the need to create new state revenues was the expansion and reorganization of corn production for military purposes in the Cochabamba Valley. This region was the largest single corn-producing area in the highlands. One of the later kings removed the native population and set up a large state enterprise (more than 2,000 warehouses), to which some 25 highland groups were sent on rotation, lineage by lineage. Each ethnic group was responsible for particular strips that were traced across the valley by Cuzco surveyors. In 1575 the Spanish viceroy Francisco de Toledo used this Inca precedent to establish the repartimiento system that provided labour for the silver mines at Potosí.

INCA TECHNOLOGY AND INTELLECTUAL LIFE

The intellectual tradition of the Inca emerged from their detailed and efficient knowledge and use of an extremely challenging environment. No system of writing, in the European sense, has been discovered, and the question remains as to how long-distance communication was achieved.

Beyond oral transmission, the most promising domain for research is in textiles. In the highlands very few have been preserved because of the humidity, but on the coastal desert many burial cloths from widely different periods have been located and studied. Their artistic qualities have fomented grave robbing on a very large scale; museums throughout the world have dozens if not hundreds of such cloths, each of great beauty and enormous sophistication.

Fibre technology went beyond burial or sacrificial textiles. Viceroy Toledo wrote to Philip II that he was sending four gigantic cloths on which maps of his Andean realm had been painted. While the letter was carefully filed in the Archives of the Indies, at Sevilla (Seville), the maps have never been located. Other uses of textiles included the quipu, used for bookkeeping and possibly also for historical recording; suspension bridges, some of which are still maintained on a regular basis by particular villages responsible for reweaving; and calendars and ceremonial accounting.

While in the field, Inca armies were rewarded with corn and cloth. One European observer was told that soldiers would rebel if they did not receive their issues of textiles and corn beer. A major manufacturing centre employing "a thousand" full-time weavers was established on the northeastern shore of Lake Titicaca. The craftspeople there were men, but every administrative centre along the Inca highway is said to have housed a group of secluded women weavers (Chosen Women); one such house, at Huánuco Pampa (administrative centre of the Huánuco region), has been located and excavated. The storehouses, full of thousands of textiles, were one of the wonders frequently mentioned by the early Spaniards in their letters.

As Tawantinsuyu grew and involved peoples of many different environments and cultures, techniques originating in any particular ethnic group were spread across the land. Prior to the Inca expansion, metals—gold, silver, copper, and their alloys—were used mainly for ornaments; and tools were made from wood and stone. Bronze tools—crowbars, chisels, axes, knives, and clubheads, to name only a few—became exceedingly common after the Inca conquest.

The remarkable Inca highway system was also noted by the earliest Spanish eyewitnesses, since these roads were in constant use, even by horses. Research since the 1950s has provided fresh insights into the engineering methods and geographic location of two parallel roads—one in the highlands, the other on the coast—the whole system adding up to at least 15,500 miles (24,945 km). While some of these roads may have been built first during the Middle Horizon and even earlier, it was during Inca times that the roads were maintained and unified into a single political and economic system. Travel units, adjusted to the pace of a loaded llama or human carrier, can still be detected along the Qhapaq Ñan, the main north–south royal road in the highlands. At the end of each day the caravan stopped at a *tambo*, a way station, which, although smaller than an administrative centre, was complete with warehouses and barracks. The maintenance of the road segment and the filling of storehouses was part of the *mit'a* responsibilities of neighbouring groups.

Measurement of both distance and surface area was done by units called *tupu*, since the Andean concern was with units of human energy expended. Somehow, two measurements that belonged to very different European systems of reckoning were part of a single Andean concern. Units of land measurement, called *papakancha*, also differed. Where the land was in continuous cultivation, as in corn country, one unit was used. Another unit was in use for highland-tuber cultivation, where fallowing and rotation was the dominant crop pattern. As one "measurer" explained to the viceroy's envoy, the papakancha was of one size when it was at a protected, lower altitude, but it could be up to seven times that size on the high, cold puna.

INCA RELIGION

Inca religion—an admixture of complex ceremonies, practices, animistic beliefs, varied forms of belief in objects having magical powers, and nature worship—culminated in the worship of the sun, which was presided over by the priests of the last native pre-Columbian conquerors of the Andean regions of South America. Though there was an Inca state religion of the sun, the substrata religious beliefs and practices of the pre-Inca peoples exerted an influence on the Andean region prior to and after the conquest of most of South America by the Spaniards in the 16th century.

INCA GODS

The creator god of the Inca and of pre-Inca peoples was Viracocha, who was also a culture hero. Creator of earth, man, and animals, Viracocha had a long list of titles, including Lord Instructor of the World, the Ancient One, and the Old Man of the Sky. Some have said that he also was the creator of the Tiwanaku civilization, of which the Inca were the cultural heirs. Viracocha went through several transmogrifications (often with grotesque or humorous effects). He made peoples, destroyed them, and re-created them of stone; and when they were re-created, he dispersed humankind in four directions. As a culture hero, he taught people various techniques and skills. He journeyed widely until he came to the shores of Manta (Ecuador), where he set off into the Pacific—some say in a boat made of his cloak, others say he walked on the water. This part of the myth has been seized upon by modern mythmakers, and, as Kon-Tiki, Viracocha was said to have brought Inca culture to Polynesia.

Viracocha was the divine protector of the Inca ruler Pachacuti Inca Yupanqui; he appeared to Pachacuti in a dream when the Inca forces were being besieged by the Chanca. Upon victory, Pachacuti raised a temple to Viracocha in Cuzco. He was represented by a gold figure "about the size of a 10-year-old child."

Inti, the sun god, was the ranking deity in the Inca pantheon. His warmth embraced the Andean earth and matured crops; as such, he was beloved by

An Aymara priest in Bolivia makes a fire offering to the sun god Inti. Considered the chief deity by the Inca, Inti was beloved for his gifts of light and warmth. Jose Luis Quintana/ LatinContent/Getty Images

farmers. Inti was represented with a human face on a ray-splayed disk. He was considered to be the divine ancestor of the Inca: "my father" was a title given to Inti by one Inca ruler.

Apu Illapu, the rain giver, was an agricultural deity to whom the common man addressed his prayers for rain. Temples to Illapu were usually on high structures; in times of drought, pilgrimages were made to them and prayers were accompanied by sacrifices—often human, if the crisis was sufficient. The

people believed that Illapu's shadow was in the Milky Way, from whence he drew the water that he poured down as rain.

Mama Quilla (Mama-Kilya), wife of the sun god, was the Moon Mother, and the regulator of women's menstrual cycles. The waxing and waning of the moon was used to calculate monthly cycles, from which the time periods for Inca festivals were set. Silver was considered to be tears of the moon. The stars had minor functions. The constellation of Lyra, which was believed to have the

THE ART OF ANCIENT ECUADOR

It is to Ecuador that one must turn for an examination of early art forms. Straddling the equator, as the name implies, this region—today the smallest republic in South America—is one of the most intriguing on the continent. For decades the region had been ignored by scholars in favour of the more glamorous Peruvian area, but in the late 20th century its tremendous antiquity began to be recognized. It now seems that ancient humans may have established their first South American foothold in Ecuador and that the region is also the site of the earliest datable pottery. From perhaps as early as 15,000 BC until about 3200 BC, when pottery was known to exist at Valdivia, there was a long, steady period of development in the region. And the development was not spotty, for the population increase was also constant.

Although the great cities and some of the major cultural activities found farther south were not found in Ecuador, there was nevertheless considerable cultural accomplishment. Weaving was done in quantity, as evidenced by Spanish accounts; and, more spectacularly, goldsmithing was a major expression of the artist's skill. Large pieces, such as crowns and breastplates, and tiny miniatures reflecting the sureness of a master's hand have been found. None of these pieces is unique; they are known in sufficient quantity to prove the existence of a longtime craft. Literally hundreds of thousands of tiny gold beads, each cast individually, have been found in the sands of La Tolita; others, slightly larger, with granulated surfaces indicating the mastery of a complex casting process, have also been recovered.

The technique of inlaying had also been mastered, and the use of emeralds and other gemstones as settings was commonplace. Platinum was worked, as in Colombia; not only was it cast but it also was frequently used in combination with other metals. Copper, too, was worked, both in its pure form and combined with tin to make bronze; occasionally, it was gilded to create a pseudo-gold finish. Heavy cast copper axes were stock-in-trade, and many smaller objects were turned out in quantity.

The pottery that emerged from the hands of the clay workers was of high quality, beautifully designed, and well finished. The modeling was powerful, and there were touches of humour. Scholars are not sure to what extent colour was used, for time and soil have removed much of it. Modeled clay effigies discovered in 1966 at Bahía de Manta are not only remarkable for their size and quantity but even more for the astonishing amount of original colour that had been preserved.

appearance of a llama, was entreated for protection. The constellation Scorpio was believed to have the shape of a cat; the Pleiades were called "little mothers," and festivals were celebrated on their reappearance in the sky. Earth was called Pachamama (Paca Mama), or Earth Mother. The sea, which was relatively remote to the Inca until after 1450, was called Cochamama (Mama Qoca), the Sea Mother.

TEMPLES AND SHRINES

Temples and shrines housing fetishes of the cult were occupied by priests, their attendants, and the Chosen Women. In general, temples were not intended to shelter the celebrants, since most ceremonies were held outside the temple proper. The ruins of the Temple of Viracocha at San Pedro Cacha (Peru), however, had a ground plan that measured 330 by 87 feet (100.5 metres by 26.5 metres), which indicates that it was designed for use other than the storage of priestly regalia.

The Sun Temple in Cuzco is the best-known of the Inca temples. Another, at Vilcashuman (which was regarded as the geographic centre of the empire), has a large temple still existing. Near Mount Aconcagua in Argentina, at the southern limit of the Inca empire, "there was a temple...an ancient oracle held in high regard where they made their sacrifices," and on Titicaca Island, one of the largest of several islands in Lake Titicaca, there was a temple of the sun.

As the Inca conquered new territories, temples were erected in the new lands. In Caranqui, Ecuador, one such temple was described by a chronicler as being filled with great vessels of gold and silver. At Latacunga (Llacta cunga) in Ecuador there was a sun temple where sacrifices were made; part of the temple was still visible when the German explorer and geographer Alexander von Humboldt sketched the ruins in 1801.

The sun temple in Cuzco, built with stones "all matched and joined," had a circumference of more than 1,200 feet (366 metres). A fragment of the wall still extant is testimony to the accuracy of the chronicler's description. Within the temple was an image of the sun "of great size," and in another precinct, the Golden Enclosure (Corincancha), were gold models of cornstalks, llamas, and lumps of earth. Portions of the land, which supported the temples, the priests, and the Chosen Women, were allotted to the sun and administered for the priests.

Along with the shrines and temples, *huacas* (sacred sites) were widespread. A huaca could be a man-made temple, mountain, hill, or bridge, such as the great *huacachaca* across the Apurímac River. A huaca also might be a mummy bundle, especially if it was that of a lord-Inca. On high points of passage in the Andes, propitiatory cairns (*apacheta*, "piles of stones") were made, to which, in passing, each person would add a small stone and pray that his journey be lightened. The idea of huaca was intimately bound up with religion, combining the magical and the charm-bearing.

The Priesthood

Priests resided at all important shrines and temples. A chronicler suggests that a priest's title was *umu*, but in usage his title was geared to his functions as diviner of lungs, sorcerer, confessor, and curer. The title of the chief priest in Cuzco, who was of noble lineage, was *villac umu*. He held his post for life, was married, and competed in authority with the Inca. He had power over all shrines and temples and could appoint and remove priests. Presumably, priests were chosen young, brought up by the more experienced, and acquired with practice the richly developed ceremonialism.

Divination

Divination was the prerequisite to all action. Nothing of importance was undertaken without recourse to divination. It was used to diagnose illness, to predict the outcome of battles, and to ferret out crimes, thus giving it a judiciary function. Divination was also used to determine what sacrifice should be made to what god. Life was believed to be controlled by the all-pervading unseen powers, and to determine these portents the priests had recourse to the supernatural. Oracles were considered to be the most important and direct means of access to the wayward gods.

One oracle of a huaca close to the Huaca-Chaca Bridge, across the Apurímac River near Cuzco, was described by a chronicler as a wooden beam as thick as a fat man, with a girdle of gold about it with two large golden breasts like a woman. These and other idols were blood spattered from sacrifices—animal and human. "Through this large idol," a chronicler wrote, "the demon of the river used to speak to them." Another well-known oracle was housed in a temple in the large adobe complex of Pachacamac near Lima.

Divination also was accomplished by watching the meandering of spiders and the arrangement that coca leaves took in a shallow dish. Another method of divination was to drink *ayahuasca*, a narcotic that had profound effects on the central nervous system. This was believed to enable one to communicate with the supernatural powers.

Fire also was believed to provide spiritual contact. The flames were blown to red heat through metal tubes, after which a practitioner (*yacarca*) who had narcotized himself by chewing coca leaves summoned the spirits with fiery conjuration to speak—"which they did," wrote a chronicler, by "ventriloquism." Divination by studying the lungs of a sacrificed white llama was considered to be efficacious. The lungs were inflated by blowing into the dissected trachea (there is an Inca ceramic showing this), and the future was foretold by priests who minutely observed the conformance of the veins. On the reading of this augury, political or military action was taken.

Confession was part of the priestly ritual of divination. Should rain not fall or a water conduit break without cause, it was believed that such an occurrence could arise from someone's failure to observe the strictly observed ceremonies. This was called *hocha*, a ritual error. The *ayllu*, a basic social unit identified with communally held land, was wounded by individual misdeeds. Crimes had to be confessed and expiated by penitence so as not to call down the divine wrath.

SACRIFICE

Sacrifice, human or animal, was offered on every important occasion; guinea pigs (more properly *cui*), llamas, certain foods, coca leaves, and *chicha* (an intoxicant corn beverage) were all used in sacrifices. Many sacrifices were daily occurrences for the ritual of the sun's appearance. A fire was kindled, and corn was thrown on the coals and toasted. "Eat this, Lord Sun," was the objuration of officiating priests, "so that you will know that we are your children."

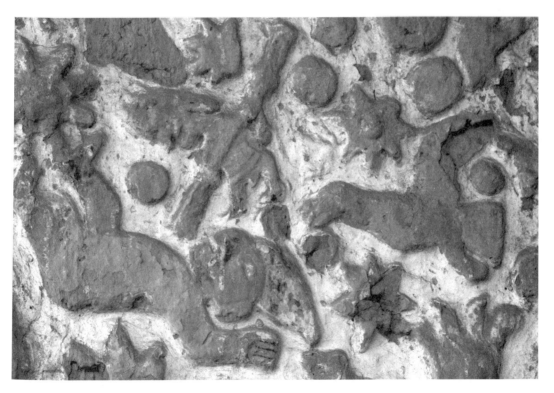

A portion of a mural in Trujillo, Peru, thought to depict a human sacrifice. Pre-Columbian civilizations sacrificed men, women, and even children to commemorate special occasions or appease the gods. Jaime Razuri/AFP/Getty Images

On the first day of every lunar month 100 pure-white llamas were driven into the Great Square, Huayaca Pata in Cuzco. They were moved about to the various images of the gods and then assigned to 30 priestly attendants, each representing a day of the month. The llamas were then sacrificed; chunks of flesh were thrown onto the fire, and the bones were powdered for ritual use. Ponchos of excellent weave or miniature vestments were burned in the offering. The Inca ruler wore his poncho only once. It was ceremoniously sacrificed in fire each day.

Humans also were sacrificed. When the need was extreme, 200 children might be immolated, such as when a new Inca ruler assumed the royal fringe. Defeats, famine, and pestilence all called for human blood. Even a Chosen Woman from the Sun Temple might be taken out for sacrifice. Children, before being sacrificed, were feasted "so that they would not enter the presence of the gods hungry and crying." It was important in human sacrifice that the sacrificed person be without blemish. Many were chosen from the conquered provinces as part of regular taxation; "blood money" was scarcely a metaphor.

FESTIVALS

The 30-day calendar was religious, and each month had its own festival. The religious calendar is explained in considerable detail by Guamán Poma de Ayala. In his letter to Philip II he offered two different versions, one centring on state ceremonies and sacrifices performed at Cuzco and the other describing the agricultural practices at the local level in the highlands. Quite different calendars prevailed on the irrigated coast, but surviving sources do not record them in any detail.

CONCLUSION

The history of the ancient Americas is not nearly as well known as that of Mesopotamia or ancient Egypt. Before the arrival of Europeans, Mesoamerica—an archaeological bridge connecting North and South America—was home to various nomadic and sedentary cultures. Mayan civilization occupied much of the northwestern part of the isthmus, from Chiapas and Yucatán, now part of southern Mexico, through Guatemala, Honduras, Belize, and El Salvador and into Nicaragua. Although the Maya were the most advanced pre-Columbian civilization in the hemisphere, they were never unified. And unlike the Aztec and Inca empires, their autonomous city-states remained independent, presaging the political fragmentation that would characterize Central America to the present day. What unity existed was cultural rather than political.

The Olmec culture and other Mexican influences substantially affected the development of Mayan civilization, while central Mexican Nahuatl influence challenged the Maya and stretched along the Pacific coast, notable especially among the Pipil of El Salvador and the

Chorotega and Nicarao of Nicaragua. In Panama and Costa Rica, South American Chibcha influence was prevalent, while Caribbean cultural patterns penetrated the coastal plain from Panama to Honduras.

The Andean civilizations owe their existence to two agricultural circumstances in particular—their ability to exploit thousands of quite different ecologic pockets, each with its own microenvironment, and the use of daytime heat and nighttime cold to develop food preservation techniques. They also developed a set of values that soon was elaborated into an economic and political ideal. Every Andean society—be it a tiny, local ethnic group of 20 to 30 villages in a single valley or a large kingdom of 150,000 people, such as the Lupaca—tried to control simultaneously a wide variety of ecologic stories up and down the mountainsides. Some of them were many days' march from the political core of the nation. If the society was small, the outliers (herders, salt winners above the core, and maize, cotton, or coca leaf cultivators in the warm country below) would be only three or four days away. When the political unit grew large and could mobilize and maintain several hundred young men as colonists, the outliers could be 10 or even 15 days' walk away from the core.

The Inca state, or Tawantinsuyu as it was known to its own citizens, was perhaps the largest political or military enterprise of all. The Incas expanded and projected on earlier, pre-Inca solutions and adaptations. In the process, many tactics that had worked well on a smaller scale became inoperative; others were reformulated in such ways that their original outline was barely recognizable.

Beyond the strategic colonies set up on an expanded model, the Inca did not interfere too much with the lives of the many local groups that they had incorporated into Tawantinsuyu. Most of the cultures that existed in Ecuador, Peru, Bolivia, Argentina, and Chile before the Inca expansion can be identified. In fact, because the European invasion beginning in 1532 was mostly concerned with breaking the resistance of the Inca overlords, frequently more is known about the pre-Inca occupants than about Cuzco rule. Inca power was broken and decapitated within 40 years of 1532. The ethnic groups, many of which (like the Wanka or the Cañari) sided with Europeans against the Inca, were still easy to locate and identify in the 18th century.

Appendix: Selected Gods of the New World

BACAB

In Mayan mythology, the name Bacab refers to any of four gods, thought to be brothers, who, with upraised arms, supported the multilayered sky from their assigned positions at the four cardinal points of the compass. (The Bacabs may also have been four manifestations of a single deity.) The four brothers were probably the offspring of Itzamná, the supreme deity, and Ixchel, the goddess of weaving, medicine, and childbirth. Each Bacab presided over one year of the four-year cycle. The Maya expected the Muluc years to be the greatest years, because the god presiding over these years was the greatest of the Bacab gods. The four directions and their corresponding colours (north, white; east, red; south, yellow; west, black) played an important part in the Mayan religious and calendrical systems.

CHAC

Chac, the Mayan god of rain, was especially important in the Yucatán region of Mexico where he was depicted in Classic times with protruding fangs, large round eyes, and a proboscis-like nose.

Like other major Mayan gods, Chac also appeared as four gods, the Chacs. The four gods were associated with the points of the compass and their colours: north, white; east, red; south, yellow; west, black. At Chichén Itzá, in Post-Classic times, human sacrifice became associated with the rain god, and the priests who held the arms and legs of the sacrificial victims were termed *chacs*.

In Post-Classic Mayan and Toltec ruins, reclining figures known as the Chacs Mool are thought to represent the rain god. Following the Spanish conquest, the Chacs were associated with Christian saints and were often depicted on horseback.

CHALCHIUHTLICUE

The Aztec goddess of rivers, lakes, streams, and other freshwaters was Chalchiuhtlicue (also spelled Chalchihuitlicue). Her name in the Nahuatl language means "She Who Wears a Jade Skirt." She was also called Matlalcueye, meaning "She Who Wears a Green Skirt." In Aztec cosmology she was the wife (in some myths, sister) of the rain god Tlaloc. It was in her reign that maize (corn) was first used. Like other water deities, she was often associated with serpents.

Not to be confused with Chalchiuhtlicue was Huixtocihuatl (Salt Lady), the goddess of salt water, of the salters guild, and of dissolute women. She is generally considered to be a sister of Tlaloc.

CHICOMECÓATL

Chicomecóatl was the Aztec goddess of sustenance and, hence, of corn (maize), one of the most ancient and important goddesses in the Valley of Mexico. Her Nahuatl name means Seven Snakes, the number seven being associated with luck and generative power. She was often portrayed as the consort of the corn god, Centéotl. Chicomecóatl is depicted in Aztec documents with her body and face painted red, wearing a distinctive rectangular headdress or pleated fan of red paper. She is similarly represented in sculpture, often holding a double ear of corn in each hand.

COATLICUE

Coatlicue, whose Nahuatl name means Serpent Skirt, was the Aztec earth goddess. She was the symbol of the earth as both creator and destroyer and the mother of the gods and mortals. The dualism that she embodies is powerfully concretized in her image: her face is of two fanged serpents and her skirt is of interwoven snakes (snakes symbolize fertility); her breasts are flabby (she nourished many); her necklace is of hands, hearts, and a skull (she feeds on corpses, as the earth consumes all that dies); and her fingers and toes are claws. Called also Teteoinnan ("Mother of the Gods") and Toci ("Our Grandmother"), she is a single manifestation of the earth goddess, a multifaceted being who also appears as the fearsome goddess of childbirth, Cihuacóatl ("Snake Woman"; like Coatlicue, called Tonantzin ["Our Mother"]), and as Tlazoltéotl, the goddess of sexual impurity and wrongful behaviour.

HUITZILOPOCHTLI

Huitzilopochtli (or Uitzilopochtli) was the Aztec sun and war god and one of the two principal deities of Aztec religion. He is often represented in art as either a hummingbird or an eagle.

Huitzilopochtli's name is a cognate of the Nahuatl words *huitzilin*, "hummingbird," and *opochtli*, "left." Aztecs believed that dead warriors were reincarnated as hummingbirds and considered the south to be the left side of the world; thus, his name meant the "resuscitated warrior of the south." His other names included Xiuhpilli ("Turquoise Prince") and Totec ("Our Lord"). His *nagual*, or animal disguise, was the eagle.

Huitzilopochtli's mother, Coatlicue, is one aspect of the Aztecs' multidimensional earth goddess. She conceived him after having kept in her bosom a ball of hummingbird feathers (i.e., the soul of a warrior) that fell from the sky. According to tradition, Huitzilopochtli was born on Coatepec Mountain, near the city of Tula.

Huitzilopochtli's brothers, the stars of the southern sky (Centzon Huitznáua, "Four Hundred Southerners"), and his sister Coyolxauhqui, a moon goddess, conspired to kill him. He foiled their plot and exterminated them with his weapon, the *xiuh cóatl* ("turquoise snake").

Huitzilopochtli is presented as the deity who guided the long migration the Aztecs undertook from Aztlan, their traditional home, to the Valley of Mexico. During the journey his image, in the form of a hummingbird, was carried upon the shoulders of priests, and at night his voice was heard giving orders. Thus, according to Huitzilopochtli's command, Tenochtitlán, the Aztec capital, was founded in AD 1325 on a small, rocky island in the lake of the Valley of Mexico. The god's first shrine was built on the spot where priests found an eagle poised upon a rock and devouring a snake, an image so important to Mexican culture that it is portrayed on the national flag of Mexico. Successive Aztec rulers enlarged the shrine until the year Eight Reed (1487), when an impressive temple was dedicated by the emperor Ahuitzotl.

The Aztecs believed that the sun god needed daily nourishment (*tlaxcaltiliztli*) in the form of human blood and hearts and that they, as "people of the sun," were required to provide Huitzilopochtli with his sustenance. The sacrificial hearts were offered to the sun *quauhtlehuanitl* ("eagle who rises") and burned in the *quauhxicalli* ("the eagle's vase"). Warriors who died in battle or as sacrifices to Huitzilopochtli were called *quauhteca* ("the eagle's people"). It was believed that after their death the warriors first formed part of the sun's brilliant retinue; then after four years

they went to live forever in the bodies of hummingbirds.

Huitzilopochtli's high priest, the Quetzalcóatl Totec Tlamacazqui ("Feathered Serpent, Priest of Our Lord"), was, with the god Tlaloc's high priest, one of the two heads of the Aztec clergy. The 15th month of the ceremonial year Panquetzaliztli ("Feast of the Flags of Precious Feathers") was dedicated to Huitzilopochtli and to his lieutenant Paynal ("He Who Hastens," so named because the priest who impersonated him ran while leading a procession around the city). During the month, warriors and *auianime* (courtesans) danced night after night on the plaza in front of the god's temple. War prisoners or slaves were bathed in a sacred spring at Huitzilopochco (modern Churubusco, near Mexico City) and were then sacrificed during or after Paynal's procession. The priests also burned a huge bark-paper serpent symbolizing the god's primary weapon. Finally, an image of Huitzilopochtli, made of ground maize (corn), was ceremonially killed with an arrow and divided between the priests and the novices; the young men who ate "Huitzilopochtli's body" were obliged to serve him for one year.

Representations of Huitzilopochtli usually show him as a hummingbird or as a warrior with armour and helmet made of hummingbird feathers. In a pattern similar to that found in many hummingbirds, his legs, arms, and the lower part of his face were painted one colour (blue) and the upper half of his face was another (black). He wore an elaborate feathered headdress and brandished a round shield and a turquoise snake.

INTI

Inti, also called Apu-punchau, was the Inca sun god. He was believed to be the ancestor of the Inca. Inti was at the head of the state cult, and his worship was imposed throughout the Inca empire. He was usually represented in human form, his face portrayed as a gold disk from which rays and flames extended. Inti's sister and consort was the moon, Mama-Kilya (or Mama-Quilla), who was portrayed as a silver disk with human features. Among the 20th-century Quechua people, Inti is occasionally confused with Christ or God.

Inti-raymi was one of a cycle of *raymi*, or "festivals." Held in June (after the Spanish conquest, in May or June to coincide with the feast of Corpus Christi), Inti-raymi honoured the sun god and was celebrated with animal sacrifices and ritual dances.

ITZAMNÁ

Itzamná (whose Mayan name means "Iguana House") was the principal pre-Columbian Mayan deity, ruler of heaven, day, and night. He frequently appeared as four gods called Itzamnás, who encased the world. Like some of the other Mesoamerican deities, the Itzamnás were associated with the points of the compass and their colours (north, white; east, red; south, yellow; west, black).

Itzamná was sometimes identified with the remote creator deity Hunab Ku and occasionally with Kinich Ahau, the sun god. The moon goddess Ixchel, patron of womanly crafts, was possibly a female manifestation of the god. Itzamná was also a culture hero who gave humankind writing and the calendar and was patron deity of medicine.

IXCHEL

Ixchel (Ix Chel) was the Maya moon goddess and the patron of womanly crafts. She was often depicted as an evil old woman and had unfavourable aspects. She may have been a manifestation of the god Itzamná. She was also the mother of the Bacabs.

MICTLANTECUHTLI

Mictlantecuhtli was the Aztec god of the dead, usually portrayed with a skull face. With his wife, Mictecacíhuatl, he ruled Mictlan, the underworld. The souls of those whose manner of death failed to call them to various paradises (i.e., for those dead by war, sacrifice, childbirth, drowning, lightning, and certain diseases) made a four-year journey, fraught with trials, through the nine hells of Mictlan. In the last, where Mictlantecuhtli lived, they disappeared or found rest.

OMETECUHTLI

The Aztec deity Ometecuhtli (Nahuatl: "Two-Lord") was the "Lord of the Duality", or Lord of Life, who represented one aspect of the cosmic duality of the Aztec tradition. With his female counterpart, Omecíhuatl ("Two-Lady" or "Lady of the Duality"), Ometecuhtli resided in Omeyocan ("Two-Place" or "Double Heaven"), the 13th and highest Aztec heaven. The opposing factors in the Aztec universe included male and female, light and dark, motion and stillness, and order and chaos. Ometecuhtli was the only Aztec god to whom no temple was erected, nor was any formal cult active in his name. Seeing him as remote in the heavens, the Aztecs assumed he would never interact with them directly, but they were aware of his presence in every act of ritual and in every rhythm of nature.

As part of the Ometéotl complex, representing a single creative theme, Ometecuhtli is depicted by symbols of fertility and adorned with ears of corn. He was believed to be responsible for releasing the souls of infants from Omeyocan in preparation for human births on earth. Despite the paramount importance of the Ometéotl deities within the hierarchy of the heavens, other lesser gods with their own distinct personalities held dominion over specific aspects of Aztec life and were regarded as autonomous in their actions.

PACHACAMAC

Pachacamac was the creator deity worshipped by the pre-Inca maritime population of Peru. It was also the name of a pilgrimage site in the Lurín Valley (south of Lima) dedicated to the god and revered for many centuries. After the Inca conquered the coast, they did not attempt to replace the ancient and deeply rooted worship of Pachacamac but instead incorporated him into their own pantheon. Pachacamac was believed to be a god of fire and a son of the sun god; he rejuvenated the world originally created by the god Viracocha and taught men the crafts. Pachacamac was also believed to be invisible and thus was never represented in art.

The ruins of the shrine in the Lurín Valley include several pyramids and temples and are partially restored. The site may have served as the central city of a coastal "kingdom" from c. 1000 to c. 1440.

TEZCATLIPOCA

Tezcatlipoca (Nahuatl: "Smoking Mirror") was god of the Great Bear constellation and of the night sky and one of the major deities of the Aztec pantheon. Tezcatlipoca's cult was brought to central Mexico by the Toltecs, Nahua-speaking warriors from the north, about the end of the 10th century AD.

Numerous myths relate how Tezcatlipoca expelled the priest-king Quetzalcóatl, the Feathered Serpent, from his centre at Tula. A protean wizard, Tezcatlipoca caused the deaths of many Toltec by his black magic and induced the virtuous Quetzalcóatl to sin, drunkenness, and carnal love, thus putting an end to the Toltec golden age. Under his influence the practice of human sacrifice was introduced into central Mexico.

Tezcatlipoca's *nagual*, or animal disguise, was the jaguar, the spotted skin of which was compared to the starry sky. A creator god, Tezcatlipoca ruled over Ocelotonatiuh ("Jaguar-Sun"), the first of the four worlds that were created and destroyed before the present universe.

Tezcatlipoca was generally represented with a stripe of black paint across his face and an obsidian mirror in place of one of his feet. The Post-Classic (after AD 900) Maya-Quiché people of Guatemala revered him as a lightning god under the name Hurakan ("One Foot"). Other representations show Tezcatlipoca with his mirror on his chest. In it he saw everything; invisible and omnipresent, he knew all the deeds and thoughts of humans.

By Aztec times (14th to 16th century AD), Tezcatlipoca's manifold attributes and functions had brought him to the summit of the divine hierarchy, where he ruled together with Huitzilopochtli, Tlaloc, and Quetzalcóatl. Called Yoalli Ehécatl ("Night Wind"), Yaotl ("Warrior"), and Telpochtli ("Young Man"), he was said to appear at crossroads at night to challenge warriors. He presided over the *telpochcalli* ("young

men's houses"), district schools in which the sons of the common people received an elementary education and military training. He was the protector of slaves and severely punished masters who ill-treated "Tezcatlipoca's beloved children." He rewarded virtue by bestowing riches and fame, and he chastised wrongdoers by sending them sickness (e.g., leprosy) or by reducing them to poverty and slavery.

The main rite of Tezcatlipoca's cult took place during Toxcatl, the fifth ritual month. Every year at that time the priest selected a young and handsome war prisoner. For one year he lived in princely luxury, impersonating the god. Four beautiful girls dressed as goddesses were chosen as his companions. On the appointed feast day, he climbed the steps of a small temple while breaking flutes that he had played. At the top he was sacrificed by the removal of his heart.

Outside of the Aztec capital, Tenochtitlán, Tezcatlipoca was especially revered at Texcoco and in the Mixteca-Puebla region between Oaxaca and Tlaxcala.

TLALOC

The Aztec rain god was Tlaloc (Nahuatl: "He Who Makes Things Sprout"). Representations of a rain god wearing a peculiar mask, with large round eyes and long fangs, date at least to the Teotihuacán culture of the highlands (3rd to 8th century AD). His characteristic features were strikingly similar to those of the Maya rain god Chac of the same period.

During Aztec times (14th to 16th century), Tlaloc's cult was apparently considered extremely important and had spread throughout Mexico. In the divinatory calendars, Tlaloc was the eighth ruler of the days and the ninth lord of the nights.

Five months of the 18-month ritual year were dedicated to Tlaloc and to his fellow deities, the Tlaloque, who were believed to dwell on the mountaintops. Children were sacrificed to Tlaloc on the first month, Atlcaualo, and on the third, Tozoztontli. During the sixth month, Etzalqualiztli, the rain priests ceremonially bathed in the lake; they imitated the cries of waterfowls and used magic "fog rattles" (*ayauhchicauaztli*) in order to obtain rain. The 13th month, Tepeilhuitl, was dedicated to the mountain Tlaloque; small idols made of amaranth paste were ritually killed and eaten. A similar rite was held on the 16th month, Atemoztli.

Tlaloc had been one of the main deities of the agricultural tribes of central Mexico for many centuries, until the warlike northern tribes invaded that part of the country, bringing with them the astral cults of the sun (Huitzilopochtli) and the starry night sky (Tezcatlipoca). Aztec syncretism placed both Huitzilopochtli and Tlaloc at the head of the pantheon. The Teocalli ("Great Temple") at Tenochtitlán, the Aztec capital, supported on its lofty pyramid two sanctuaries of equal size: one,

dedicated to Huitzilopochtli, was painted in white and red, and the other, dedicated to Tlaloc, was painted in white and blue. The rain god's high priest, the Quetzalcóatl Tlaloc Tlamacazqui ("Feathered Serpent, Priest of Tlaloc") ruled with a title and rank equal to that of the sun god's high priest.

Tlaloc was not only highly revered but also greatly feared. He could send out the rain or provoke drought and hunger. He hurled the lightning upon the earth and unleashed the devastating hurricanes. The Tlaloque, it was believed, could send down to the earth different kinds of rain, beneficent or crop destroying. Certain illnesses, such as dropsy, leprosy, and rheumatism, were said to be caused by Tlaloc and his fellow deities. Although the dead were generally cremated, those who had died from one of the special illnesses or who had drowned or been struck by lightning were buried. Tlaloc bestowed on them an eternal and blissful life in his paradise, Tlalocan.

Associated with Tlaloc was his companion Chalchiuhtlicue ("She Who Wears a Jade Skirt"), also called Matlalcueye ("She Who Wears a Green Skirt"), the goddess of freshwater lakes and streams.

TLAZOLTÉOTL

Tlazoltéotl (Nahuatl: "Filth Deity") was the Aztec goddess who represented sexual impurity and sinful behaviour. Also called Ixcuina or Tlaelquani, she was probably introduced to the Aztecs from the gulf lowlands of Huaxteca. Tlazoltéotl was an important and complex earth-mother goddess. She was known in four guises, associated with different stages of life. As a young woman, she was a care-free temptress. In her second form she was the destructive goddess of gambling and uncertainty. In her middle age she was the great goddess able to absorb human sin. In her final manifestation she was a destructive and terrifying hag preying upon youths. Tlazoltéotl was thought to provoke both lust and lustful behaviour, but she could also grant absolution to those who had so sinned. She became best known for her capacity to cleanse such sins during confessionals conducted by her priests. Thus, although she could, in one form, inspire debauched behaviour, she could also forgive sinners and remove corruption from the world. She was portrayed in an elaborate head-dress of raw cotton and in some representations wearing the skin of a sacrificial victim or in a costume that featured symbols of the moon.

TONATIUH

Tonatiuh was the Nahua sun deity of the fifth and final era (the Fifth Sun). In most myths of the Mesoamerican Nahua peoples, including those of the Aztecs, four eras preceded the era of Tonatiuh, each ended by cataclysmic destruction. Tonatiuh, or Ollin Tonatiuh, was associated with the eagle (at sunrise and sunset) and, in Aztec versions, with the deity Huitzilopochtli.

The Aztecs viewed Tonatiuh as a god constantly threatened by the awesome tasks of his daily birth at sunrise, by his death each sunset, and by the immense effort of making his journey across the sky each day. According to Aztec traditions, the gods themselves were believed to practice voluntary sacrifice, first to create Tonatiuh and then to feed him and encourage him on his path through the sky. The worship of Tonatiuh, whose sustenance required human blood and hearts, involved militaristic cults and the practice of frequent human sacrifice to ensure perpetuation of the world.

Tonatiuh is generally represented by a colourful disk. He is best known as he is depicted in the centre of the Aztec calendar, with his eagle's claw hands clutching human hearts.

VIRACOCHA

The creator deity originally worshiped by the pre-Inca inhabitants of Peru and later assimilated into the Inca pantheon was Viracocha (Huiracocha, Wiraqoca). He was believed to have created the sun and moon on Lake Titicaca. According to tradition, after forming the rest of the heavens and the earth, Viracocha wandered through the world teaching men the arts of civilization. At Manta (Ecuador) he walked westward across the Pacific, promising to return one day. He was sometimes represented as an old man wearing a beard (a symbol of water gods) and a long robe and carrying a staff.

The cult of Viracocha is extremely ancient, and it is possible that he is the weeping god sculptured in the megalithic ruins at Tiwanaku, near Lake Titicaca. He probably entered the Inca pantheon at a relatively late date, possibly under the emperor Viracocha (died c. 1438), who took the god's name. The Inca believed that Viracocha was a remote being who left the daily working of the world to the surveillance of the other deities that he had created. He was actively worshiped by the nobility, primarily in times of crisis.

XIPE TOTEC

Xipe Totec (Nahuatl: "Our Lord the Flayed One") was the god of spring and new vegetation and patron of goldsmiths. He was venerated by the Toltec and Aztec. As a symbol of the new vegetation, Xipe Totec wore the skin of a human victim—the "new skin" that covered the earth in the spring. His statues and stone masks always show him wearing a freshly flayed skin.

Representations of Xipe Totec first appeared at Xolalpan, near Teotihuacán, and at Texcoco, in connection with the Mazapan culture—that is, during the Post-Classic Toltec phase (9th to 12th century AD). The Aztecs adopted his cult during the reign of Axayacatl (1469–81). During Tlacaxipehualiztli ("Flaying of Men"), the second ritual month of the Aztec year, the priests killed human victims by removing their hearts. They flayed the bodies and put on the skins, which were dyed yellow and called *teocuitlaquemitl* ("golden clothes"). Other victims were fastened to a frame and put to death with arrows; their blood dripping down was believed to symbolize the fertile spring rains. A hymn sung in honour of Xipe Totec called him Yoalli Tlauana ("Night Drinker") because beneficent rains fell during the night; it thanked him for bringing the Feathered Serpent, who was the symbol of plenty, and for averting drought.

XIUHTECUHTLI

The Aztec god of fire, thought to be the creator of all life, was Xiuhtecuhtli (Nahuatl: "Turquoise [Year] Lord"). He was also called Huehueteotl, or "Old God," a reflection of his relative age in the Aztec pantheon. In association with Chantico, his feminine counterpart, Xiuhtecuhtli was believed to be a representation of the divine creator, Ometecuhtli.

One of the important duties of an Aztec priest centred on the maintenance of the sacred fire, making sure that it would burn perpetually. A new fire was ritually kindled during the dedication of new buildings. The two festivals of Xiuhtecuhtli coincide with the two extremes in the climatological cycle, the heat of August and the cold of January. Once every 52 years, at the end of a complete cycle in the calendar of the Aztecs, fire was ceremonially transferred first from temple to temple and then from temples to homes.

The god of fire appears in various representations and guises, one of which depicts him as a toothless old man with a stooped back, carrying an enormous brazier on his head. His insignia was the Xiuhcóatl, or serpent of fire, characterized by a nose of horn, decorated with seven stars.

XOCHIQUETZAL

Xochiquetzal (Nahuatl: "Precious Feather Flower") was the Aztec goddess of beauty, sexual love, and household arts who is also associated with flowers and plants. According to Aztec mythology, she came from Tamoanchán, the verdant paradise of the west. Originally the wife of Tlaloc, the rain god, she was abducted for her beauty by Tezcatlipoca, the malevolent god of night, who enthroned her as goddess of love. In some areas she was identified with Chalchiuhtlicue, goddess of freshwater.

GLOSSARY

alluvial Use of sedimentary material deposited by rivers, consisting of silt, sand, clay, gravel, and organic matter.

calpixque A name give to ancient Aztec tax collectors.

calpulli A unit of several Aztec households grouped together by territory and social interactions; a "ward" or neighbourhood.

chinampas Gardens planted on man-made islands built for agricultural purposes.

codices Sacred Aztec texts that gave an account of deities and religious ceremonies.

cosmogony The study of the origin and composition of the universe.

danzantes Dancers shown in stone-carved reliefs found by archaeologists in an outdoor courtyard of the Monte Alban site.

endogamy The custom of marrying within one's own tribe or socio-political group.

eschatology Theology dealing with death and final matters.

hieroglyphic Written in or belonging to a system of writing mainly in pictorial characters.

lacustrine Located near, or affiliated with, a lake.

lapidary Someone who works with precious or semiprecious stones; a jeweler.

leiden plate A jade plaque upon whose face is inscribed the Mayan calendar; one of the earliest examples of the complete calendar.

lintel A beam fitted across an opening of a building, such as those found in a door or window frame.

logograms A written symbol that stands for a whole word.

macehual The largest societal class in Aztec culture made up of commoners—a majority of the population.

mayeques The lowest caste of Aztec culture, composed of serfs who worked the land at the will of its owner.

Mesoamerican A term that defines the indigenous peoples of Mexico and Central America prior to the 16th century.

metates The upper of two millstones used by Mesoamericans to grind grain.

nagual A personal guardian spirit believed by some Mesoamericans to live in the guise of animals.

obsidian A natural glass, formed by the rapid cooling of volcanic lava, used to create many Mesoamerican stone tools.

pipiltin The upper class of nobles and royalty in the Aztec civilization.

puna Treeless basin land located high in the Andes mountains.

quipu A multicoloured Inca accounting and record-keeping device constituting one long main rope and several secondary and tertiary cords that represented numbers.

stela A standing stone slab used in the ancient world primarily as a grave marker, but also for dedication, and commemoration.

syllabary A collection of written symbols that represent the syllables of the words within a particular language.

talus Sloped land formed when rock and mineral debris accumulate at the base of a precipice.

tecomate A globular, neckless jar.

tecuhtli A title Aztec commoners could achieve if they performed nobly and took prisoners during battle.

teosinte A genus of tall grass native to Mexico, Guatemala, Honduras, and Nicaragua.

BIBLIOGRAPHY

MESOAMERICAN CIVILIZA-TIONS—GENERAL WORKS

The comprehensive, multivolume series "Handbook of Middle American Indians," especially vol. 2–3, Gordon R. Willey (ed.), *Archaeology of Southern Mesoamerica* (1965), and vol. 10–11, Gordon F. Ekholm and Ignacio Bernal (eds.), *Archaeology of Northern Mesoamerica* (1971), is indispensable. Summaries of more recent developments are found in Jeremy A. Sabloff (ed.), *Archaeology* (1981), vol. 1 in the series "Supplement to the Handbook of Middle American Indians." Historical sources include Francis Augustus MacNutt (trans. and ed.), *Letters of Cortes: The Five Letters of Relation from Fernando Cortes to the Emperor Charles V*, 2 vol. (1908, reprinted 1977); and Bernal Díaz Del Castillo, *The True History of the Conquest of New Spain*, 5 vol., ed. and trans. by Alfred Percival Maudsley (1908–16, reprinted as *The Conquest of New Spain*, 4 vol., 1967). Also useful are Muriel Porter Weaver, *The Aztecs, Maya, and Their Predecessors: Archaeology of Mesoamerica*, 2nd ed. (1981); Jacques Soustelle, *The Four Suns: Recollections and Reflections of an Ethnologist in Mexico* (1971; originally published in French, 1967), and *Arts of Ancient Mexico* (1966; originally published in French, 1966); Suzanne Abel-Vidor et al., *Between Continents/Between Seas: Precolumbian Art of Costa Rica* (1981); Anna Benson Gyles and Chlöe Sayer, *Of Gods and Men: Mexico and the Mexican Indian* (1980); Michael D. Coe, *Mexico*, 3rd rev. ed. (1984); and Joyce Kelly, *The Complete Visitor's Guide to Mesoamerican Ruins* (1982).

THE MAYA

General books on the Maya include J. Eric S. Thompson, *The Rise and Fall of Maya Civilization*, 2nd enl. ed. (1966, reprinted 1977); Michael D. Coe, *The Maya*, 4th rev. ed. (1987); Norman Hammond, *Ancient Maya Civilization* (1982); and Sylvanus G. Morley and George W. Brainerd, *The Ancient Maya*, 4th ed., rev. by Robert J. Sharer (1983). The rise and decline of Maya civilization are discussed in Richard E.W. Adams (ed.), *The Origins of Maya Civilization* (1977); and T. Patrick Culbert (ed.), *The Classic Maya Collapse* (1973, reprinted 1983). Other helpful volumes include John S. Henderson, *The World of the Ancient Maya* (1981), an ethnohistory. A basic work on Maya hieroglyphic writing is J. Eric S. Thompson, *Maya Hieroglyphic Writing: An Introduction*, 3rd ed. (1971). Later research in the field can be found in David Humiston Kelley, *Deciphering the Maya Script* (1976); Elizabeth P. Benson (ed.), *Mesoamerican Writing Systems* (1973); and Linda Schele and Mary Ellen Miller, *The Blood of Kings: Dynasty and Ritual in Maya Art* (1986). For the complex subject of ancient Maya religion, J. Eric S. Thompson, *Maya History and Religion* (1970), is an indispensable introductory guide. Native and early historical sources include Daniel G. Brinton (ed. and trans.), *The Maya Chronicles* (1882, reprinted 1969), and *The Annals of the Cakchiquels* (1885, reprinted 1969); *Popol Vuh: The Sacred Book of the Ancient Quiché Maya,* trans. from the Spanish work of Adrián Recinos by Delia Goetz and Sylvanus G. Morley (1950, reprinted 1978); Ralph L. Roys (trans.), *The Book of Chilam Balam of Chumayel* (1933, reprinted 1967); Diego De Landa, *Landa's Relación de las cosas de Yucatán,* trans. into English and ed. by Alfred M. Tozzer (1941, reprinted 1978); and Munro S. Edmonson (trans. and ed.), *The Ancient Future of the Itza: The Book of Chilam Balam of Tizimin* (1982). Jacques Soustelle, *Mexico,* trans. from French (1967), deals with the relation of Maya and other ancient Mesoamerican religions. Economic and demographic features are treated in Peter D. Harrison and B.L. Turner II, *Pre-Hispanic Maya Agriculture* (1978); and Wendy Ashmore (ed.), *Lowland Maya Settlement Patterns* (1981). Also useful is Henri Stierlin, *Art of the Maya: From the Olmecs to the Toltec-Maya* (1981; originally published in French, 1981).

POST-CLASSIC PERIOD

Bernardino De Sahagún, *General History of the Things of New Spain: Florentine Codex,* trans. from Nahuatl and ed. by Arthur J.O. Anderson and Charles E. Dibble, 13 vol. in 12 (1950–82), is the first full translation of this 16th-century Spanish writer of Aztec culture and is particularly informative on Aztec religion. J. Eric S. Thompson, *Mexico Before Cortez: An Account of the Daily Life, Religion, and Ritual of the Aztecs and Kindred Peoples* (1933), is a shorter survey. Also useful is Jacques Soustelle, *The Daily Life of the Aztecs: On the Eve of the Spanish Conquest* (1962, reissued 1970; originally published in French, 1955); Richard A. Diehl, *Tula: The Toltec Capital of Ancient Mexico* (1983); Nigel Davies, *The Toltecs, Until the Fall of Tula* (1977), and *The Toltec Heritage: From the Fall of Tula to the Rise of Tenochtitlán* (1980); and Burr Cartwright Brundage, *The Fifth Sun: Aztec Gods, Aztec World* (1979), and *The Phoenix of the Western World: Quetzalcoatl and the Sky Religion* (1982).

ANDEAN CIVILIZATIONS— GENERAL WORKS

A comprehensive and still useful survey is provided by the articles in *The Andean Civilizations,* vol. 2 of Julian H. Steward (ed.), *Handbook of South American Indians,* 7 vol. (1946–59, reprinted 1963). Introductions include John Howland Rowe and Dorothy Menzel (eds.), *Peruvian Archaeology: Selected Readings* (1967); Luis G. Lumbreras, *The People and Cultures of Ancient Peru* (1974; originally published in Spanish, 1969); and Richard W. Keatinge (ed.), *Peruvian Prehistory* (1988). John A. Mason, *The Ancient Civilizations of Peru* (1968, reprinted 1979); John V. Murra, *Nathan Wachtel,* and Jacques Revel (eds.), *Anthropological History of Andean Politics* (1986; originally published in French in issues 5-6 of *Annales, Economies, Societés, Civilizations,* vol. 33, 1978); and Shozo Masuda, Izumi Shimada, and Craig Morris (eds.), *Andean Ecology and Civilization: An Interdisciplinary Perspective on Andean Ecological Complementarity* (1985), are also useful. The material culture admired by the Spanish observers from the first days of the invasion is discussed in such works as Christopher B. Donnan (ed.), *Early Ceremonial Architecture in the Andes* (1985); Ann Pollard Rowe (ed.), *The Junius B. Bird Conference on Andean Textiles, April 7-8, 1984* (1986); and Andrea M. Heckman, *Woven Stories: Andean Textiles and Rituals* (2003).

THE INCA

The works of the chroniclers are available in modern English translations or in modern critical editions: Pedro de Cieza de León, *The Incas,* trans. by Harriet de Onis, ed. by Victor Wolfgang von Hagen (1959, reprinted 1967); Garcilaso de la Vega, *The Incas: The Royal Commentaries of the Inca, Garcilaso de la Vega, 1539-1616,* trans. by Maria Jolas from the critical annotated French edition of Alain Gheerbrant (1961, reissued 1971; originally published in French, 1959); and Felipe Guamán Poma de Ayala, *El primer nueva corónica y buen gobierno,* trans. from Quechua by Jorge L. Urioste, ed. by John V. Murra and Rolena Adorno, 3 vol. (1980). Comprehensive histories include Alfred Métraux, *The History of the Incas* (1969; originally published in French, 1963); George A. Collier, Renato I. Rosaldo, and John D. Wirth (eds.), *The Inca and Aztec States, 1400-1800: Anthropology and History* (1982); and John Hemming,*The Conquest of the Incas,* rev. ed. (1983). The following works study special aspects of the Inca civilization: Gary Urton, *At the Crossroads of the Earth and the Sky: An Andean Cosmology* (1981); Maria Ascher and Robert Ascher, *Code of the Quipu: A Study in Media, Mathematics, and Culture* (1981); Frank Salomon, *Native Lords of Quito in the Age of the Incas: The Political Economy of North-Andean Chiefdoms* (1986); Craig Morris and Donald E. Thompson, *Huánuco Pampa: An Inca City and Its Hinterland* (1985); Sally Falk Moore, *Power and Property in Inca Peru* (1958, reprinted 1973); John V. Murra, *The Economic Organization of the Inka State* (1980); John Hyslop, *The Inca Road System* (1984); and Graziano Gasparini and Luise Margolies, *Inca Architecture* (1980; originally published in Spanish, 1977).

INDEX

A

Abaj Takalik, 33
Acamapichtli, 78
Acapana, 130
Acarí Valley, 127
Acropolis, 35, 133
afterlife, 62–63, 67, 104–106
agriculture, 16, 19–20, 21, 22, 29, 39, 51, 74–75, 89–91, 92, 94, 96, 110, 111, 115, 116, 117, 118, 151, 160, 169
Aguas Calientes, 134
Ah Mun, 66
Ah Puch, 66–67
Ahuitzotl, 79
alpacas, 111–112, 143
altars, 27, 33, 42, 48, 52, 53, 55, 81, 99
Amazon Basin, 113
Anales de Cuauhtitlán, 80, 88
Ancasmayo River, 155
ancestor worship, 70, 93
Ancón, 119
Andes, 108–115, 116, 117, 124, 130, 132, 140, 143, 146, 148, 153, 165
Antiquities of Mexico, 61
Apo Mayta, 147, 149
Apu Illapu, 163
Apurímac River, 165, 166
Apurlé, 138
architecture, 31–32, 35, 39–40, 45–46, 48, 50, 52–53, 54, 55, 57, 65, 77, 81–82, 117, 118, 120, 122, 124, 130, 133, 138–139, 165
Archives of the Indies, 161
Arevalo phase, 29
Argentina, 107, 108, 135, 142, 154, 155, 165, 169
astrology, 61, 79, 99
astronomy, 17, 60, 61, 63, 64, 67, 69, 77, 102, 117, 163–164

Atacama Desert, 114–115
Atahuallpa, 144, 156–157, 158
Avenue of the Dead, 38, 39
Axayacatl, 79
Ayacucho Basin, 116, 156
Ayarmaca, 147
Aymara, 112, 114, 140, 150, 154, 159
Azcapotzalco, 78–79
Azcatitlan, 87
Aztecs, 17, 40, 41, 42, 46, 61, 62, 63, 65, 69, 72, 73, 74, 77, 78–79, 81, 84–106, 168

B

Bacabs, 63, 64, 69
Bahía de Manta, 164
ball courts, 42–43, 45, 50, 53, 69, 97, 98
ball games, 25, 42–43, 45, 50, 69, 98
Barra phase, 21
Basin of Mexico, 78, 79, 93
bas-relief designs, 55
beans, 19, 20, 74, 75, 116, 118
Belize, 21, 28, 168
Belize City, 83
Berlin, Heinrich, 58
Berns, Augusto, 132
Bingham, Hiram, 132, 133, 134
Bolivia, 107, 135–136, 144, 148, 155, 169
Bolivian High Plateau, 114
Bolontiku, 65
Bolon Tzacab, 62
Bombon, 156
Bonampak, 53, 67
bronze, 135–136, 154, 155, 161, 164
Building J, 32
burial cloths, 160–161
burial traditions, 27, 31–32, 35, 40, 44, 45, 46, 51, 52, 54, 57, 62, 67, 106, 116, 117, 131, 160–161

C